EDUCATION AND SOCIAL CHANGES IN BIHAR

(1900-1921)

A Survey of Social History of Bihar from Lord Curzon to Non-cooperation Movement

Dr. SHREEDHAR NARAYAN PANDEY
Lecturer in History
Ganesh Dutta College, Begusarai
(Lalit Narayan Mithila University)

MOTILAL BANARSIDASS
Delhi :: Patna :: Varanasi

Indological Publishers & Booksellers
Head Office : BUNGLOW ROAD, JAWAHAR NAGAR, DELHI-7
Branches : 1. CHOWK, VARANASI-1 (U.P.)
2. ASHOK RAJPATH, PATNA (BIHAR)

ISBN 0 8426 0986 5

First Edition : Varanasi, 1975

The publication of the thesis was financially supported by the Indian Council of Historical Research; and the responsibility of conclusions reached is entirely that of the author and the Indian Council of Historical Research accepts no responsibility for them.

Printed in India
At the Asian Printing Works, Varanasi and Published by Sundarlal Jain, for Motilal Banarsidass, Chowk, Vạranasi (U. P.)

CONTENTS

PREFACE

This book forms a part of my thesis approved by the Patna University for Ph. D. degree.

The pioneers in the field of writing Indian History were the British Historians. But it was not expected of them to write on the social history of India. Most of the British historians did not even touch upon the social and educational developments of Bihar. Even those like W. W. Hunter or O' Malley[1] who did it just remained on the periphery of the problem. Hunter's *Statistical Account of Bengal* and Risley's Volumes, the *District Gazetteers and the Census Reports* provide enough data about the growth of education and the composition of caste structure no doubt, but they hardly provide any conclusion.

The works of British authors like Dodwell, V. A. Smith and Roberts and others on modern India were concerned with the political history. They naturally ignored social developments especially in the different regions of India. *The Cambridge History of India* and the *Oxford History of India*, for example, are primarily concerned with the political and the administrative developments. Moreover, their authors suffered from administrative prejudices or even an imperialist bias. They were naturally little interested in the social history of the people of India on a regional scale.

Attempts have been made by some Indian scholars like B. Sahay,[2] to present history of education in Bihar. But Sahay, being a government officer in the British days suffered from certain limitations : he had his administrators' prejudices and could not therefore criticise the government policies. Moreover, he took a long time and tried to stuff his book with facts, providing no analysis, let alone any word on social reaction. A couple of unpublished research works on *Education in Bihar* of the nineteenth century do not take into account the social developments during that period.

1. History of Bengal, Bihar and Orissa.
2. B. Sahay, History of Education in Bihar under British Rule, 1928

During the last two decades, specially after independence a few regional histories have been produced, e.g. Dr. K. K. Datta's volumes on the *History of Freedom Movement in Bihar*, R. K. Choudhury's *History of Bihar*, V. C. P. Choudhury's *The creation of Modern Bihar*, J. S. Jha's *History of Darbhanga Raj*, and so on; but none of them has delved deep into the social and educational problems of the first two decades of the twentieth century. Dr. Datta's book is devoted exclusively to the history of the freedom sturggle. R. R. Diwakar, once a Governor of Bihar after independence, edited a comprehensive volume on the history of Bihar—*Bihar Through the Ages*. But it was supposed to be a general survey of long period, covering more than three thousand years. Most of these books have not utilized the primary sources or the contemporary newspapers and periodicals for portraying the background of the political and social awakening in Bihar in the present century.

In a word, no objective and complete treatment of the educational and social problems of Bihar in the first two decades of the present century has been undertaken so far.

For the sake of an objective study in this work both primary and secondary sources have been utilised. The source material of this period, various official documents, reports and monographs by British and Indian writers have been examined. The progress of education has been based on the government reports; but they have been supplemented by the material from the memorials, the proceedings of the education department, the Legislative Council proceedings and the contemporary newspapers. The biographies, autobiographies, memoirs, resolutions and proceedings of public bodies have helped the reconstruction of the social history of this period a good deal.

The selection of the date has been guided by two factors: The period of Lord Curzon is a landmark in the history of education in modern India. In 1900, the Secretary of State drew the attention of the government to the necessity of the continuance of Government control in education. This year Curzon set on reforming the whole pattern of education that existed at that time. That is why the present study of the educational development in Bihar begins from 1900. In the field of social history also, this period was equally significant : with the beginning of the present century, new progressive trends like breaking of social barriers and taboos in Bihar's social life began.

The new social consciousness continued to grow to new political dimensions during the first two decades of the present century till its culmination in the non-co-operation movement of 1921.

I am very much obliged to Dr. J. C. Jha, the Reader, Department of History, Patna University, presently Professor of Indian Studies, University of Trinided (West Indies) for agreeing to work as my supervisor and I am also grateful to Dr. R. S. Sharma, the then University Professor and Head of the Department of History, Patna University for encouraging me in the project. I express my gratitude to Dr. K. K. Datta, former Vice-chancellor, Patna University, who with his profound knowledge of Modern India has offered me many valuable suggestions from time to time.

My thanks are due to the staff of National Archives, New Delhi, Bihar State Central Records Office, Patna, National Library, Calcutta, West Bengal State Record Office, Calcutta, Sinha Library, Patna, Patna University Library, Patna Departmental Library, Department of History, Patna University, Shrinandan Library, Chapra and Khublal Singh Library, Begusarai.

I must express my gratitude to the authorities of the G. D. College, Begusarai, who granted me leave, without which it was not possible to complete this work. I express my thanks to my wife, Mrs. Sharada Pandey M.A. for her valuable cooperation. I am very much indebted, in particular, to the chairman of the ICHR who took keen interest in the publication of this book and I am thankful to the authorities of the ICHR for providing financial assistance in bringing out this volume. My thanks are also due to shri J. P. Jain, the proprietor of Motilal Banarsidass, for taking up the publication and bringing it in time.

ABBREVIATIONS

B. D. G.	..	Bengal District Gazetteers
		Bihar District Gazetteers
B. O. D. G.	..	Bihar & Orissa District Gazetteers
B. O.	..	Bihar & Orissa
B. P. A. T.	..	Bihar Provincial Association Tracts
C. P.	..	Curzon Papers
D. P. I.	..	Director of Public Instruction
Deptt.	..	Department
Ed.	..	Educational
Intr.	..	Introduction
Govt.	..	Government
J. B. R. S.	..	Journal of Bihar Research Society
Offg.	..	Officiating

CHAPTER I

INTRODUCTION

State of Education and Society in Second-half of the Nineteenth Century

Bihar came into contact with the British quite early through their trading activities, but their political domination began in 1760 with the grant of Mir Kasim. The decisive battle of Buxar which confirmed the verdict of Plassey (1757) was fought on the soil of Bihar in 1764 With the British victory at Buxar followed by the grant of **diwani** in 1765, Bihar along with Bengal passed under direct British rule. The East India Company gradually consolidated its gains and envolved a new administrative machinery in this region during the post-Buxar years, Bihar forming an integral part of Bengal.

Initially the British thought that the Indian people must be left to follow their own system of faith and morals. They were sympathetic towards the attempts made to revive Indian learning, but entertained no idea of introducing any new system of education. It was in 1781 that the East India Company took the initiative in the field of Education, but this was confined to vernacular education only. This initiative was naturally taken in Calcutta, the head-quarters of the Company and Banaras, an ancient seat of Hindu learning and Culture[1]. As a part of their general social policy the British Indian government continued the system of education it found in vogue in Bihar.

The state of indigenous education in Bihar prior to 1835 can be gleaned from the detailed and authentic reports of F. Buchanan. According to this report in Purnea there were 643 elementary schools and 110 Sanskrit Schools. In the district of South Bihar, there were 27 Sanskrit Schools and 291 Persian and Arabic Schools. In the district of Tirhut there were 80 Hindi Schools, 56 Sanskrit

1. The Calcutta Madarsa was started in 1781 while the Sanskrit college in 1791.

Schools and 238 Persian and Arabic Schools. In Sanskrit Schools all the teachers were Brahmins. Out of 80 teachers in the 80 Hindi schools of the district of Tirhut, 77 were Kayasthas, 2 were Gandhvanik and one was Brahmin[1]. Adam's report on Vernacular Education in Bengal and Bihar gives an account of Sanskrit, Persian and Arabic education. It mentions two classes of schools :

(1) Elementary Schools teaching only vernacular.

(2) Indigenous schools where the medium of instruction was Sanskrit or Persian and Arabic.

In short, during the early days of its administration in India the East India Company's Government followed till 1813 a policy of **laissez faire** in education because being a commercial institution it had no concern with educational and social matters. It remained busy in promoting its economic gains and consolidating its political supremacy. There were only some isolated and individual attempts made for the revival of old indigenous educational institution or the establishment of new ones got the revival and cultivation of the already existing Hindu and Mohammaden learning, which were then found to be in a progressive state of decay.

In Bihar. as elsewhere proposals to encourage Hindu and Mohammedan learning, were made quite early. In his Minute of 6 March 1811 Lord Minto recommended that for the advancement of Hindu learning and literature, a college should be established at Bhour near Bhowara in Tirhut and a Mohammedan college might be established at Bhagalpur.[2] But nothing came out of this recommendation before 1873 when the Dharma Samaj Sanskrit Vidyalaya was established at Muzaffarpur.

English was first introduced by private enterprise to meet the local demands of individuals or small communities. In 1819 the Calcutta Book Society[3] set on foot the project of establishing school, both English and Vernacular all over the country. It commenced its work from Calcutta, which was made a centre of educational

1. F. Buchanan, **An Account of the District of Purnea** in 1809–10 pp. 176–177
2. H. Sharp, **Selection from Educational Records**, Part–I, (1781–1899), p–19
3. See History and Culture of the Indian People, Vol. X. Part II. pp. 31–32

activities. It could not, however, establish any school in Bihar. In fact, there were no English Schools in Bihar established through private enterprise.

Even so, Bihar formed an integral part of Bengal and was in close touch with Calcutta on account of the Supreme Court established in that city to decide appeals from the courts in Bihar, the movement in favour of English education in Calcutta and the influx of English educated Bengalis from Calcutta and its suburbs into Bihar prepared the ground for English education in Bihar.

The people who already had some means of availing themselves of oriental learning but were handicapped for want of English education eventually began to demand more facilities for English education. The Government moved in this direction by devising a scheme in 1835. Two educational circles were established–one at Bhagalpur and the other in Bihar. It was proposed to have a central college with as many zila schools as there were districts in the circle.[1]

Institutions to impart English education began to spring up at different places. According to Adam, one school for English education was started at Purnea in 1835. The Patna High School established in the same year was usually regarded as the parent institution of the Patna College. R. B. Chapman, Inspector of schools, in Bihar wrote of it in 1855 as being 'the first English School in Bihar.........established under government auspices at Patna and standing alone for ten years.[2]

There was intense activity on the educational front with the coming of W. Taylor, an enthusiastic Commissioner of Patna. He found that there was less enthusiasm among the people of Bihar for the acquisition of knowledge; indeed, there was 'a strong and inveterate dislike for it both among Hindus and Mohammedans.'[3] To remove this dislike and general apathy it was absolutely necessary, he thought, to exert the strongest available influence. All influence in these districts, he wrote to the D. P. I., "does and will for

1. B. Sabay, op. cit., P–24
2. Letter of R. B. Chapman cited in Sarkar and Jha, **History of the Patna College,** p–5
3. Taylo to W. Gordon Young, D. P. I., 31 January 1856

a century atleast to come, radiate townwards."[1] Taylor further saw that there was "no adequate means of communication between the Government and the people through which such influence could have been exercised."[2] It was all the more necessary that the Zamindars' co-operation should be obtained by all means to achieve the desired end.

Since the people were accustomed to look to the landlords for guidance, Taylor thought, it was only through that such influence could be brought to bear. Therefore, Taylor started a dialogue between the Government and the principal landlords of the four districts in his division and received assurance of support and co-operation from them. Guarded with this assurance Taylor took steps to establish a few schools in some of the principal towns and villages within their estates. This would be followed by the foundation at Sadar stations of normal teachers' vernacular training schools for the future schools. He also suggested that educated people should get preference in the Government services.

After the resolution of 1859, a beginning was made by establishing Zila school at Patna, Arrah and Chapra and the Hill school at Bhagalpur. In 1863, the district of Deoghar, Motihari, Hazaribagh and Chaibasa got one school each.[3] The school at Deoghar was transferred to Dumka when it became the headquarters of the Santhal Parganas.

In the beginning the zila schools opened by the Government were not popular. People were not inclined to send their children to these schools. Even so, social prejudices stood against the progress of modern education in Bihar. The officiating Collector of Gaya saw that the Government schools of the district were not functioning well owing to the backwardness of the parents who did not allow their children to attend the classes. The guardians used to withdraw their wards frequently, thus interrupting their studies.

Patna had the advantage of being the administrative headquarters of Bihar. Naturally enough, all educational experiments were initiated here. The first attempt to impart higher education in Bihar was made here by the middle of the nineteenth century.

1. Ibid.
2. Ibid.
3. Educational proceedings (Government of Bengal), August 1863, nos. 76–80, pp. 43–45.

There was little response to higher education among the people of Bihar, presumably because of the abhorrence of all contact with European ideas and intercourse. This is why attempts to start a college at Patna failed twice during the first half of the nineteenth century. Gradually however, public interest in higher education was evinced, partly as a result of the introduction of English in the chief appellate court and, partly due to the extension of the railways.

The Government proposed to establish a college at Patna, entrusted Mr. Rogers, the then Headmaster of the collegiate school, with the responsibility of organising it, and granted affiliation to proposed college.[1] At last the Patna College was opened with five students only in 1863. Unfortunately, the college did not attract much attention in the early days of its existence. But things changed with the appointment of J. W. Mccrinolle, a famous indologist on 11 February 1867 as the Principal of the college. Its activity further increased with the addition of the department of Law in May 1864 with one lecturer, viz., Nobin Chandra De.

Donations started coming. One Syeed Wallayat Ally Khan donated Rs. 5,000 to the college.[2] Once the college was on a secure financial footing C. F. Cockburn, Commissioner of Patna, wrote to the government that this college should be separated from the school and located near the opium godowns.[3]

Eventually on the occasion of the visit of the lieutenant Governor, Cecil Beadon (1862-1868) to Patna, it was decided that pending the construction of a new and suitable building for the college, the magistrate's cutchery might be available for the use of the upper classes.[4]

By the end of the nineteenth century the Patna college became one of the premier colleges of the Bengal Presidency, the number of its pupils increased and the results were also satisfactory. At the

1. Educational Proceedings (Govt. of Bengal), September 1862, no. 30.
2. The Darbhanga Raj and the Bettiah estate also contributed Rs. 6,000 and Rs. 4,000/–respectively to the new college: Vide Edn. Proceedings April 1863, and November 1863, no. 19.
3. C. F. Cockburn to the Secretary, Govt. of Bengal, 22 January 1863.
4. Ibid.

outset the college had an insignificant number of Bihari students, but by 1899 there were 216 Biharis as against 85 Bengali students, the total number being 235.[1]

In the beginning the people of Bihar were more averse to higher collegiate education than to school education. But the growing appreciation of the advantage of higher education by the Biharis, a re-orientation of their general outlook [and the Government policy of diffusing more education among them than before, led to the rise in their proportion in the college classes from 1873-74 onwards.

The second college that rose in Bihar was the Tej Narayan Jubilee college which was affiliated in 1887 as a second grade college and in 1890 as a first grade college.[2] It was started by Tej Narayan Singh, a local Zamindar. It was maintained entirely by subscriptions and donations supplemented by the receipt from fees. Ladli Mohan Ghosh, a medical practitioner in Bhagalpur, did much for the growth of this college.

The next college that sprang up was the Bihar National College founded by Bisheshwar Singh,[3] Zamindar of Kulharia in the district of Shahabad. It was affiliated in 1889 as a second grade college and as a first grade college in 1892.[4]

---

1. Educational Proceedings (Govt. of Bihar), 1900, nos : 28-29, p. 41.
2. O Malley, Ed. B. D. G. Bhagalpur, p. 155.
3. Bisheshwar Singh : **Bisheshwar Singh** (1849 1899) and Saligram Singh (1852-1905)

   Both brothers born at a village in the Shahabad district; first read in the Aarrah Zila School; joined the Patna Collegiate School, joined the Presidency college for graduation; Bisheshwar left his studies without graduating himself, passed the District Court Law Examination, joined the Patna Bar, spent the rest of his life there, occupying a high position in public life. Saligram Singh graduated in 1874, joined the Law College in Calcutta; obtained his degree in law in 1877; joined the Calcutta Bar; attained a leading position at the Calcutta Bar; was elected a member of the Legislative Council of the province of Bengal, Bihar and Orissa, served there for two years; both brothers formed the first batch of delegates from Bihar to join the session of the Indian National Congress held in Calcutta in 1886, they founded the Bihar National Congress at Patna : Saligram Singh was a fellow of the Calcutta University; he took an active interest in the proceedings of the Senate; was also for several years an elected member of the syndicate; Bihar National College is a monument of the two brothers.
4. Educational Proceedings (Govt. of Bengal) September 1892, Nos. 59-63

It was in Monghyr that the fourth college of Bihar was started. It was named the Diamond Jubilee college to commemorate the diamond jubilee of the rule of Queen Victoria. This college was the result of an amalgamation of Raja Kamleshwari Prasad Sinha's High English school and the Victorial Jubilee school with the Monghyr Zila school in 1897. C. R. Marriott, the Collector of Monghyr, was instrumental in bringing about this amalgamation. The college was affiliated in 1898 as a second grade college.[1]

As there was no provision for higher education in North Bihar up to 1899, those students who wished to join a college were obliged to go either to Patna, to Bhagalpur or to Calcutta. The rapid spread of education in this part of the state led the Bhumihar Brahman Sabha to hold a meeting in March 1899 at which it was decided to establish a college at Muzaffarpur.

The college was actually opened on July 1899.[2] It was affiliated at first upto Intermediate standard in Arts and in 1900 it was upgraded to Degree standard.[3] This new institution fulfilled a distinct need of the districts north of the Ganges.

The Bhumihar Brahmin College of Muzaffarpur owed its creation to Babu Langat Singh, a public spirited Zamindar, and its later position as a first grade government college to T. R. Greer, a Commissioner of the Tirhut Division.

Next to the zamindars and civilians in the field of education, came the missionaries. St. Columa's College at Hazaribagh was started as a philanthropic work of the Dublin University Mission and its object was the uplift of the aborigines. It was started in 1899 with 23 students and with a donation of Rs. 3,000 from Raja Ram Narayan Singh of Ramgarh.[4]

There is no mention of any public girls schools in Buchanan's reports nor does Adam make any mention of them. According to a Government report there was not only a very general ignorance among females but also a thorough want even of the agency

1. A Pedler to the Government of Bengal, 6 September 1904.
2. Educational Proceedings (Govt. of Bengal) August 1899 Nos. 52-61
3. Educational Proceedings (Govt. of Bengal), Decemer 1900 Nos. 9-19
4. Educational Proceedings (Govt. of Bengal), September 1899, Nos. 27-31.

which should teach females to read and write.[1] In the period that followed Wood's despatch (1854) practically nothing was done in respect of female education : not a single school was opened for the education of girls either by the government or by private individuals. The few schools that were established for the education of girls were all in the hands of Christian missionaries. The normal schools established at Chapra and Arrah for the training of teachers also languished within a short period.

Want of female teachers, the Hindu conception of the duties of a woman, and **parda** were some of the hindrances to the growth of female education in the region towards the end of the 19th century.[2]

The only institutions for the education of girls in Bihar was the Bankipur female High School founded by some leading Bengalis of Patna like Sri Prakash Chandra Roy and his wife Aghore Kamini in 1857. Since it was under the influence of the Brahmo-Samaj, it could not attract Bihari students. It was a pity that no Bihari girl student attended this school.[3]

Various steps were taken to educate females, such as separate schools for them by male teachers, separate schools for them by famale teachers, the collection of grown-up women at central places for their education by a lady teacher, the teaching of grown-up girls and women at their own houses by a lady peripatetic teacher.

The most important measure in this field was the establishment of the Badshah Razavi's Training College for imparting training female teachers at Patna. This institution owed its existence to the liberality of Badshah Nawab of Patna and to the interest of Syed Hasan Imam, and Earle and Maude, Commissioners of the Patna Division. Part of the credit went to the Tikari Raj for it provided accommodation for in its own places at Patna. Even so, the state of female education in Bihar towards the close of the nineteenth century was far from satisfactory as the **parda** system still kept women in seclusion.

1. Educational Proceedings (Govt. of Bengal), April, 1873. p-11
2. Review of Education in Bengal, 1892-97
3. Educational Proceedings (Govt. of Bengal), April, 1873, p-11

A woman who lost her husband led a life of enforced widowhood. Prohibition to re-marry was very strict though only among upper castes-Brahmins, Rajputs, Kayasthas, Babhans and some Baniyas. Among the lower caste Hindus, however, more than three-fourths of the young widows could re-marry. **Sati** (burning of widows on the funeral pyre of their husbands) was still in vogue.

The census reports of the 19th century refer to the practice of early marriage. This along with **parda** retarted the progress of female education. Yet another obstacle to female education was the wrong notion prevalent among the common masses that educated girls become more independent than ignorant ones. Another obstacle was the superstition that widowhood was inevitable if girls would get higher education.

The condition of the people and the state of social and intellectual progress were enquired into by the government agencies in the latter part of the nineteenth century. They held that while race and health improvement was an essential requisite for the solid physical foundation of a community or nation, educational progress or intellectual develoment was the integral and component part of its social progress.

In Bengal, at the close of the nineteenth century the total number of students represents only 15·4 percent of the total population of school going-age, the boys representing 28·9 percent of the males and the girls 1.9 percent of the female population of school going-age. There were 44 colleges at work in Bengal.[1] But the province of Bihar had only five colleges and the percentage of students much behind Bengal. Even though Patna was the first among the districts of Bihar to receive English education, the percentage of literacy among the people of Patna city was 6·4 (12·3 males and 0·6 females) at the close of the last century.[2]

Epidemics like Plague, Cholera and Fever caused great hindrance to the social and educational development. Indeed, plague had become an annual visitation which caused heavy mortality.[3]

1. **Moral and Material Progress and Condition of India, 1899-1900, P.171**
2. O'Malley (Ed.) B. D. G. Patna, P-172
3. **Imperial Gazetteer of India,** Vol. II Bengal, p-15

After 1854, the government began to establish schools. It was reported in 1866 that education in Patna district was progressing well. Indeed, there arose a great demand for English knowing Indians and therefore most people earnestly wished their children to take modern education. This is why every important place had a vernacular school and every principal town an English school.[1]

There were altogether 758 schools in the Patna Division, according to Inspector's report of 1872. This number did not include the indigenous schools.[2] In 1870-71, there were 23 Government and aided schools attended by 1,530 students in the Patna district alone. In 1880-81 there were 3 aided and 4 unaided High schools with a total attendance of 781 boys and the number of Middle Vernacular schools 16, Lower Vernacular schools 46 and Primary Schools 1,633.[3]

After Patna, Muzaffarpur came second. True, the rate of literacy in the Muzaffarpur district was higher than other districts of North Bihar, but it was considerably below the average of Bengal : only 3.9. percent of the Muzaffarpur population could read and write.[4] The number of schools in Muzaffarpur rose from 314 to 1,782 in 1875 and the number of pupils from 7,027 to 20,726.[5] This phenomenal rise was brought about as a result of the recommendations of the Indian Education Commission, popularly known as Hunter Commission. It encouraged private bodies to participate in the task of education.

Saran sent out a large proportion of emigrants, perhaps more than any other district in Bengal outside Chotanagpur. In the first years of this century more than a tenth of the population of the district were away from home. Naturally enough, the number of females was recorded highest in the district. Infant marriage, a common practice in Bihar, was much less common here than in other districts of the province. There had been a marked falling

1. J. W. Dalrymple to the Govt. of Bengal, 20 August, 186 ;
2. S. C. Bayley to the Govt. of Bengal, 1 November, 1872
3. O'Malley (Ed) **B. D. G.** Patna, P-172
4. **Imperial Gazetteer of India, Vol. II, Bengal, p-118**
5. P. C. Roy Choudhry, (Ed), **B. D. G.** Muzaffarpur p-179,

off during the last two decades of the nineteenth century in the proportion of married persons, and also in the number of children. Thus there was a preventive check on the growth of population in this district.[1]

Education was in a backward state in the majority of the districts of Bihar. In Saran[2] and Darbhanga literacy was only 3·5 percent, in Gaya 3.6 percent, in Champaran 2·3 percent and the great majority of the population in Monghyr district were illiterate as only 2.9. percent were able to read and write.[3]

Education was exceptionally backward in the Purnea district as only 3 percent were literate at the close of the nineteenth century.[4] One of the districts which was making progress and trying to overcome backwardness was Bhagalpur. Here 66 male per thousand and 1 female per thousand were literate at the time of the census in 1901. But in 1891, 61 males and 1 female per thousand were returned as literate.[5] In fact, there had been a steady progress in the direction of literacy during the last twenty years of the nineteenth century.[6] There was one Arts College, 19 secondary, 962 primary and 337 special schools. A Santhal boys' school and a Santhal girls' school near the estern border had a large attendance, while all the primary schools in the south of the district were attended by boys of aboriginal races.[7]

The other districts of South Bihar were much more backward in education, and not even 3 percent of the population was able to read and write. The Collector of Shahabad reported "Education is backward, owing a great measure to the character of its population. Shahabad is peopled largely by Rajputs and this class of men take little or no interst in intellectual pursuits"[8]

1. **Imperial Gazetteer of India**. Vol. II. p-15
2. However, the Chapra School was in a very satisfactory condition : Educational Proceedings, February 1867, p-15
3. See W. W. Hunter, **Statistical Account of Bengal**, Vols. XI, XII & XV
4. Imperial Gazetteer of India, Bengal, p-188
5. O' Malley (Ed.) B. D. G., Bhagalpur, pp. 155–56.
6. **Ibid.**
7. Imperial Gazetteer of India, Vol. II. Bengal, P. 174
8. J.W. Dalrymple to the Govt. of Bengal, 20 August. 1866.

The social condition of Santhals, nay of all the tribal people, was different from the rest of the population. The Santhal and other **Adivasi** girls were married as adults mostly to men of their own choice. Pre-marital sexual intercourse was tacitly recognised, it being understood that if the girl became pregnant the young man was bound to marry her. In case of his attempt to evade this obligation, he was severely beaten and in addition his father was required to pay a heavy fine. Christian missionaries had much influence in Chotanagpur and the Santhal Parganas The Christians numbered 9,875 of whom 9,463 were local people, including 7,064 Santhals. The largest numbers were to be found in the sub-divisional headquarters where the Scandinavian Lutheran Mission called the Indian Home Mission had been at work for over forty years and maintained 29 mission stations and 2 schools [1]

The Chotanagpur division was the home of numerous non-Aryan tribes, who were never completely subjugated either by the early Aryan invaders or by the Pathans and Moghul Emperors or indeed by any outside power until the advent of the British. They had preserved in their mountain fastnesses an individuality in respect of tribal organization, religion and language. The most distinctive of the tribes represented were the Santhals in Hazaribagh, Manbhum and Singhbhum, the Mundas in Ranchi, the Oraons in Ranchi the Hos in Singhbhum, the Bhumijes in Manbhum and Singhbhum. A remarkable increase in number of Christian took place during the last decad of the nineteenth century. In Ranchi christians numbered 1,24,958 at the end of the nineteenth century, whereas ten years before this there were only 75,693 Christians.[2]

According to a Government report of 1870 Chotanagpur was still much behind the rest of Bengal so far as education was concerned. However, the progress made in this field between 1865 and 1870 was remarkable when compared to the 'stagnation of the previous period.'[3] Since the people, high and low, showed no interest in education the number of schools for an area equal to England's was negligible: in 1860's Ranchi had only one Govern-

1. **Imperial Gazeteer of India**. Vol. II, Bengal, p.225

2. **Idid.**, p. 325

3. E. T. Dalton to R. Thompson, cited in Educational Proceedings. November, 1870 No. 12, p. 45

ment school and one Lutheran Mission boarding school with little attendance, Purulia one and Chaibasa one. Dalton, the Chotanagpur Commissioner, thought that "arrogance, exclusiveness, bigotry, and superstition restrained the zamindars from giving heed to the advice constantly pressed on them by the local authorities"[1]. The lower classes however, were gradually impressed by the liberal educational policy of the Government.

The work carried on by the German mission was chiefly educational. The Free Church of Scotland opened a branch of its Santhal Mission at Pachamba near Giridih in 1871, and maintained a dispensary and schools. The Dublin University Missionary, established at Hazaribagh in 1892, maintained a boys high school, an upper primary school and a first Arts College, in addition to dispensaries at Hazaribagh.[2]

The district most backward in education was Palamu, where only 1.9 percent of the population could read and write. In Manbhum district the material progress of the people was accelerated due to the opening up of the country by railways and the growth of coal industry. The Jharia coalfield attracted a large number of labourers, chiefly from Hazaribagh, North Bihar and the United Provinces. The Hos of Singhbhum had the practice of late marriage, owing to the excessive bride-price which was the customary. The population of the district was polyglot.

The main occupation of the people in Bihar as a whole has been agriculture. The percentage of population engaged in agriculture in the nineteenth century varied between 65 percent to 80 percent. The vast mass of population lived in villages. But a change was visible in the second half of the nineteenth century. A beginning of professional and technical institutions was made which indicated change in future. The students of Bihar first received technical instruction in the Engineering College at Calcutta and the Roorki College. Then a survey school was attached to the Patna College in 1864, which was affiliated in 1876 to the Sibpur Engineering College. In 1890 the Patna Survey school

1. Educational Proceedings, (Govt. of Bengal) November, 1870 No. 12, p-15
2. **Imperial Gazetteer of India. Vol. II Bengal, p-321.**

was transferred from the Patna College building to the new premises. In 1896 the Survey School was amalgamated with the Bihar Industrial School and the new institution at Bankipur was entitled the 'Bihar School of Engineering'[1] It owed its origin to a fund raised by the residents of Bihar to commemorate the visit of King Emp r to Patna in 1876.

At Ranchi there was a private Missionary school since 1870. It was recognised in 1890–91 and taken over by Government in 1894.[2] The manufactures of the people were carried on by manual labour. There were no factories. In the beginning social organization in Bihar was against factories.

In the early nineteenth century there were traditional industries too carried on by the hereditary artisans at their private workshops Patna was famous for its gold and silver, embroidery, Nabinagar for its blankets, Arval for its bleached and glazed paper of fine texture, Khagra-Kishanganj for its brass and bell metal utensils, Kharagpur for its silver ornaments, Lalganj for its carpentry, Monghyr for its ammunition work and gun factory, Bihar subdivision for weaving, Saran and Champaran for their saltpetre, Chotanagpur for its mineral wealth, Purnea for **Bidar**.

The construction of railway lines in the second half of the nineteenth century brought rapid change in the life of the people. It paved the way for the industrial education of the people. The unskilled labourers of these tracts learnt the various works of railway construction under European Engineers. A stimulus was given by the railway works to the carpenters, blacksmiths and masons. The railway workshop at Jamalpur and railway headquarters at Samastipur and Katihar emerged as towns of industrial activities. The locomotive workshop at Jamalpur did more for industrial education than any number of industrial schools could have done. Jamalpur contained an institute comprising a library, reading and billiardrooms, an entertainment hall and a swimming pool. It had a church and aided schools for European and Indians.[3]

---

1. **Report on Technical and Industrial Education in Bengal.** (1888-1908) para-7, p-11
2. **Ibid.**, para-3 p-20
3. **Imperial Gazetteer oidj In ep engal**, Vol. BII, p. 158-5

The Dehri workshop was established in 1873. It employed hundreds of carpenters and blacksmiths of Shahabad who learnt the technique of constructing canals while labourers learnt canal making. The Tribeni canal likewise afforded instruction to the labourers of Saran and Champaran.

The first medical institution set up by Government was the Medical School at Patna on June 1874 under the supervision of Richard Temple. In 1892 this school was thrown open to female students admitted free of charge and granted Rs. 10/- from Provincial Revenues.

Thus new education was introduced to a society which was based on caste-system. The caste rigidity was still very strong and intercaste marital connections were not permissible. Below the castes there were many sub-castes observing the same rigidity. Interdining among members of different castes and sub-castes was not at all in practice. Women were kept in seclusion, specially women of higher castes. Infant marriage was universal. Marriage of widows of the higher castes was not permissible. There was no social intercourse between high and low castes.

The percentage of English-educated persons remained very low. But some of the educated people in Bihar distinguished themselves in the social life of this period and became important factors in bringing about social changes.

The growth in the number of literates in Bihar began to have its effect by the eighties of the 19th century. The demand for higher education and more share in governmental jobs increased. The more enterprising among Biharis began to cross the seas for studying in England. Among the Bihari Hindus the lead in English education was taken by the Kayasthas, who were traditionally service-holders and did not entirely depend upon land for their livelihood. The Bhumihars and Rajputs who formed the bulk of the landed aristocracy and land holding peasantry followed suit. The Brahmins also took to English education, although their response varied because of local conditions.

The demand for higher education led to the opening of more colleges through public contributions by the end of the century. The public at large now began to take a more active interest in the spread of education. The English schools and colleges helped the formation of the Bihari educated middle class. The leaders of Bihar public life at the beginning of the 20th century were the product of these schools and colleges established in the second half of nineteenth century.

CHAPTER-II

EDUCATION UNDR CURZON

NEW DEVELOPMENT IN EDUCATION :

The end of the nineteenth century witnessed a rapid increase in the number of students throughout India. Between 1886 and 1901 the number of college students throughout India increased from 11,501 to 23,009 and that of pupils in secondary Schools from, 4,29,093 to 6,33,728. And the outlay on education by the government and localboards rose from Rs. 132.80 lakhs in 1885 to Rs. 177.04 lakhs in 1901. But the general tendency to regard schooling simply as a means of qualifying for clerical or professional employment retarded the primary instruction among the masses. At this juncture Governor-General Lord Curzon arrived who combined enthusiastic idealism with abounding energy and great insight into the details of administration. Fearing no problem, however thorny he gradually set himself to grapple with the thorniest problem of all[2].

Curzon came to India when a new change in the political life of his country was taking place. The expansion of education had led to political consciousness and opening for a new horizon, giving

1. The Cambridge History of India, Vol. VI. p. 348.
2. Ibid., p. 349.

a momentum to the national movement. The work of national awakening and regeneration had no doubt been started by the Indian National Congress, but its influence was also limited to the educated classes, 'the microscopic minority'.

It was the group of educated men, which used to express their views relating to administration, education and economic affairs in the form of resolutions of Indian National Congress. It was felt, however, that a storm was gathering on the political horizon of India. There arose a new school of nationalism believing in the revolutionary activities when pistols and bombs were frequently used against British officers. In Poona a youngman named Damodar Chapekar shot dead a British official and this incident echoed throughout the British empire, and the machinery of the empire was alerted against the Indian youth. George Hamilton, Secretary of State for India, wrote to Curzon to keep a tighter hand over education, both as regards its objects, and control of administration.[1]

Curzon appointed a Commission to enquire into the conditions and prospects of the Universities in India. The University Act of 1904 was passed on the basis of the recommendation of this Commission. The main purpose of the University Act of 1904 was to confer upon the universities of India a working constitution and to invest them with general powers which were required to enable them to control and supervise higher education in accordance with the principles and policy approved by the Government of India. The main result of the Act was to make the control and supervision of the Government over university more direct and effective.

No doubt, Curzon was trying to suppress the revolutionary trends in India, but impartial and uninterested persons would admit that a reform was urgently needed. Indeed, Curzon's educational policy guided the education of India for many years.

EDUCATION IN BIHAR DURING THE PERIOD 1899 to 1905

In the last decades of the nineteenth century the elementary education of the masses received much attention. The primary education was given priority in the terms of reference of Education Commission 1882. Moreover, the proposals of this Commission,

1. George Hamilton to Curzon, 18 May 1899, C. P.

which influenced the subsequent government policy, were those relating to the expansion of primary education. In 1885 Ripon inaugurated the scheme of Local Self-Government. The control of primary education passed from the District Magistrate to the District Board. The development of grants-in-aid system and the stimulation of private enterprise in the field of primary education began.

The beginning of the twentieth century opened a new chapter in the history of education in India. In 1900 the Secretary of State, George Hamilton drew the attention of the Government to the necessity of the continuance of Government control, guidance and assistance of higher education [1] But the educational policy of 1904 reiterated the views of the Commission of 1882 in regard to the importance of primary education. In the Simla Conference of 1901 Curzon said : "The teaching of the masses in the vernacular had shrivelled and pinned since the cold breath of Macaulay's rhetoric passed over the field of Indian languages and text books."[2] This Conference condemned the payment-by-results 'as uncertain in operation and tending to encourage cramming.' The Government of India accepted the views of the Simla Conference and ordered that the results-grant-system was to be stopped as soon as possible. It was replaced by a system of payment in which attendance, building, circumstances of the locality, teachers, nature of instruction and outlay from other sources would all be taken into consideration in assessing the grant. As a result of this decision payment-by-results was abolished in 1902-03. The Government of India made a special educational grant of 10 lakhs in 1902-03 to assist the carrying out of the recommendations of the Simla Conference.

The majority of primary schools in Bihar were situated in Board areas, though they were controlled by the department. The report of the Director of Public Instructions in 1901 said that the relation between the District Boards and Education Department was harmonious. The suggestions and recommendations made by

1. George Hamilton to Curzon, 18 May 1899, C. P.
2. Proceedings of Simla Conference, September 1901 (Quoted in Education Proceedings, Government of Bengal, January 1904, No. 12-13, P-18).

the Deputy Inspectors generally received due consideration from the District Board. Local Boards in some districts of Bihar were also entrusted with the administration of the primary fund and the control of the primary education. The Local Boards, which had the charge of primary education in the beginning of this century, were the Local Boards of Monghyr and Bhagalpur in the Bhagalpur Division.

The recommendation of the Indian Education Commission of 1882 added a new controlling body to the Department of Public Instruction. The control and administration of primary and middle schools was given to the local bodies. The Local Self-Government Act of 1885 was put into force in sixteen districts of Bihar including Patna District on 1 October 1885. But by the year 1887-88 all the regulation districts came within the purview of the Act. With the introduction of this Act the district committees of the regulation districts were abolished. The Government middle and primary schools came under the control of the District Boards, but the District Committee continued to function in the non-regulation district.

In 1899-1900 the number of primary schools in the Bengal Presidency decreased by 205 or 0·4 per cent, but their strength increased by 9,438 or 0.76 percent. The average number of pupils in a *Pathshala* also rose from 25·5 to 26 percent[1]. The decrease was due to the elimination of weak schools. It was supported by the fact that the number of primary schools of the upper classes, which served as a connecting link between primary and secondary schools, increased by 68 or 1·6 percent. The divisions of Bihar which showed an increase in the number and strength of upper primary schools were Bhagalpur and Chotanagpur. The Patna division showed an increase in the number of schools but a decrease in the number of pupils. The number and strength of lower primary schools declined in the division of Patna and Bhagalpur, but it increased in the Chotanagpur division.[2]

The following table shows the state of lower primary schools in the three divisions of Bihar between 1898 and 1900.[3]

1. **Report on Public Instruction in Bengal** (1899-1900), p. 72.
2. *Ibid.*, p. 72.
3. *Ibid*, p. 88.

TABLE No. 1

Divisions :	1898–99		1899–1900	
	Schools.	Boys.	Schools.	Boys.
Patna	5,668	150,052	5,599	147,235
Bhagalpur	3,410	76,834	3,379	75,343
Chotanagpur	2,148	55,435	2,198	57,699

The decrease in the number of schools in the Patna division was 69, while that of Bhagalpur 31. The Director in his report expressed satisfaction that inspite of these losses there was an advancement of strong schools year by year. This decline was mostly confined to those weak schools which had less than 29 pupils.

In the Patna division, the number of upper primary schools was 233, the Bhagalpur division had 277 such schools, and Chotanagpur division possessed 142 upper primary schools.[1]

The following table classified the primary schools for boys in each division according to the numerical strength.[2]

TABLE No. 2

Division	Total No. of schools.	Total No. of schools with 50 students.	Pupils	Total No. of schools with less than 50 and more than 40 students.	Pupils
Patna	233	144	7,159	68	2,996
Bhagalpur	277	85	5,279	73	3,210
Chotanagpur	142	59	3,590	41	1,702

Table No. 2 continued (given below)

Division:	Schools with less than 40 and more than 30 students		Schools with less than 20 & more than 10 students	
	Schools.	Pupils.	Schools.	Pupils.
Patna	12	314	—	—
Bhagalpur	46	1,146	11	180
Chotanagpur	7	186	1	18

1. *Ibid.*, p.87
2. *Ibid.*, p.84

The weak schools and their attendance had diminished, while the strong ones, viz., those with attendance of 30 to 40 and 40 to 50 were steadily progressing. The schools of the strongest class, viz., those with 50 pupils and more, generally developed into middle schools and hence those showing losses were frequently converted into secondary schools.[1] But the primary education for the masses was not treated with all the importance it deserved, inspite of the recommendations of the Wood's Despatch and the Indian Education Commission of 1882: both had declared that primary education deserved the greater care of the state and a larger claim on public money than higher education, yet the grant sanctioned to primary education was inadequate for its proper expansion and improvement. It was realised that a large increase in the cost of primary education was inevitable and the limited resources of the local bodies were unable to meet two-thirds of the cost of primary education. Therefore, the Government Resolution of 1904 accepted the proposition that 'active extension of primary education is one of the most important duties of the State'. Presumably this was the result of public consciousness about the importance of primary education: in fact, there was a growing demand for more schools and compulsory primary education.[2]

The Government now decided to give larger grants to primary education, and this view was duly incorporated in the Government Resolution of March 1904.[3]

There was an increase in the number of secondary schools by 5 in Bengal (which included Bengal, Bihar and Orissa) in the beginning of this century. The number of pupils increased to 233,074 from 230,433 : this was an increase of 1.1 percent.[4] Secondary schools were of two classes—high and middle. The former taught upto the Matriculation standard of the Calcutta University and the latter a standard short of this called the middle scholarship standard. Middle schools again were either middle English or middle vernacular schools. Secondary schools of all

1. *Ibid.*, p. 85
2. Raja Ram Singh, The growth and evaluation of educational administration in Bihar (1946-P. U.), pp. 16-17.
3. *Ibid.*
4. **Bengal Administration Report** (1900-01), p. 212.

classes, taken together declined by 30 or 1.2 percent but the pupils increased by 5,895 or 2.6 percent. High English schools increased by 43 schools and 12,274 pupils. On the other hand, middle English schools had decreased by 24 with 3,216 pupils and middle Vernacular schools by 49 with 3,163 pupils.[1]

The middle vernacular schools were becoming unpopular mainly because English had come to be. established as a better means for employment. To a promising boy there was little prospect if he obtained a middle vernacular school certificate. At the same time, it required a longer time for a student, who read in a middle vernacular school upto the middle standard, to come to the Entrance Examination. It was, therefore, better to read in an English school from the very beginning. Thus the unpopularity of middle vernacular school was due to the following facts :—

(1) English education was considered more helpful in getting livelihood.

(2) Middle examination pass-certificate holders were no longer allowed to enter the vernacular medical schools or to go in for the Mukhtarship examination—the lucrative avenues of employment were closed to them.

The Inspector of Schools, Patna division wrote : 'Pure vernacular education is not valued by the people nor it is paying. The desire for an English education has become universal, and people even in rural tracts are anxious to give their children such an education. In view of these facts, I believe, there will be no objection to the gradual conversion of all middle vernacular schools into middle English schools'.[2]

The District Magistrate of Shahabad also wrote : 'The introduction of English in these (middle vernacular) schools will not only make them more popular, but would secure the supply of the sort of teachers most in demand for primary schools.'[3] The Government initiative had led to the opening of zila schools in all the district headquarters. In 1900 the number of high English

---

1. **Report of Director of Public Instruction,** Bengal (1899–1900), pp.51–52. The figures include the secondary schools of Bengal, Bihar and Orissa of this period.

2. Report on Public Instruction in Bengal (1899–1900), p. 55.

3. *Ibid.*

schools managed by the Department and by the Municipalities or joint committees did not increase, but these schools gained in strength Moreover, the aided high schools increased : one new school in Patna and 2 in Bhagalpur. The aided schools were distributed as follows : Patna-9, Bhagalpur-11, Chotanagpur-3. The unaided high schools also increased throughout Bengal but Patna lost one school. These schools were thus distributed : Patna-22, Bhagalpur-8, and Chotanagpur-2 during this period. Thus the total number of aided and unaided high schools in Bihar was 55.[1]

The suspicion about English education, which was universal in the 19th century in Bihar, was now gone. Now people were much more inclined to get English education than in the past.

The aided middle English schools were distributed as follows : Patna-24, Bhagalpur-21 and Chotanagpur-35. The unaided middle English schools were 28 in all these divisions of the province. Patna had 14, Bhagalpur-9 and Chotanagpur-5.[2]

The Government high schools were either collegiate schools or branch schools under the control of Principals of colleges to which they were attached; or zila schools of first, second or third class according to the strength of 300 and upwards, between 300 and 175, and less than 175. In 1900 Patna City School was transferred to the second class, because its strength had been reduced from 309 to 242.

Curzon touched all branches of Indian education. The immediate result of the University Act 1904 was to reduce the number of affiliated colleges which in 1902 stood at 192 for British India.[3] Even so, in Bihar the number of colleges remained static during the early years of the 20th century.

In the beginning of this century there were 11 Government, 7 aided and 25 unaided colleges with 1 municipal college working in Bengal.[4] In Bengal the number of students attending Arts college increased from 7,204 to 7,868. The share of Bihar in this growth of higher education was negligible. Higher education was not only

1. *Ibid.*
2. *Ibid.*, pp. 62–63.
3. Education in India (1902-1907), p. 37, In 1902 the number of Arts colleges in India was 188 which was reduced to 161 in 1907.
4. *Ibid.*, p. 31.

top-heavy, but unevenly distributed. Initially colleges, like joint-stock companies, were established in the Presidency towns, specially in Calcutta which had the maximum degree of concentration.[1] After sometime they were started at other places too, but they remained confined to the provincial headquarters and chief towns for many years.

Bihar had only six Arts colleges. At Patna, the Patna College was a Government college while the Bihar National College was a private college. The Tej Narayan Jubilee College at Bhagalpur was also a private college. The Dublin University College at Hazaribagh was a missionary institution aided by the Government. And the remaining two private colleges, the Bhumihar Brahmin College at Muzaffarpur and the Diamond Jubilee College at Monghyr were unaided.

The Table No. 3 given below gives a picture of the strength of students in these colleges towards the close of the last century.[2]

Th· falling of the numerical strength of the Patna College was not accompanied by any corresponding increase in the figures of the Bihar National College, which was a first-grade college working at the same time. In the early years of the present century, the Bhumihar Brahmin College had 65 students mostly drawn from the districts north of the Ganga.

TABLE No. 3

College	Number of students 1896	1897	1898	1899	1900
1. Patna College	193	188	216	235	205
2. Dublin University Mission College	—	—	—	—	24
3. T. N. J. College	114	165	142	178	173
4. B. N. College	145	185	266	256	263
. Monghyr Diamond Jubilee College	—	—	—	—	70
6. Bhumihar Brahmin College	—	—	—	—	65

1. D. B. Mira, op, cit. p. 305.
2. **Report on Public Instruction in Bengal** (1899- 1900). p. 31."

The following table shows variation in the number of students in the different colleges during this period.[1]

TABLE No. 4

Name of Colleges	Number on the Rolls on the 31st March of 1902	1903	1904	1905
1. Patna College	149	151	133	146
2. T. N. J. College, Bhagalpur	173	147	138	166
3. B. N. College, Bankipur	107	138	169	180
4. Dublin University Mission College, Hazaribagh	36	29	21	73
5. B. B. College, Muzaffarpur	154	121	71	105
6. Diamond Jubilee College, Monghyr	27	34	39	26

The total number of students reading in three most important colleges of Bihar--the Patna College, the Biha · National College and the Tej Narayan College in 1900 was 641, but it was reduced to 492 in 1905. On the other hand there was an increase in three new colleges of Bihar.

The Government colleges in Bengal sent up 632 students, the aided colleges 432 and the unaided ones 1,936 for the examinations in 1900. The Government colleges passed 50 percent of their students, and the aided and unaided 37 and 33 percent respectively. But the Patna College did the worst, percentage of pass being 26 percent only. Among the aided colleges the Dublin University Mission College did it best with 82 percent pass. This was the only institution of higher learning in the Chotanagpur division. It gave considerable impetus to the progress of higher education in the division, which was predominated by aborigines.[2]

In 1900 out of 205 students on the rolls of the Patna College, 161 were Biharis, 53 Bengalis and 1 European.[3] This was a marked change from the situation found in the nineteenth century when the Patna College remained dominated by Bengalis. The Patna College

1. **Report on Public Instruction in Bengal (Supplement), (1905-1906), p. 10.**
2. **Report on Public Instruction Bengal (1899-1900), p.36.**
3. **Report from the Principal of Patna College (1899-1900).**

was undoubtedly developing as the premier educational institution in Bihar, but it had not taken the same position as that of some of the other important Arts Colleges of Bengal at the turn of the last century. Even so, the Patna College had been described next to the Presidency College in 1905.[1] It was much improved and its expansion scheme took shape in 1905, laying down the line of development for many years to come.

A proposal to establish a model Government college and secondary school at Ranchi came up for discussion during this period at a Conference held at the private room of the Lt. Governor of Bengal, Andrew Fraser on 4 April 1904.[2] Many eminent persons and Government officers attended it. The Lt. Governor expressed his desire to establish a model Government College and a secondary school outside Calcutta in some good climate on the lines laid down by the Universities Commisson Report, which had been passed as the Indian Universities Act. He observed that a residential college and school should be opened at Ranchi. This should be the best college and school that the Government could establish and they should serve as a model for future institutions. All the suggestions regarding the building of hostels, class rooms, etc. of the proposed college at Ranchi were generally agreed to. It was decided that the proposal to establish a separate school for the sons of zamindars, which had been under consideration in Bengal for some time past, should be finally abandoned. The sons of zamindars should be educated just as the sons of other ordinary gentlemen.

A meeting of the noblemen, landed gentry and professionals and businessmen was held at Belvedere, the official residence of the Governor-General at Calcutta on 17 September 1904 in connection with the proposal to establish a model Government college and a Government econdary school at Ranchi.[3] This was attended by Asutosh Mukerjee, Maharaja Rameshwar Singh Bahadur of Darbhanga, Maharaja Sir Ravaneshwar Prasad Singh Bahadur of Gidhour, Syed Khurshid, Nawab of Patna City and Syed Shurffuddin

1. J. N. Sarkar & J. C. Jha op., cit., p. 93.
2. Proceedings of Government of Bengal, General Department (Education), May 1906, Nos.5–6, p. 95.
3. *Ibid.*, No. 7, p. 95,

of Patna along with 60 other gentlemen of Bengal. Raja Ramnarain Singh Bahadur of Khaira, Monghyr, Raja Surendra Narain Singh of Barwari, Bhagalpur, M. S. Zafar, Nawab of Gaya along with 56 other persons expressed sympathies with the object of the meeting, regretting their unavoidable inability to attend it.

The Lt. Governor expressed the hope that the leading lights of Bihar would help the scheme for a model Government college and a secondary school outside Calcutta put forward by him. The demand for such an institution had been made by zamindars more than once. The Mohammadan community of the province was also pressing for an institution exclusively for their children. But the Lt. Governor ruled out his support for such an institution and declared that he did not believe in exclusive education. He further said: 'The third class to which I refer is composed of successful professionals and businessmen...who have to send their sons away from home for their college education.'[1]

The site for the college was fixed at Ranchi. Though this proposal could not materialise during this period, the interest taken by the various sections indicate a change in the attitude of Biharis.

In Bihar *Parda* was a great stumbling block to the growth of female education. The female education among the Mohammadan residents of Patna was carried on by *Atus* or *Parda-Nashin* ladies who did not stir out in public. In Patna city during this period there were 10 to 15 *Atus* who taught girls that went to them. There was a female *Madarsa* in Patna city opened by Mussammat Rashidan, a literate lady, wife of Maulavi Mohammad Yehia, a pleader. But this school was closed after sometime. Individual efforts for female education among Bihari Hindus met with greater difficulty; in 1900–01 at Bahpura, a big village near Bihta station, a Kayastha lady, who taught girls could not get sufficient number of students, while at Arup, a village near Bikram in the Dinapur subdivision, a Babhan lady teaching girls with the help of '*Guru*' had great difficulty in getting Hindu female teachers.[2]

1. Proceedings of Government of Bengal, General Department (Education) May 1906, No. 70, pp. 96–97.
2. Proceedings of the Government of Bengal, General Department (Education), April-1906, Nos. 6–7, p. 59.

Eventually, the problem of spreading female education in Bihar caught the attention of the Lt. Governor of Bengal, Andrew Fraser. He sought opinion from literate citizens and officials of the Education Department in Bihar. This resulted in the formulation of a scheme for promoting female education in Patna. A. Pedler, Director of Public Instruction, Bengal referred the proposals to foster female education in Bihar to the Secretary, Government of Bengal.[1]

The following experiments were proposed :[2]

(a) **Zenana Education by house to house visitation** :

One Mohammadan lady was appointed for the purpose. She taught only the girls of her religion. The Inspector of Schools recommended that a Hindu female teacher for Hindu girls should be appointed.

(b) **Zenana education by central gatherings** :

In Patna city a centre was established for this purpose under a qualified Mohammaden lady teacher. The owner of the house, in which this school was located, refused to lend rooms, as a result of which the school collapsed.

(c) **Training class for native mistresses** :

There was such a class attached to the Bankipur Mission Girls' School. This school was working satisfactorily, according to the report of the Director and Inspector.

(d) **Establishment of Secondary and High Schools for girls** :

The premier institution for the education of girls was Bankipur Female High School. The average number of girls in this school was 50, but all of them were Bengalis. Since this institution was under the influence of the Brahmo-Samaj it could not attract the Bihar population. Moreover, the Commissioner of Patna was not satisfied with the management of this school. The Director of Public Instruction, while discussing female education in Bihar, remarked about this school, "It has not been doing good work since its establishment". So a middle English school for 'Parda-nashin' girls was sanctioned for such girls of Bihar who observed *parda*.[3]

1. *Ibid.*, p. 60.
2. The Director of Public Instruction, Bengal to Bengal Government, Calcutta, 16 January, 1906.
3. Proceedings of Government of Bengal, General Department (Education), April 1906, Nos. 8-9, pp. 60-61.

Unfortunately, there were many social prejudices against female education in Bihar. Realising these prejudices, Purnendu Narayan Sinha, a prominent public figure and Government pleader at Patna said that the question of female education should be dealt with cautiously in Bihar. He wanted to proceed on the lines of least resistance by finding out the existing materials and improving them.[1] The Government, therefore, tried to encourage female education through *Parda-schools*, and the Director of Public Instructions tried to get *Parda-nashin* girls and Hindu lady teachers. A system of monthly stipend of Rs. 5 together with a capitation grant of annas 4 for each girl receiving instruction was proposed for Atus to give incentive to female education.[2]

But even this moderate scheme did not cut much ice because of the conservatism prevailing in the society. In 1901 there were 65' girls schools with 939 pupils, and in 1905 there were one high school, one middle English school, and one model primary school for girls which were teaching 57, 47 and 35 girls respectively in the Patna district while 456 girls were receiving instruction in the boys' schools. There were 2 peripatetical lady teachers teaching 27 females under their tuition on 31 March 1904, 4 pupils taught while studying in the training schools for mistresses opened in 1904–05.[3]

The Patna branch of the Calcutta Central Mohammadan Association presented an address to the Lt. Governor during his visit to Bihar. This address was mainly occupied with proposals for the improvement and advancement of female education. The question of female education in Bihar came prominently before the public in 1904 when the Director of Public Instruction visited Bankipur Female School on 9 August. Plans to attract Bihari girls to this school were discussed. The Commssioner of the Patna division moved in this matter and appointed a committee of the following gentlemen :

1. Nilambar Prasad
2. Gajadhar Prasad

---

1. Purnendu Narayan Sinha to the Private Secretary to Lt. Governor of Bengal, 24 July, 1905.
2. A. Pedler to the Bengal Government, 16 January, 1906.
3. L. S. S. O'Malley, (ed.), B. D. G. Patna, p. 172.

3. Brahmadeo Narayan
4. Nareswar Sahay
5. Hasan Imam
6. Hakim Nasirul Haque
7. Brij Bansi Sahay.

According to W. Billing, Inspector of Schools, Patna division, there were 60 girls in high schools, 41 in middle English schools, 37 in upper primary schools and 1,511 in lower primary schools totalling 1,649 pupils. In 1903–04 there were 1,045 girls and in the year proceeding the number of girls was 1,265 and in 1901–02 there were 1,100 girl students in the whole division.[1] There was a peripatetic teacher for Patna town, who was required to work solely among the Hindus. In 1905 she was teaching 26 girls in 12 Hindu families. On 24 April 1905 the Government sanctioned the scheme for the education of Mohammadans : three classes of *Maktabs,* liberal subsidies and an inspecting Maulvi were established. On 31 October 1905 the Government sanctioned a middle school for Hindu *Parda-nashin* ladies at a monthly cost of Rs. 285.[2]

Thus it is evident that the Government was doing all that was possible to advance the cause of female education, both Hindu and Mohammadan. But there was great difficulty in getting qualified teachers, especially Hindus. There was no dearth of female Brahmo or Christian teachers. But the orthodox Hindus and Mohammadans were still hesitant in putting their girls under them. The Inspector of Public Instruction remarked : "Bihar is ready enough to receive female education, but it is not yet prepared to let her educated females to act as teachers, nor are there many qualified for the work."[3] In fact, the prejudice against ladies taking teaching profession retarded the female education in Bihar. Attempts were therefore made to get trained female teachers from United Provinces, where there was no such prejudice.

1. Proceedings of Government of Bengal, General Department (Education), April 1906, Nos. 6–7, p. 59.
2. *Ibid.*, p. 62.
   Ibid., Nos. 8–9, pp. 60–61.
3. *Idib.*

Missionaries were doing laudable work during this period for the advancement of education in Bihar specially in the field of female education. In the Santhal Parganas missionaries were running some of the best middle and primary schools for aboriginal boys and girls. They created a written Santhali language and published many books suitable for use in primary schools[1]. Since the latter part of the nineteenth century they were running twelve Mission schools[2]. The three separate Missions–the Lutheran Mission, the S. P. G. Mission and Roman Catholic Mission–were managing many boys and girls schools independent of each other at Ranchi. The Lutheran Mission had a high school, a girls school at Ranchi and 32 primary schools at out-stations. The St. Paul's high school at Ranchi was its most important institution. This Mission maintained 28 boys' schools, 11 girls' schools and 46 mixed schools throughout the Ranchi district[3]. Apart from the High School at Ranchi, the Catholic Mission had no less than 230 boys' schools in Chotanagpur, majority of which were in the Ranchi district. There was also an industrial school managed by the missionaries which opened in 1894.[4]

But the oldest Missionary school in Bihar was the St. Joseph's High School at Bankipur which was opened as early as 1853. The second school was the St. Michael's High School situated between Bankipur & Dinapur.[5] The Railway Workshop at Jamalpur attracted missionaries' attention. They established one technical school there which was originally a night school. The Dublin University Mission at Hazaribagh was running the St. Columba's Collegiate School along with the college founded by it.[6]

The Missionary schools were mostly patronised by Europeans or Anglo-Indians. But the people in Bihar were still allergic to the missionary schools. The main areas of missionary influence, however, were the towns of Chotanagpur and the Santhal Parganas. A. Pedler, the D. I. P. of Bengal wrote to the Government of

1. O'Malley, (ed,) and S. C. Mukherjee, (revised), B. D. G. p. 361.
2. K. K. Basu, Missionary Education in Santhal Parganas, JBRS, Vol, XXX, Part II, p. 180.
3. M. G. Hallet, (ed.), B. O. D. G., pp 233–234.
4. *Ibid*, 239.
5. O'Malley, (ed.), B. O. D. G., Patna, p. 156.
6. *Ibid*, Hazaribagh, p. 79.

Bengal : "It is, of course, most noble and devoted on the part of the missionary bodies and of the lady missionaries who have undertaken this field of work to strive to educate and elevate Indian girls, but the preponderance of the missionary element in female education has possibly its drawbacks, and it is probable that girl pupils would be much more numerous in our girl schools, which are subsidised by Government, if parents did not fear that in addition to receiving secular education, their children's religious belief would be shaken. Were this fear removed, I believe, a great improvement could have been effected both in the number of girls attending girls' schools in towns and also in the educational work done in zenanas."[1]

It was felt that the Government initiative in the field of female education was essential. Not even the school at Bankipur was attracting Bihari girls. In fact, this school had not a single student really belonging to the province of Bihar in the higher classes. The Bihari girls of whom there were some in the lower classes, always gave up their studies quite early. It was only the more or less temporarily residing Bengali population and almost entirely those of Brahmos whose children attended the higher classes of the Bankipur school. It was felt that girl schools or high schools might be established in such advanced towns at Bhagalpur and Muzaffarpur. But it was apprehended that the local people would not be ready to send their daughters and the students would be entirely from among the daughters of Bengali pleaders practising in these towns.[2] So the Director of Public Instruction decided to start the girl education from the primary stage. He sought permission to establish model girl schools for the primary stage. He wrote : "These schools should not be influenced by such considerations as the backwardness of the district, as our object is to stimulate a desire for female education by providing facilities where none at present exist. It is only in the case of girl schools in higher stage contemplated by the Government of India that the selection of advanced localities is essential, since no such schools can thrive in places where there do not already exist a large number of girl schools in various stages

1. Proceedings of the Government of Bengal, General Department, (Education), 1904, No. 31, p. 213.
2. A. Pedler to Bengal Government, 1 February 1902.

upto middle standard."[1] The Government sanctioned money for this proposal.

It was decided to open 37 additional model primary schools for girls during the years 1904-05. In Bihar one such school was opened in each of the following districts—Gaya, Champaran, Muzaffarpur, Monghyr, Bhagalpur, Purnea, Ranchi, Singhbhum, manbhum and Palamau.[2]

The education department of the Government of Bengal considered other branches of education as special instruction (section) during the period. These covered (1) Law classes attached to Arts colleges (2) Medical Institutions (3) Arts Schools and Industrial Schools (4) Training Schools for masters and mistresses.

There was no institution in Bihar exclusively devoted to the teaching of Law. Law classes were attached to some of the first-grade Arts Colleges, which were attended by students who desired to qualify for the B. L. or the Pleadership examination.

In Bihar Law classes were attached to the Patna College, Tej Narayan Jubilee College and Bihar National College. In the beginning of this century the average number of law students in the Patna College was 25 and the average monthly roll number was 29. The expenditure of this college was met purely from private funds. The amount realised from fees and fines in 1900 was 1,780 and it sufficed for expenditure. The Tej Narayan Jubilee College, Bhagalpur, had an average of 40 students and the expenditure from fee and fines was 1,630. The third college, the Bihar National College, had 113 pupils in law classes and its expenditure was 4,988.[3]

There was during this period only one Medical College in Bengal, viz., the Calcutta Medical College. Bihar had a Medical School named the Temple Medical School, Bankipur established in 1874. The average number of students in this school was 151 and

1. Ibid., 11 July 1902
2. Ibid., 2 February, 1904
3. Proceeding of Government of Bengal, General Department (Education), 1900, p. 104

the total expenditure of the school was Rs. 24,993. The most important change was made in the management of this school when at the turn of the last century it passed from the hands of Director of Public Instruction to those of the Inspector General of Civil Hospitals, Bengal. The Director quoted the following lines from the report of the Inspector General of Hospitals : "I found at my first inspection of the Temple Medical School at Bankipur that there was no opportunity for the male students to see anything of women or their special diseases, as all female were treated in a separate institution. Such one sided training is obviously most injurious. I therefore, gave orders that a certain number of women should be treated in the General Hospital".[1]

The Bihar School of Engineering formally opened on 11 July 1896 by the Lieutenant Governor of Bengal was under the management of the Principal of the Patna College, assisted by a Board of Visitors. The number of students on 31 March 1900 was 90 which increased to 105 in 1903 as against 110 in the previous year. Of these 83 were Biharis (Hindus and Mohammadens), 20 domiciled Bengalis, 1 Hindu from the United Provinces and 1 European.[2]

In 1904 a hostel was built and in the following year it was found that this had developed a marked degree of corporate and social life amongst the students.[3]

There had been repeated requests from the leading citizens of Patna to raise the status of the school, converting it into an Engineering College. The history of the school showed steady advancement. And it was natural that Bihari educated men desired to have an Engineering College. This school was the result of their own initiative : it had originated through an endowment subscribed by the Biharis. Naturally enough, there was preference for the sons of the soil in the matter of admissions. To add to the local initiative the Government sanctioned a grant of Rs. 4,884 towards the construction of the Hostel.[4]

---

1. **Report on Public Instruction**, Bengal, 1899-1900, p. 109
2. **Report on Public Instruction in Bengal, 1902-03, para 6, p. 30**
3. **Technical and Industrial Instruction in Bengal (1888-1900)** para-7, p. 11
4. A. Pedler to the Director of Public Instruction, Bengal, 4, Nov. 1903.

At one time there was a proposal to transfer the Sibpur Engineering College in Bengal to Ranchi. There were eight firstgrade training schools managed by the Government of Bengal in 1900, the Patna Training School being one of them. The Patna Normal School (established on 1 October 1863 with 2 students) used to give training to the teachers of elementary vernacular schools. Later an English department was attached to it for the training of teachers in Anglo-Vernacular schools.[1] But it was abolished very soon. The Patna Training school, a first grade training school, gave training to Matriculates and F. A.s for the job of school teachers. The course of instruction extended over a year, and was both theoretical and practical. The practical instruction was carried on in the middle school attached to the training school. Text books were prescribed by the department and an examination was held annually to which not only students of the teachership classes, but also all graduates and such undergraduates who had at least three years experience as teachers were admissible. Three grades of certificates were granted by the department to the successful candidates, first grade certificate being granted to graduates while second and third grade certificates were given to First Arts and Matriculation stage students.[2]

The Government Training School of lower grade at Motihari prepared teachers for the primary schools of Champaran. It consisted of two classes, the higher teaching the second class standard of middle vernacular schools and the lower teaching the upper primary standard. Both classes received instruction in the art of teaching. The students of the upper class appeared at the 'Guruship' examination. At the examination in 1900, 3 out of 4 candidates sent up were successful. Of 7 candidates sent up for the upper primary examination only one passed.[3]

The lower grade Government Training School at Daltonganj had 11 pupils. Since this school did not pass any pupil at any examination, the Inspector suggested its transfer to a more suitable place.

---

1. B. Sahay, op. cit., p. 336
2. Report on Public Instruction in Bengal, 1899-1900, p-101
3. Ibid., p-96

The Ranchi Training school, however showed a higher percentage of success during this period.[1] It passed 18 candidates out of 20. The standards for the Patna and Ranchi training schools were brought into uniformity in the beginning of this century. Therefore the Government decided to arrange a common examination for two schools.[2]

The total number of training institutions in Bengal increased from 33 to 61 and pupils from 1,285 to 1,471 in 1902-03. There were four unaided training schools, three for male and one for females in the Bhagalpur Division.[3] The only unaided training school for mistresses had 15 students in 1903. It was a school for the training of native female teachers at Banagoria in the Bhagalpur division.[4]

A proposal for the establishment of a Central Training School at Bhagalpur came in 1905. A. Pedler requested the Government to instruct the Inspector of Works, Bhagalpur, to procure plans and estimates for the building.[5] Hornell was selected to be in-charge of the Central Training School. With a view to improving the efficiency of schools for boys training schools for primary school teachers were sanctioned at 134 sub-divisional headquarters of the districts of the province of Bengal. Thus all the sub-divisional headquarters of Bihar got one such school.[6]

In south Bihar elementary technical schools also existed. The Chotanagpur division had 11 technical schools during this period, 9 aided and 2 unaided. The aided schools received small grants either from the district fund or the departmental primary grant. Most of these schools taught blacksmith's work. Three of these schools deserve special mention : (1) the school at Beniadih located in Giridih had 40 students, (2) the Chaibasa school under Anglican Mission had 16 pupils and (3) the third was the Ghatshila school.[7]

1. **Ibid.**, p-98
2. **Ibid.**, p-97
3. **Ibid.**, (1902-03), p-24
4. **Ibid.**, p-27
5. Proceedings of the Government of Bengal, General Department (Education) July, 1906, no. 6, p-13
6. Reports on Public Instruction in Bengal, 1902-03, P-20
7. **Ibid.**, p-35

In the Hazaribagh district there were four technical schools. The Giridih school was occasionally helped by the Railway Company. This school was doing useful work and was able to supply all the skilled native labour required in the colliery. The schools at Hurlung, Bagda and Chitrapur had 12, 15 and 22 students respectively. These taught only blacksmith's work.[1]

The Ranchi Industrial School was a Government institution. It had 43 pupils in 1900, all of them belonging to aboriginal races. The school was maintained by Government grants supplemented by the sale-proceeds of articles manufactured in the school and the interest on the assets of the *Chutia Fair Fund.*[2] The christian influence in this area was very much marked.

The number of students in this school on 31 March 1901 was 46 and 50 in 1902. This did not include the students of Ranchi Zila school who learnt manual work in this industrial school.

The students got stipends, the rate varying from Re. 1/–to Rs. 3/– a month. They were taught carpentry, and blacksmith's work, carriage painting, free hand drawing, practical geometry and elementary arithmetic.[3]

The industrial school at Ranchi was established by the Government in the year 1876. In 1901, J. S. Slater, Principal, Civil Engineering college visited the school, and submitted a note on the development of the school through the introduction of machinery in it. The Commissioner of Chotanagpur represented to the Government that the main hope of advancement for the Kols was in being able to obtain technical instruction for getting employment in the mines and workshops which were being developed rapidly. So the conversion of this school into a school of sub-overseer standard was urged.[4]

The most remarkable feature of the period was the introduc-

---

1. Ibid., (1900-01), pp. 32-33
2. Ibid., p-30
3. Reports on Public Instruction in Bengal, 1902-03, p-33
4. A. Earl, Secretary to the Government of Bengal, to the Government of India, Calcutta, 24 February, 1904

tion of the new scheme of vernacular education in the primary and secondary schools in 1902. Under this scheme the system of teaching all subjects through the medium of English in the lowest classes in all types of schools was discontinued. The Government sanctioned five lakhs rupees for the expansion of primary education during this period.

The other noteworthy event of this period was the Government order for the formation of a system of school committee similar to those formed in the Central Provinces for schools of different classes in Bengal. Different rules were framed and approved for the formation of committees of management for aided upper primary schools in Bengal. But it was not considered expedient to form committees for the lower primary schools.[1]

By the end of the period important changes took place in every branch of education. True, there was a falling off in the attendance in primary schools in 1904-05 throughout Bengal but this decrease of 2.5 percent was attributed to failure of crops and the prevalence of disease.[2]

There was a decrease in the number of secondary schools also during this period. The decrease was mainly in the case of vernacular schools. The public examination for the middle standard was now abolished.

The most important event in the history of collegiate education during this period was the commencement of the new Universities Act. A new Senate of the University was formed and, when the Director reported that the committees were appointed, the work of producing a new body of regulations began. The state of affairs in the Patna College improved and the scheme for a model college at Ranchi advanced further with liberal subscriptions.[3]

In the Bhagalpur division, the education of the aboriginals was encouraged by the Government. The tribal pupils were 8,267 in 1903, of whom 826 were Christians. The largest increase

1. **Report on Public Instruction in Bengal**, 1992-03, p-10
2. **Report on Public Instruction in Bengal**, 1904-05, p-134
3. **Ibid.**, p-136

took place in the Santhal Parganas. A special grant from the provincial revenues of Rs. 9,500 per annum was placed at the disposal of the Deputy Commissioner of this district for the promotion of the Santhals' education.[1]

Missionary organisations were actively engaged in spreading education among aboriginal population. The total number of aboriginal pupils in the Chotanagpur division was 21,561 of whom 6,539 were Christians.[2]

An attempt was made to improve the system of education in Singhbhum district also, with a view to spreading education among the aboriginals. The medium of instruction in the Chaibasa Zila School was Bengali, which was not suitable for 'Ho' boys. Thomson, the Deputy Commissioner of Singhbhum, made efforts to increase the number of literate Hos. He recommended that the teaching staff in the Chaibasa schools should consist of greater part of Biharis or others whose mother tongue was Hindustani. He pointed out that Hindustani should be the Principal Language in the Chaibasa Zila School. He requested the Director of Public Instruction to give preference in admission to local inhabitants. The Director of Public Instruction accordingly took an initiative to give such a privilege to the children of local people.[3]

In 1901 a reformatory school at Hazaribagh was made over to the Education Department. It was placed under the supervision of a Board of Management which worked under the general control of the Director of Public Instruction, Bengal. The number of students here in 1900 was 213 and the boys admitted to the school in 1904 was 101. The training of boys was mainly in agriculture.[4]

---

1. **Report on Public Instruction in Bengal**, 1902-03, p. 43
2. **Ibid.**, p-43
3. Slater, Offg. Director of Public Instruction to Bengal Government, 17 March, 1902.
4. **Annual Report on the Reformatory School**, (Ed. Proceeding 1906, no. 13. p-37)

★

CHAPTER III

PRIMARY EDUCATION (1906-1921)

This was a period of great activity on different fronts and there was considerable progress in the field of education. The scheme for vernacular education, the organization of the Calcutta University, the deliberations of numerous conferences that were held and the strengthening of education services were some of the striking features at the beginning of this period. During this period there was significant change in the educational field. In 1910 Government showed their sense of increasing importance of education and transferred it from the Home Department to the newly created Department of Education. The increase in the number of primary schools and students in 1906 was 1.1 percent and 2.1 percent respectively.

At the end of the year 1906-07 there were 33-954 primary schools for boys attended by 9,07,222 boys and 40,233 girls.[2] But the number of schools in the different parts of the province varied considerably. In the Burdwan division for example which had an area of 13,949 square miles, there were 8,509 primary schools for the boys, whereas in the Chotanagpur division, which with the feudatory states of Kharsawan and Saraikela had an area of 27,703 square miles, there were only 2,799 primary schools.[3]

The following table shows the distribution of primary schools in different districts of Bihar in the beginning of this period.[4]

---

1. Report of Public Instruction in Bengal, 1905-06, 0-20
2. Report on the Progress of Education in Bengal, 1906-07 (Government of Bengal, Education Proceeding, 1908, p-16
3. Ibid. the Burdwan division included areas of Bihar aso
4. Proceedings of Government of Bengal, General Department, (Education), 1905

Districts :	Number of schools in 1904-05
Patna	1,180
Gaya	904
Shahabad	489
Champaran	673
Muzaffarpur	907
Darbhanga	929
Monghyr	929
Bhagalpur	861
Purnea	665
Santhal Pargana	781
Hazaribagh	485
Ranchi	763
Palamau	264
Singhbhum	340

The following table gives a picture of the number of pupils in primary schools in different divisions of Bihar from 1906 to 1911.[1] (From 1906 to 1908 Patna Division included the areas of Tirhut.)

Divisions :	1906-07	1907-08	1908-09	1909-10	1910-11
1. Patna	204,588	209,857	88,999	89,656	93,447
2. Tirhut	—	—	133,347	134,353	135,182
3. Bhagalpur	93,348	91,391	103,910	108,269	107,334
4. Chotanagpur	82,345	77,840	77,203	84,102	83,524
Total :	380,281	379,088	403,459	416,380	419,487

By the end of 1911, there were 21,990 primary schools for boys with 613,359 pupils in Bihar & Orissa. Of these pupils 5,478 were reading in Government schools, 10,377 in Board and Municipal schools, 5,043 in Native State Schools, 463,007 in aided schools and 124,454 in unaided schools. Of the total number of pupils 566,599 were boys and 46,760 girls.[2] The number of primary

1. Report on Public Instruction in Bengal, 1910-11 (Supplementary tables) no. 3

2. Report of Bihar and Orissa Administration, 1911-12, p-227

schools in six years, from 1905-06 to 1911-12 increased more than twice.[1] The report on the administration of the territories included in the province of Bihar and Orissa gives much information on educated 760,874 students.[2]

The increase was the largest under the head of primary schools. The proportion of pupils to the estimated population of school going age was 15.6 percent in 1911-12, an increase of 1.1 percent over the previous years figure of 14.7[3]

Of the various public institutions 352 with 19,412 pupils were under Government management, 217 with 18,373 pupils were placed under the management of district boards and municipalities, 182 with 7,983 pupils were under native states, 18,186 with 554, 548 pupils were in aided and 7,025 with 160,543 pupils were unaided.[4]

The total expenditure was Rs. 55,75,514 in 1911-12. The cost to provincial revenues increased from Rs. 14,75,024 to Rs. 19,53,474 and in native states revenue from 1,05,320 to Rs. 1,07,392 but the cost to district funds decreased from Rs. 7,28,244 to Rs. 7,22,107 and to municipal funds from Rs. 53,591 to Rs. 51,507. The expenditure from fees rose from Rs. 15,27,504 to Rs. 17,32,332 and from other sources from Rs. 9,25,957 to Rs. 10,08,602. The total direct expenditure during the year (1911-12) was Rs 39,07,349. and the indirect expenditure Rs. 10,63,165. Out of the direct expenditure Rs. 18,76,240 was spent on primary schools and Rs. 2,82,833, Rs. 10,30,528 and Rs. 7,17,748 went to college, secondary and special instruction respectively.[5] The indirect expenditure was most on the construction of buildings of different institutions.

Female education in Bihar was mostly limited to the primary stage in the beginning. The education of girls was not carried

---

1. Ibid.
2. Report on the Administration of the territories included in Province of Bihar & Orissa, 1911-12, p-225, Para-3
3. Report on the Administration of the territories included in the Province of Bihar and Orissa, 1911-12, p-225, Para-3
4. Ibid.
5. Report on the Administration of Bihar and Orissa, 1911-12, p. 225, Para-4

beyond the primary stage in any district, except Patna and Ranchi : the former had the advantage of administrative headquarters and the latter was influenced by missionary activities. Girls were reading in separate girls' schools and in boys' schools also. There was no prejudice against girls being taught by a male teacher provided he was a resident of the same village. Referring to the want of progress in respect of the education of women, A. Pedler observed : "The chief cause for the slow progress of this branch of education are : (1) the conservatism of a great portion of the people, (2) the fact that the education of their female children was a matter of great indifference to a large proportion of parents and guardians, as they usually did not take the same amount of care and interest in the education of their female wards as they did in that of boys, (3) the system of early marriage which presented an almost insurmountable barrier to education beyond the primary stages, (4) the want of educated female teachers, (5) the want of a system for educating Zenana ladies and (6) the want of adequate state aid and aid from other public funds." This statement presented a true picture of female education in Bihar. But the beginnings of a new trend were felt even in those early years. Miss Brook, the Inspectress of schools, in her report for 1904-05 observed : "I found from the visiting Zenanas and from the expression of native opinion that there was no prejudice against the education of girls, but a strong feeling against any relaxation of the *parda* system for higher caste girls. This is supported by the fact that recently a meeting of the more educated classes was held at Muzaffarpur with a view to opening a strictly *parda* school for the Hindus. In some parts of Bihar education would have been welcomed if it had not brought with it male officials in the Girls' schools. What was needed was a far greater extension of the ZENANA system of teaching for higher caste girls as a preliminary step to schools, and for lower class girls strictly parda schools. These would necessarily have to be wholly inspected by women."[1]

In November 1911 Gokhale presented an important Bill in the Imperial Legislative Council to make primary education free

1. **Report on Public Instruction in Bengal**, 1905-06, p. 34

which would make the primary education compulsery. The speech which Gokhale delivered while introducing the Bill on Elementary Education was essentially the speech of a statesman. Mazharul Haque[1] from Bihar supported this Bill with a great force in the Imperial Legislative Council. He suggested even to impose fresh taxation for it and wanted to extend it to female primary education. He said that this resolution, if accepted, would raise Indians high and the stigma of backwardness would go. But the Government did not accept this proposal on various grounds; the paucity of funds being the most prominent.

The opposition to Gokhale's Bill centered round the question of want for the purpose. But in Bihar there were many instances, when the District Magistrate as Chairman of the District Boards diverted the money to other works. Mylyall, the District Magistrate of Muzaffarpur for example, reduced the grant for primary education by many thousands and diverted the money in other works. In Tirhut Division the District Boards were dominated by indigo-planters. It was therefore felt during this period that

---

1. **Mazharul Haque. : Mazharul Haque (1866-1930)**

Born in December 1966 at a village in the Patna District took distinguished as an eminent lawyer : took admission in the Patna College; went to Lucknow andjoined the Canning college in 1887; went to Aden in 1888 and London in 1888; called to Bar in July 1891; was enrolled as an advocate of the Calcutta High Court; begun practice at Patna; but in 1892 accepted the post of Munsif in Oudh; resigned in 1892, returned to Bihar; resumed his practice at Chapra; made a name for himself; joined the Muslim League to bring it near the National Congress; presided over the session of the League in 1915; opposed the separate electorate in Municipalities and local boards; removed himself to Patna in 1908; was twice elected to the Old Imperial Legislative Council; was the Chairman of the Reception Committee of the Patna Session of Indian National Congress in 1912, was elected to accompany a deputation to London in 1904, was ready to help Mahatma Gandhi in Champaran Mission; in 1920, gave up his practice and joined the non-co-operation movement; started an English Weekly called **THE MOTHERLAND**; was sentenced to imprisonment for the months while editing this paper, moved to his home and lived a retired life till his death; built for himself, outside Patna a hermitage called **SADAQUAT ASHRAM** which soon became the chief centre of Congress activities.

the element of election should be introduced in the boards. The educated people of Bihar urged to have a non-official Chairman in the District Boards. Bihar, it was felt, was backward in the sphere of primary education, mainly due to two reasons : the inadequate amount set apart for the purpose of primary education, and the indifference of some officials.

There had been a campaign for compulsory education in India and Gokhale's Bill aroused much enthusiasm among Indians. Local Governments and people were demanding more funds for the expansion of education. All this led to the announcement of the Educational Resolution of the Government of India of 1913. The Government, it was said, would assist Local Governments by large grants as funds became available to extend a comprehensive scheme of education in several provinces.[1]

This period was really significant for the educational development in Bihar as in other parts of India. Three events had the greatest effect on the progress of education : the formation of the new province in 1912, the outbreak of war in August 1914, and the announcement of a large additional grant for education from the imperial revenues in 1912, 1913 and 1914. The creation of Bihar as a separate province gave an impetus to the advancement of education. The educational needs of Bihar were subordinate to the more advanced parts of Bengal. New schemes for the expansion and improvement of education were initiated by imperial grants.

The events in the history of education in the province during the period 1912-1917 may be summarised on the following lines :[2]

The controlling and inspecting staff was strengthened, an Assistant Director of Public Instruction was appointed. The number of Inspectors, Deputy Inspectors, Inspectresses and Assistant Inspectors was increased. The new rules regarding the new grants-in-aid and scholarships and the rule under the Local Self-Government were framed.

---

1. Indian Statutory Commission, 1929, p. 16
2. The First Quinquennial Review on the Progress of Education in Bihar and Orissa (1912-1917) Chapter I, p-1

The beginning of a policy of establishing primary schools under the direct management of local bodies was a major event of this period. The following statistics show the progress of primary education.[1]

Class of Institution :	1911-12 Schools	1911-12 Pupils	1915-16 Schools	1915-16 Pupils	1916-17 Schools	1916-17 Pupils
Middle Vernaculars :	133	9,304	125	11,034	130	11,635
Upper Primary	1,475	74,475	1,687	88,698	1,729	91,475
Lower Primary	18,927	493,328	19,539	503,002	20,429	527,746
Recognised Maktabs	1,525	48,408	1,774	45,435	1,020	25,078
Recognised Sanskrit Pathshalas	—	—	53	998	96	2,050
TOTAL :	22,060	617,515	23,178	649167:	23404:	657,980

The figures include schools and pupils of Orissa also.

EXPENDITURE

Year :	Provincial Revenues	Local Funds	Municipal Funds	Fee, endowment- and subscription	Total
	Rs.	Rs.	Rs.	Rs.	Rs.
1911-12	1,47,017	4,54,030	29,701	11,79,715	18,10,463
1915-16	2,59,066	9,52,103	69,063	13,88,605	26,18,037
1916-17	2,46,353	9,94,467	73,603	14,20,731	27,35,234

The Middle Vernacular schools were becoming so unpopular that the Deputy Commissioner of the Santhal Parganas remarked : "The trying to foster Middle Vernacular Schools is like an attempt to galvanize a dead horse."

The decrease in the number of *Maktabs* in 1916-17 was due to the change of classification : 823 of these institutions were shown as primary schools. The *Sanskrit Pathshala* which adopted the departmental syllabus, became eligible for aid during this period. The increase in expenditure from local funds during this period was remarkable. The fall in the expenditure from provincial revenues in 1916-17 was due to the fact that the Government Model *Maktabs* were handed over to the management of Local Bodies.

1. Ibid, p-71

To improve matters, a committee was appointed by the Government in March 1914 to examine the question of development of primary education in the province. This committee recommended that the jurisdiction of Local Bodies should be confined to vernacular schools. It recommended the formation of managing committees for primary schools, whenever possible. It felt that the greatest hindrance to the expansion of primary education had been the distance of schools from most of the villages. It was therefore resolved that schools should be located in such a way that no boy should have to walk more than a mile to attend a lower primary school.[1]

The Committee thought that the state of education in the municipalities was not satisfactory. The appointment of an Education Committee to advise the Commissioners was recommended. This Education Committee was expected to suggest special measures to encourage the education of the depressed classes whether by opening special schools or otherwise. It laid down certain principles in connection with the buildings for primary schools. In short, the recommendations of this Committee covered a wide ground. It was related to the inspecting staff, the training of staff and scholarship.

The number of vernacular schools remained almost static, but that of the pupils was increasing. The number of Government schools had fallen from 17 to 14. The aided school at Lalganj was wrongly shown as Government school on previous occasions, while the school at Dehri-on-Sone was handed over to the District Board and that at Mohulia in Singhbhum was made an aided Middle school. The number of schools managed by Local Bodies increased from 75 to 76, while that of the aided schools increased from 29 to 34.[2]

The following table gives a picture of the primary schools in various districts of Bihar during the period 1912-1917.[3]

---

1. **Ibid.** p-71
2. **Ibid.**, pp. 72-73
3. **Ibid.**, p. 76

Name of the District.	Primary School 1911–12	1915–16	1916–17	Boys attending Primary Schools. 1911-12	1915-16	1916-17
1. Patna	1,236	1,291	1,284	34,005	34,936	34,929
2. Gaya	1,330	1,496	1,537	41,258	40,203	41,083
3. Shahabad	910	992	959	26,032	29,048	28,737
4. Saran	747	1,015	1,088	24,223	29,969	31,830
5. Champaran	754	842	810	16,615	19,872	19,813
6. Muzaffarpur	1,275	1,264	1,239	36,350	33,724	33,857
7. Darbhanga	1,601	1,478	1,438	55,207	44,724	45,929
8. Monghyr	1,111	1,291	1,345	28.188	32,250	32,255
9. Bhagalpur	948	1,014	1,096	23,829	25,431	28,418
10. Purnea	897	959	990	22,362	22,541	24,406
11. Santhal Pargana	954	974	992	24,612	27,781	29,139
12. Hazaribagh	507	660	603	13,650	16,270	16,568
13. Ranchi	960	1,268	1,142	24,020	29,908	26,388
14. Palamau	397	353	380	7,935	8,270	8,851
15. Manbhum	785	467	1,036	26,236	28,098	28,860
16. Singhbhum	353	375	382	11,270	11,033	10,948

Thus the only areas in which there was rapid development were the Bhagalpur division and the districts of Saran, Hazaribagh aud Manbhum. The number of pupils was also rising in the districts of Patna and Palamau, though in the Patna district there was a fall of 7 schools-in 1916-17. In other districts there was a fall in the number of schools. The decrease in Gaya was attributed to a severe attack of Plague in 1912-13 and 1913-14. In other districts the setback was attributed to inadequacy of funds.

There were 605,204 boys in Bihar at the Primary stage in 1916-17 of whom 57.2 percent were in the first year infant class and 46-2 percent were in the next three classes and only 6.6 percent in the upper primary stage. These figures disclosed that about half of the boys who attended the school, did not go further than infant classes and thus they received no real education. The parents used to remove their children from the school where they derived no benefit. This fact affected the progress of primary education. The Primary Education Committee considered this problem and suggested that the remedy was to ensure that no teacher should teach more than 30 pupils or two classes.[1]

The problem of the expansion and improvement of primary education was taken up in 1916-17. The great hindrance was finance which the provincial government could not provide. Even so, a general policy was laid down. The report on the Committee on primary education rightly pointed out that the education "required for the children of cultivators and of other people of similar occupations is of an extremely simple kind"[2] The Government agreed with this view : "the lower primary course gives the bare minimum of educations."[3] Consequently, the primary education was divided into two parts—(a) higher standard of education given in upper primary and middle vernacular schools and (b) lower standard provided by lower primary or infant schools.[4] The schools for imparting advanced primary instruction were to be set up primarily on a pressing demand for them, but such an education was to be easily accessible in all parts of the district. Local bodies were to try to provide one upper primary school for every 25 square miles, and one middle vernacular school for every 125 square miles.[5]

The problem of lower primary education was of a different nature. The Committee on primary education suggested that this should be made universal, whereas the Government of India wished that the existing number of pupils should be doubled. The Bihar Government discussed the problem at length and came to the conclusion that it was not enough to increase the number of boys reading in primary schools ; "it was equally necessary to see that they receive a proper education."[6] In 1914-15, it was

1. **Ibid.**, p-75
2. **Educational Proceedings** (Govt. of Bihar & Orissa), 1916, no. 20, p-93
3. **Ibid.**
4. **Ibid.**
5. **Ibid.**
6. **Educational Proceedings** (Govt. of Bihar & Orissa), 1916, no. 20, p-93

pointed out, there were about 440,000 boys in the infant classes, 140,000 in the lower primary classes, and 20,000 in the upper primary classes. This indicated that one-half of the boys in primary schools never rose above the infant classes, and failed 'to derive any lasting benefit from their attendance at school.'[1] This was confirmed by the Census report of 1911 which recorded that 59 persons per mile of the age-group 15 to 20 were literate as compared to 186 per mile in the age-group 10 to 15 who were in middle schools. This might be either because they could not stay long enough at the primary school, or failed because of insufficient teaching or many boys were taken away even before they completed four years at schools.[2]

Every district officer and Chairman of District Boards was directed to pay more attention to primary education for the moral and material progress of the cultivator. The Government orders said : "Whether he would encourage him to resist the oppression of bad zamindars or of corrupt subordinate employees of Government, whether he would cause him to understand the record-of-rights, whether he would bring him into co-operative societies, whether he would induce him to try new seeds, implements or improved agricultural methods or to protect his cattle against disease, or his family against maleria and plague, at every step he is confronted with the same difficulty, the ignorance and illiteracy of the masses, which make them suspicious of every change and easy prey to every oppressor and imposter"[3] Therefore the first concern of the district authorities was to be more active in the implementation of the programme of primary education among the masses.

The following figures will show the number of primary schools and pupils in the districts of Bihar in 1918.[4]

---

1. **Ibid.**
2. **Ibid.**
3. **Education Proceedings (Govt. of Bihar & Orissa) 1916, no. 20, p-93**
4. **Edueation Proceedings (Govt. of Bihar & Orissa), 1921, no. 82, p-179**

Districts	Area in Sq. Miles.	No. of boys Primary age group	No. of middle verna-cular schools	No. of Pri-mary schools.	Boys in Primary schools.
Patna	2,121	80,978	13	1,284	35,390
Gaya	4,714	106,129	14	1,473	39,098
Shahabad	4,353	90,495	19	995	30,608
Saran	2,683	106,433	20	1,077	33,001
Muzaffarpur	3,036	136,020	22	1,300	37,915
Darbhanga	3,348	141,267	25	1,434	46,599
Monghyr	3,961	104,348	26	1,419	36,958
Bhagalpur	4,226	105,787	21	1,153	30,423
Champaran	3,531	94,201	11	772	20,625
Purnea	4,998	101,642	11	1,067	25,978
Santhal Pargana	5,479	93,343	x	1,004	28,705
Hazaribagh	6,986	62,910	9	627	16,196
Ranchi	7,102	67,675	11	1,158	27,315
Palamau	4,916	34,116	7	385	9,896
Manbhum	4,147	78,854	17	1,013	29,093
Singhbhum	3,938	34,121	x	388	12,003

The total number of primary schools of Bihar and Orissa were 23,052 in 1917. Out of a total population of 34,045,290 only 635,123 were getting instructions in these schools. The total cost in these schools was Rs. 27,94,096, the cost of educating each pupil being Rs. 4-9.4.[1] The proportion of primary education was still very low, presumably because this education had been transferred to local bodies and municipalities much earlier.

Sri Krishna Sahay introduced a primary Education Bill in Legislative Council in January 1918.[2] The object of this Bill was to make a provision for the extension of primary education in the province. It was drafted on the basis of the bill that had been drafted by Gokhale in 1910-11. It was discussed and supported by many distinguished members in the Legislative Assembly.

1. Report on the Administration of Bihar & Orissa, 1918-19, p. 103
2. Proceeding of the Legislative Council of Bihar and Orissa, 1918, p. 49

Sharat Chandra Sen, Lachchmi Prasad Sinha, Purnendu Narayan Sinha and many others including Rai Bahadur Dwarkanath gave a whole-hearted support to this Bill.[1]

But this Bill was opposed through a memorial signed by leading landed aristocracy of Bihar. Sri Krishna Sahay wrote an open letter to the Darbhanga Maharaja who was heading the list of signatories. The important ground on which the bill was opposed was that the bill would interfere with the social and religious life of the people. One more ground of opposition was that the superior castes would come in contact with the untouchables. Sri Krishna Sahay urged the Darbhanga Maharaja to withdraw his opposition and support it.[2]

In spite of the opposition from certain quarters, the Bihar and Orissa Primary Education Bill was passed in November, 1918. In January 1919 the Bihar and Orissa Primary Education Act came into force. It was an act to provide for the extension of primary education in the province of Bihar and Orissa. Its aim was to enable municipalities, district boards and similar rural authorities with the sanction of local Government to make the primary education of children between six and ten years of age within their jurisdiction compulsory.[3] It gave local board authorities power to impose a cess to be called education cess with the sanction of the local Government. This was a great step towards the spread of mass education.

Even so, in 1918 there was no remarkable progress in primary education, though the number of students in the province increased to 663.915.[4]

The middle vernacular schools remained static at 130, but their students decreased from 11,635 to 11,476 in 1918. The number of upper primary schools rose from 1,729 to 1,738 and that of

---

1. Ibid., pp. 57-61
2. The Searchlight, 22 August 1918
3. Bihar & Orissa Gazette No. 1,26 February, 1919 Part-IV, pp. 1-7
4. Report on the administration of Bihar & Orissa, 1917-18, p. 103

pupils from 91,471 to 92,880. On the other hand the lower primary schools showed a decline.[1]

The report entitled 'India in 1920' prepared by William stated that only 3.36 percent of the total population of British India was under instruction in education institutions, of which only 5.6 percent was from male population and 1.2 percent from the female population. In Bihar the percentage was even less-4.7 percent of the male population, and 0.65 percent of the female population by 1921. Thus the total percentage of literacy of the masses had reached only 2.43 percent during the first twenty years of this century.[2]

The total number of primary schools between 1914 and 1920 in India increased from 1,23,000 to 1,50,000 and that of pupils from 4.9 to 5.9 millions. In Bihar and Orissa, however, during the same period the number of schools increased from 23,408 to 25,793 and of students from 650,426 to 781,446.[3] There was no doubt an attempt to extend the sphere of primary education. But these were also years of exceptional economic crises and financial difficulties. An increase of 2,000 primary schools and over 68,000 primary students was in no way a bad progress.[4]

There was however a sharp decline between 1920 and 1921 in primary education in the province, primary schools of all classes during this period lost their students. The total number of primary schools decreased from 23,120 to 22,591 and that of their pupils from 655,554 to 644,169. This decrease was confined to unaided schools which showed a fall of 535 schools with 13,436 pupils. On the other hand there was an increase of 5 schools with 2,651 students in the managed and aided primary schools.[5]

In spite of the opposition of the landed aristocrates the primary Education Act was passed with a provision for implementing compulsory education. But by 1921 only the Ranchi Municipality

---

1. **Report on the Administration of Bihar & Orissa**, 1917-18, p-101
2. G. E. Owen, **Bihar & Orissa**, 1921, p. 112
3. G. E. Owen, op. cit., p-113
4. Ibid
5. **Report on the Progress of Education in Bihar & Orissa**, 1920-21, p. 12

took advantage of this Act. The reluctance of other municipalities to follow the example of Ranchi was due to their fear of the odium which would follow the imposition of cess. There was a feeling among upper castes that the extension of education might make it difficult to obtain menial and other labour at the prevailing rent.

The table in Appendix will show the state of primary schools in Bihar from 1916-17 to 1921-22.[1]

The development of primary education remained limited in spite of its transfer to local bodies. The transfer of responsibility for the expansion of primary education to local bodies could not possibly succeed because of the composition of district boards and municipalities based on a highly restricted franchise and weighted by nominated members was not such as would feel impelled to spend money on the needs of the poor. Moreover, even if such a sense of social responsibility had been present the resources of local bodies were meagre. The main concern of the district boards was in the spread of secondary education which benefitted the children of their members and not in the extension of primary education to the poor areas.[2]

The first cause of the slow progress in pimary education was the grinding poverty of the great majority of the population which prevented them from starting schools, from sending their children to ones started or to keep them there for more than a couple of years since child labour was valuable economically both in domestic chores and outside work.[3]

Primary schools for boys and girls declined by 533 or 2.1 percent and pupils by 11,700 or 1.6 percent during this period.[2] This decrease occurred in spite of the attempt on the part of the Government and local bodies to extend primary education, pri-

---

1. Appendix-B
2. V. B. Singh, (ed.), **The Economic History of India**, 1857-1956, p. 737 Also see, Huge Tinker, **Local Self-Government of India and Pakistan and Burma** and C. H. Philips (ed.), **Politics and Society in India**
3. V. B. Singh, (ed.), **The Economic History of India**, 1857-1956, pp. 735-36.

marily due to certain economic reasons. The Director of Public Instruction reported that the decline was confined to unaided schools, probably partly due to the rise in prices.

According to an enquiry conducted by Government of Bihar and Orissa in 1920-21, a very large number of boys were kept away from schools.[1] The reason was that parents of such boys were not able to pay even minimum charges of the schools. There was other side of the picture also. The large number of boys of a tender age belonging to lower castes were employed by upper castes. They were forced to earn at very early age. Indeed, the zamindary system was a great hindrance to the spread of mass literacy in Bihar.[2]

CHAPTER IV

SECONDARY EDUCATION
(1906-1921)

The three important stages of education in all the ages had been primary, secondary and higher education. These three stages were recognised from the very beginning in modern India. The primary stage of education is the means of educating masses, whereas the secondary education is the gateway to higher education.

There were one thousand four hundred and fortyone secondary schools for boys in the whole of Bengal in 1906-07. Of those, 1,032 were English and 409 vernacular schools.[3]

---

1. G. E. Owen, op. cit., p-11
2. Ibid., p-114
3. Reprt on the Progress of Education in Bengal 1906-07 (Educational Proceedings, 1908) p-11

But the average number of English schools also varied considerably in different parts of the province. The Burdwan division headed the list with an average of 67 English schools, next came the presidency division (excluding Calcutta), with an average of 61.2 ; then Patna with an average of 12.7 : and Chotanagpur with an average of 10.2. Calcutta had 80 English schools.[1]

There were 13 High English Schools for boys with a total attendance of 2,192 pupils (in 1906) in the Patna district ; of these schools two were maintained by the Government and four received grants-in aid ; the rest were unaided institutions.[2]

The schools maintained by the Government were the Patna Collegiate school and the Patna City school and those aided by it were the High School at Bihar, Dinapur and Khagaul and Ram Mohan Roy Seminary at Patna. Of the unaided High schools, one the Bayley High school, was at Barh, other, the Aryan High school at Dinapur, and five were within Municipal limits of Patna, viz., the Bihar National Collegiate school, T. K. Ghosh's Academy,[3] and the Anglo-Arabic, Anglo Sanskrit and Diamond Jubilee School. Besides these, there was a High school for girls.[4]

In 1906 there were 5 Middle English Schools with 210 pupils and 6 middle vernacular schools with 318 pupils, in the Patna district. Of the 5 Middle English Schools, one was maintained by the district board, 2 were aided by the same body, one was aided by Government and the other was an unaided school, of the 6 middle vernacular schools one was under the direct control of the Education Department, while the rest were district board schools. There was also a Middle English School for girls.[5]

In Patna there was a High School for girls at Bankipur, which was the only secondary school for girls in Bihar. This

---

1. **Ibid.**
2. **O'Malley, (ed.), B. D. G. Patna, p-172**
3. **Rajendra Pd., the late President of India and a prominent Bihari Leader, had his schooling here as well as at zila school, Chapra,**
4. **O'Malley, (ed.), B. D. G. Patna, p-172**
5. **Ibid.**

school received a departmental grant-in-aid of Rs. 110/- per month for a long time. In 1905 the Director of Public Instruction reported that the Bankipore Girls School had entirely failed to attract Bihari girls. It was also reported that the financial condition of the school was very unsatisfactory and the staff was inadequate.[1]

In 1906 in Bankipore High School for girls, out of 54 girls, 40 were Bengalis and only 12 Biharis and 2 were inhabitants of other provinces.[2] Parda was a great hindrance in the expansion of female education in Bihar. The Director of Public Instruction therefore recommended that a separate school solely for the education of such Bihari girls, who did not wish to associate with Bengali girls might be started. It was decided to withdraw the grant from the High School and replace it by a Middle English School by the Government with effect from January, 1906. It was proposed to conduct the new school strictly on Zenana lines. But for want of suitable teachers it was found impossible to open the new school soon.

In 1906 a new Director of Public Instruction took up the cause of female education in Bihar. He did realise the necessity of establishing a separate school for Bihari girls on strictly *Zenana* lines but he did not approve of his predecessor's decision to close the existing High School at Bankipore. He agreed with the view of the Inspector of Schools, Patna division, that if this school was closed female education in Bihar would lose ground not to be regained for years. The Commissioner of the Patna Division, Maude, wrote in a similar vein, 'I look on this little school as an object-lesson to the people of Bihar planted in their chief city in order to show them that girls can be educated without even a strict *parda* system...and it would be a very great pity if it were removed by the closure'.[3] Thus the Bankipore High English School was allowed to continue and the grant which the Director of Public Instruction got was not sufficient in order to keep the school in a

1. A. Earle, To Bengal Govt., General Department, 28 October, 1906
2. Ibid.
3. A. Earle to the Government of Bengal, 28 October, 1906

state of efficiency. The Government therefore sanctioned the restoration of the old grant, and increase was assured on condition of financial and teaching improvement.[1] The Government further sanctioned the opening of a Middle English School at Bankipore to meet the urgent need of the Hindu girls. This scheme was blocked, owing to the fact that suitable teachers could not be produced. According to the Directory of Public Instruction it was a wrong start because without providing for qualified teachers such schools could not succeed.

This led to the formulation of establishing training colleges for women teachers on strictly *Parda* lines. At an informal conference held at Belvedre on 15 March 1906 and presided over by the Lt. Governor it was decided to establish a training college at once. Sayed Badshah Nawab Rizvi of Patna had offered a permanent endowment for the promotion of female education. This donation brought an income of Rs 7,500/- a year which provided a great impetus to the proposed scheme. This followed subscriptions from other enlightened and educated men of Bihar. The Maharani of Bettiah placed a large house along with a big compound for the accommodation of the college and the practising school.[2]

The district which stood next to Patna in the number of High Schools was Bhagalpur. There were seven High Schools with 1,454 pupils in this district during this period. And the number of Middle schools both English and Vernacular, was 11 with 907 pupils in 1908-09.[3] In this district the number of boys of school-going age was about 154,130. In 1907-08 only 15.4 percent of those were attending school and in 1908-09 only 19.9 percent.[4] In Shahabad there were 6 High schools, 6 Middle English schools and 12 Middle Vernacular schools in 1910-11. These schools had 1,037, 433 and 785 students respectively on their rolls in the same

---

1. T. W. Richardson, Secretary to Government of Bengal, to Director of Public Instruction, 28 November 1906.
2. A Earl to the Government of Bengal, 13 May, 1906
3. O'Malley, (ed.), B. D. G. Bhagalpur, p-156
4. Ibid.

year.[1] The Muzaffarpur district contained five High Schools; three of which were situated at Muzaffarpur town, viz., the Zila school with 264 students, the Bhumihar Brahman Collegiate school with 326 students and the Mukherjee Seminary with 342 students. Other two schools were at the outlying sub-division headquarters, Hajipur and Sitamarhi and they had 129 and 218 students respectively.[2]

There were 7 Middle English schools, two of which were in the Muzaffarpur town, viz., the Methodist Mission Girls School and Dharma Samaj School. The first was aided by Government and the second was aided by the Municipality. Of the remaining five schools, four were aided by the district board and were situated in the interior of the district. The last one, even though situated at the headquarters station, was not an aided school.[3]

The number of Middle Vernacular Schools was 7 and all such schools were situated in the interior of the district. One at Lalganj was managed by Government, four were under the direct management of the district board and two were maintained by the Darbhanga Raj.[4] There were 353 students in the MiddleEnglish and 352 students in the Middle Vernacular Schools.

The opening of the Methodist Mission Girls School in 1906 marked the real beginning of female secondary education in North Bihar. But for quite sometime it was attended solely by native Christian girls. It received a grant-in-aid of Rs. 77/- a month from the Government. The girl education of the district, however, was mainly confined to the primary stage. There was no prejudice against girls being taught by a male teacher provided he was a resident of the same village. Only the Mission Girls School had female teachers on its staff, all other girls schools had male teachers. But during this period a *PATHSHALA* for native girls,

---

1. O' Malley, (ed.), **B. O. D. G. SHAHABAD, p-146**
2. O' Malley, (ed.), **B. D. G. Muzaffarpur. p-134**
3. O' Malley, (ed.), **B. D. G., Muzaffarpur, p-134**
4. **Ibid, pp. 134-135**

called the Chapman Pathshala, after the then District Judge, was opened in Muzaffarpur town with a female teacher. This school had 50 girls, the majority of whom were Bengalis. It taught upper primary course. There were two model girls schools in the district, one at Gangaya and the other at Sursand, which had 39 and 31 pupils respectively in 1905-06.[1]

In the district of Saran there were 20 secondary schools attended by 2,366 students, including 6 High Schools, 3 Middle Schools and 11 Middle Vernacular schools. There were 1,507 pupils in High Schools. The Zila school at Chapra was maintained by Government, and two were Government aided viz., the Victoria Memorial High School at Siwan and the High School at Gopalganj. The other three schools were unaided : the Saran Academy and the Collegiate School at Chapra and the Eden High School at Hathua. All the Middle English Schools received grants-in-aid from the Government. They were situated at Amnaur, Aphar and Revelganj and had 146 students. Among the middle vernacular schools ten were maintained by the District Board and one was under the private management. The number of students in these schools was 113.[2]

There were 6 High schools in Darbhanga district of which four were at Darbhanga, viz., the North Brook School, the Darbhanga Raj School, the Saraswati Academy and the Bengali High English school, and two were situated in the subdivisional headquarters: Samastipur and Madhubani. These were Watson High English School at Madhubani with 246 pupils, and Samastipur High English School with 188 pupils.[3]

The second class of school, Middle English School were 8 in all in this district. All the schools of this class were in the interior of the district. One at Samastipur, though aided by the district board, was maintained by the municipality; three at Dighra, Rashik and Jogiara were aided by the district board, and

---

1. O' Malley, (ed)., B. D. G. **Muzaffarpur**, p-136
2. O' Malley, (ed.), B. D. G. **Saran**, p-140
3. O' malley, (ed), B. D. G. **Darbhanga**, p-137

the remaining three at Narhan, Dalsingsarai and Tajpur were maintained entirely by the Narhan estate.[1]

On the other hand, the number of middle vernacular schools was 6, and they were maintained entirely by the Darbhanga Raj.

In the district of Champaran there were 2 High Schools. 7 Middle English Schools and two Middle Vernacular schools.[2] The total number of students in these schools was 1,124 in 1907.

The secondary education was imparted in the district of Gaya to 1,123 students in 4 high schools. Of these four schools, three viz., the zila school, the town school and the Sahibganj school were situated at Gaya and the fourth was situated at Tekari Raj with the exception of the Gaya Zila School, all were private schools unaided by the Government.[3]

The 9 Middle English schools of Gaya were distributed as follows: one each at Gaya and Daudnagar was aided by Government; one each at Arwal, Aurangabad, Deo, Jahanabad, and Nawada was aided by the district board and one each at Bhaidaiya and Fakirpur was unaided. The popularity of Middle vernacular schools was on the wane; in fact, the number of such schools had fallen to 7.[4]

The zila school of Monghyr was maintained by the Government and the aided schools were at Jamalpur, Begusarai and Jamui. The town School in Monghyr was, however, unaided. The distribution of middle schools was 7, Middle English and Middle Vernacular school with 547 and 408 students respectively.[5]

The progress of education in the Ranchi district during this period was remarkable, and the credit for it must go to the Christian missions. Though there was no college in the district, there were four flourishing High English schools with more than 1500

1. Ibid
2. B. O. D. G. Champaran, p-130
3. O' Malley, (ed.), B. D. G., Gaya p-196
4. Ibid., pp. 196-97
5. Ibid., Monghyr, p-194

boys. The Ranchi Zila school, maintained by the Government, was under the charge of a European Head Master of the Indian Educational service. This school was rapidly growing in size and popularity. New school building including hostels were constructed on a site in the compound of the house formerly occupied by the Commissioner of the division. The other three schools were maintained by the three missions, who were assisted by annual grants from Government and also received special grants to enable them to erect new school buildings and boarding houses. The names of these schools were the Lutheran Mission School, St. Paul's High school maintained by S. P. G. Mission and St. John's High school maintained by the Roman Catholic Mission.[1]

There were thirteen Middle English schools of which three (at Gumla, Khunti and Jharia) were well maintained. That at Bundu was aided by the district board, another was aided by the Ranchi municipality and five were aided by the Government. Three of the latter, as well as the three which were unaided, were under the management of one or another missions. There were five Middle Vernacular schools in this district of which one was attached to the Ranchi Training school and one was maintained by the Government. The remaining schools were maintained and managed by the district board. The Missions were not at all interested in the development of vernacular and therefore had no Middle vernacular schools.[2]

There was only one High School, viz., the zila school at Chaibasa which had 230 pupils in 1908. There were 7 Middle English schools situated at Jagannathpur (maintained by Government), Chaibasa (an aided school managed by the society), Chakradharpur (a railway aided school), Ghatshila (aided), Bahargora (aided) and also at Kharsawan and Saraikela, the last two being unaided schools maintained by the chief of the state. The third class of secondary schools consisted of 6 Middle Vernacular schools maintained by the Government and situated at Asura, Dumaria,

---

1. M. G. Hallet, (ed.), **B. O. D. G.**, **Ranchi** pp., 219
2. **B. O. D. G. Ranchi.** pp. 220-221

Haludpukur, Chitmiti Mahulia and Purnea. The number of students in all the 14 secondary schools was 13,331 in 1908.[1]

There were 3 High schools in Purnea district. One of these, the Purnea Zila school, was maintained by the Government and the other two viz., the High Schools at Aroria and Kishanganj were Government aided. There were 7 Middle English schools, of which two in the Purnea town and Katihar were aided by Government and four, situated at Barsoi Churli, Forbesganj and Manihari were aided by the district board. An unaided school at Champanagar was closed during this period. The number of Middle Vernacular schools was six, five of these at Abadpur, Amtola, Dasgram, Dholbaja and Kasba were managed by the district board and one at Patni was aided by it. The total number of students in all the secondary schools was 1,108.[2]

In the Palamau district there was only one High English school, the Zila school at Daltonganj. There other four Middle English schools aided by Government were situated at Daltonganj, Hussainabad, Garhwa and Nagaruntari. And 4 Middle vernacular schools managed by the district board were situated at Hariharganj, Haidarnagar, Bisrampur and Lesliganj. One such school was managed by the Daltonganj Municipality.[3]

In the town of Hazaribagh the Zila school and the St. Columba's Collegiate school were imparting secondary education. A third High School was situated at Giridih in the Hazaribagh district. The number of Middle English School was 7 whereas that of Middle vernacular four only.[4]

There were 5 High schools in the Santhal Parganas of which Dumka Zila School with 174 boys on the rolls was managed by the Government. The other four schools, which were situated at Deogarh, Godda, Jamtara and Pakur were aided schools. In 1908 they had together 572 students on the rolls. Moreover, there were 11 Middle schools, with an attendance of 837 pupils ; of which 7

1. O' Malley, (ed.), **B. D. G. Singhbhum**, p-204
2. **Ibid.**, Purnea, p-170
3. P. C. **Tallents**, (ed.) B. O. D. G., Palamau, p-173
4. **Ibid.**, Hazaribagh, p-197

were aided and 4 were unaided schools. The number of middle vernacular schools was 14 with 514 boys and 286 girls.[1]

The district of Manbhum contained 25 secondary schools with 2,248 students. The number of High schools was six of which only the Zila school at Purulia was maintained by the Government. This school had 272 students in 1908-09. Two schools, i.e., those at Chirkunda and Raghunathpur, with a total of 259 pupils were aided by Government. The other two schools—one at Jharia with 88 students and Pandra with 118 students were established by Raja Durga Singh and Rani Hingam Kumari respectively. The remaining High school with 366 students was called the Victoria Institution situated at Purulia. There were 19 Middle schools of which 12 were Middle English and 7 were Middle vernacular schools.[2]

In 1911-12 Bihar and Orissa had 440 secondary schools for Indian boys attended by 53,954 pupils. Of these pupils 7,803 were reading in Government schools, 7,900 in board schools, 2,538 in Native States Schools, 21,911 in aided schools and 13,742 in unaided schools. Classified according to stages of instruction 11,732 were reading in the higher stage, 12,290 in the middle stage, and 29,932 in the primary stage.[3]

The High and Middle English schools numbered 304 and had 44,442 pupils and Middle vernacular secondary schools numbered 136 and were attended by 9,512 pupils in 1911-12. A comparison of these figures with those of 1910-11 shows that the number of English schools had increased by eight and their pupils by 4,699, but the vernacular schools had decreased by four.[1]

In 1911 at the Matriculation examination 1,533 candidates appeared, of whom 908 or 59.2 percent passed. The total expenditure on secondary schools in this year amounted to Rs. 9,50,868 of which Rs, 8,73,583 was spent on English secondary-High and Middle English schools and Rs. 77,285 on Middle Vernacular

---

1. O' Malley, (ed.), **B. D. G. Santhal Parganas**, p-241
2. Ibid., Manbhum, p-259
3. **Report on Administration of Bihar & Orissa 1911-12, p. 226**
4. **Report on Administration of Bihar and Orissa. 1911-12, p. 226**

Schools. In this expenditure on English secondary schools provincial revenues contributed Rs. 1,60,332, district funds Rs. 32,297, municipal funds Rs. 6,400, native states revenues Rs. 30,830, fees Rs. 4,53,445 and subscriptions, endowments, etc. Rs. 1,90, 279.[1]

The expenditure on vernacular secondary schools was contributed as follows—provincial revenues Rs. 10,346, native states revenues Rs. 1,183, district funds Rs. 31, 958, municipal funds Rs. 857, fees Rs. 20,282 and subscriptions, endowments, etc., Rs. 12, 659. The average cost of educating a boy in a High English school was Rs. 25.4, in a Middle English school Rs. 12.02 and in Middle Vernacular school 8.1.[2]

The improvement and development of secondary education continued during this period. The number of matriculate students had increased in a remarkable manner during the period. The following table gives a picture of the expansion of secondary education in the province of Bihar and Orissa :

High Schools	**1911-12**	**1915-16**	**1916-17**
Number of schools	91	94	100
Number of pupils	24,392	33,392	34,734
Direct Expenditure	Rs. 6,31,871	Rs. 9,29,733	Rs. 9,85,724
Middle English Schools[3]			
Number of school.	188	222	226
Number of pupils	16,959	22,302	23,415
Direct Expenditure	Rs. 1,77,764	Rs. 3,52,769	Rs. 3,99,108

Eleven schools received recognition during the period 1912-17 of which the following nine schools were in Bihar—Nawadah High School, the Gaya Model School, the Foley Rajput High English

1. Ibid.
2. Ibid.
3. N. L. Hallward to the Government of Bengal, 8 January 1913. In 1913 there were in all 133 Middle English Schools in Bihar, of which 24 were maintained by the District Boards, 83 were aided by the Boards, 25 were unaided, and one, a school for aborigines in Chotanagpur was aided directly by the government.

School at Chapra, the Pusa Government High School, the Madhepur High School in Darbhanga, the aided High school at Muzaffarpur, the Nagendrabala Academy at Chapra, the Preparatory School at Monghyr and Dhanbad High School. The Diamond Jubilee School in the Patna City and the Bengali High School at Laheriasarai were closed. The number of Government Schools (including those of Orissa) rose from 21 to 22 owing to the opening of the school at Pusa. The increase in the number of aided schools was five and that of unaided schools three. The number of pupils rose with a very rapid speed during this period (1912-1917)—by 40 percent.[1]

The increase in the expenditure was also striking during this period—56 percent. The increase of allotment from tbe. provincial revenues was from Rs. 1,36,725 to Rs. 1,82,446 and that from fees Rs. 3,78,066 to Rs. 7,08,053. On the other hand the District Fund contribution disappeared in 1916-17. The municipalities concentrated on primary schools. Therefore its expenditure also fell from Rs. 2,459 to Rs. 1,080.

The increase in the fee-income of schools was also phenomenal, presumably due to the standardization in the fee rates sanctioned in 1912-13. The larger number of students also added more money to the fee income. In 1916-17 the fee-income covered 71.8 percent of the total expenditure[2]-pointer to the fact that more and more people in Bihar were inclined to get education. The parents were prepared to pay at any rate the greater part of the cost of educating their children in Secondary Schools.

The secondary schools were not sufficient to meet the demand of secondary education. The Inspector of the Patna district reported : "The large increase in the number of pupils in High schools with accommodation practically stationary, has resulted in a serious state of congestion. Almost every school is overcrowded. The remedy for this lies of course in encouraging the opening of new High Schools"[3]

---

1. The First Quinquennial Review on the Progress of Education in Bihar and Orissa (1912-17), p. 65
2. Ibid., p. 65
3. Ibid., p. 66

There was a time when schools in Bihar were closed for want of students in the last century, but now more and more schools were being demanded. Many Inspectors suggested the abolition of lower classes from High schools to accommodate more students in upper classes at the secondary stage. The improvement of Matriculation examination attracted the attention of the officials. A Departmental Committee was convened in August 1913 to examine this question. But nothing could be carried and the recommendation of the committee was suspended, till the establishment of the Patna University.[1]

In 1913-14 special classes were opened at the zila schools at Chapra, Ranchi, Motihari and Daltonganj for students who had completed the middle course in vernacular schools. A similar class was opened in the Foley Rajput School at Chapra. The students who joined the High schools from Middle Vernacular school were given special course of English for one year. These classes at Daltonganj and Foley Rajput School at Chapra worked well.[2]

The Middle English Schools were also progressing steadily. There was an increase of 38 such schools in Bihar and Orissa in which Bihar got 29 which were distributed as follows : Tirhut 11, Bhagalpur 16 and Chotanagpur 2. One new Government Middle School was opened as a practising school for the Ranchi Training School. The increase in local bodies Middle English Schools was 10 and of aided schools 28. The number of aided schools declined by one. The increase in the percentage of pupils was 38.07 percent.[3]

The secondary education in Bihar continued to develop and these years witnessed a rapid development in this field. In Bihar and Orissa hundreds of students passed the secondary school examinations every year. Though the percentage of literacy and of elementary primary education remained low, the percentage of youths in secondary schools was encouraging. The percentage of

---

1. Ibid., p. 67
2. Ibid., p. 68
3. Ibid.

youths undergoing secondary education to the total population was 18, and of those undergoing university education was ·07 only.[1]

This uneven distribution of educational development was due to the insistent demand from a limited class of higher caste Hindus for an education which would qualify them for the continuance under British rule of their hereditary careers in the administrative body of India. This was the cause of such big gap between the intelligentsia and the uneducated masses. These castes demanded and pursued the education from the beginning. But the education of masses suffered due to the indifference shown by the mass themselves.[2]

The total number of all types of secondary schools for boys and girls in Bihar and Orissa increased from 497 to 525 and the number of students increased from 73,446 to 73,842 in 1917-18. The number of high schools was 114 and that of Middle English schools 139. The following schools were permitted this year (1917) to open class XII—Gruning Soghra Waqf High school at Bihar, the Mokama Ghat High School, the Gait High School at Aurangabad, the Model Institute and Khatriya High School at Arrah, the Sursand High School at Muzaffarpur, the Katihar High School and the Maheshpur High School in Santhal Parganas.[3]

The six schools, which were recognised in 1917-18 were Gorea Kothi in Saran, the Edward Memorial Institution at Chapra, the Panchgachia School in the Bhagalpur district, the Jamalpur High School in Monghyr and the Katras High School in Manbhum. Owing to the war the number of buildings erected for High schools was not large, but a new building was completed at Nawadah and five halls were constructed for C. M. S. High school at Bhagalpur. Extensions were made to the zila school at Motihari and High schools at Banka, Kishanganj and Deoghar.[4]

---

1. G. E. Oven, **Bihar and Orissa 1921**, p. 115
2. **Report on Indian Constitutional Reforms**, p. 119
3. **Report on the Administration of Bihar and Orissa**, 1918-19, p. 103
4. **Report on the Progress of Education in Bihar and Orissa**, 1917-18·p. 10[illegible]

The number of High schools recognised as qualified to present candidates to the Matriculation examination continued to increase, having risen from 126 in 1919 to 132 in 1920. The number of candidates appearing at the Matriculation examination increased very rapidly. In 1919,3,335 appeared and next year 4,298 appeared. Of these 1,945 or 559 more than 1919 passed.[1]

The number of secondary schools of all types for boys and girls in Bihar and Orissa underwent a rapid development. At the time of the creation of the province in 1912 the number of such schools was 437 with 53,170 students, but in 1919-20 it went up to 561 with 53,170 students. This field of education had consumed about four times money since 1912, as all the expenditure increased in 1920 from $2\frac{1}{2}$ lakhs to Rs. 8 lakhs.[2] Between 1920 and 1921 three more schools, the Har Prasad Das Jain High School at Arrah, the Heycock Academy at Motihari and the Monghyr Training Academy were granted recognition. The Mrs. Perin Memorial School at Jamshedpur was recognised for the purpose of the School Leaving Certificate Examination. On the other hand recognition was withdrawn from six schools which took an active part in non-cooperation movement.[3]

Between 1920 and 1921 though three schools were added, but all the schools, both new and old, lost 10 percent students. The political condition of the period was responsible for this decline. In 1920-21 another important new development was to hold for the first time a School Leaving Certificate Examination. The object of this scheme was to initiate a special course in secondary schools. It was designed to prepare students for commercial or clerical courses. This introduction led to the unpopularity of Middle Vernacular schools, because a similar leaving certificate examination was introduced in these schools also.[4]

---

1. Patna University, Minutes of the Senate, Syndicate and Faculties 1920-21, p. 12
2. G. E. Owen op. cit., p. 116
3. Report on the Progress of Education in Bihar and Orissa 1920-21, p. 11
4. G. E. Owen, op. cit., O. 117

Secondary Schools in Bihar and Orissa.[1]

	1916 17	1920-21	1921-22
High Schools			
Number of schools	100	118	119
Number of pupils	34,734	25,269	24,645
Middle English Schools			
Number of schools	226	259	275
Number of Pupils	23,415	21,849	19,270
Middle Vernacular Schools			
Number of schools	130	158	159
Number of Pupils	11,635	11,815	11,323

The technical education in Bihar remained confined to the two schools, viz., the Bihar School of Engineering and the Temple Medical School even though there was persistent demand of educated and enlightened group of educated persons to raise their status and convert them into colleges. The strength of students in Bihar School of Engineering on 31 March 1918 was 155, but this fell to 116 in 1921. This school was greatly affected by the non-cooperation movement : a large number of students left the school and joined the National School at *Sadaquat Ashram*. But by 1922 there was a little improvement and the number of students increased to 153.[2]

During the period 1917-1921, 193 students in all left the school with certificates and 184 of these were able to secure employment. The old Board of Visitors was replaced by a strong Governing Body consisting of 17 members and considerably powers were delegated to it. A scheme to raise the school to the status of a college was placed before the Government but it could not be raised during this period. The Surveyor class was abolished owing to the difficulty experienced by passed students in obtaining employment. The overseer and sub-overseer classes were separated. The former was named the Upper sub-ordinate class and its course

1. The Second Quinquennial Review on the Progress of Education in Bihar and Orissa, p. 54
2. Ibid., pp. 92-93

was made of three years. The latter was made a course of two years and was called Lower-Sub-ordinate class.[1]

The Temple Medical School was gradually progressing. The number of students was 159 in 1917-18, 169 in 1918-19, 246 in 1919-20, 258 in 1920-21, and 267 in 1921-22.[2] There was a four year course conducted in English by the Medical Examination Board from 1917. For the first time in the history of the school two students of the depressed classes were admitted during this period.

There was an attempt to attract female students as well to the medical school. Some Government Scholarships of the value of Rs. 10 per month were awarded to female students. One such scholarship was awarded by the District Board of Patna to a deserving student of the school without any agreement or condition. The Lady Elliot Scholarship was awarded to a Mohammaden female student from Bihar who, after qualifying, undertook to work under the Lady Dufferin's Fund Association. Scholarships were also sometimes available from the Countess of Dufferin's Fund, District Boards, Municipalities and other sources.[3]

Twenty-four Government scholarships, each of Rs. 10 a month and an equal number of scholarships were awarded to male students of the Medical school in Bihar. Three scholarships were also awarded by the District Board of Patna, each of the value of Rs. 10 a month to male student. In addition to the scholarships and studentships mentioned above, four scholarships of Rs. 5 a month each was awarded to four meritorious Mohammaden students. It was paid from the Quazi Reza Hussain's Fund.[4]

In rural areas the most popular institutions were local hospitals and dispensaries established by the Government. But considerable difficulty was found in obtaining Bihari doctors particularly Hindus. In 1921 there were 155 permanent Sub-Assistant Surgeons employed in Bihar and Orissa out of which only 9 were

1. **Ibid.**
2. **Ibid.**, p. 85
3. **Ibid.**, pp. 86 87
4. **Ibid.**

Bihari and 33 Oriya Hindus and 24 Mohammedans while the number of Bangali doctors was 63 in addition to 23 domiciled Bengal-doctors. This was partly due to caste prejudice, which was still continuing among the Biharis. Moreover, while the average number of Biharis seeking admission in the Calcutta Medical College was between 40 and 60, only 18 seats were made available to them. Eventually, the situation improved when the Temple Medical School was developed, and in 1920 a large hostel was constructed.[1]

There were a few elementary technical schools under the Department of Industries in Bihar created in April 1920. The number of applications for admission in the Bihar School of Engineering in 1921 was 352. The Ranchi Industrial School continued to give elementary training of motor mechanics, chiefly to Christian aborigines. The Mission schools at Bettiah and Chaibasa also imparted training in carpentry and blacksmithy. In the Perin Memoral Technical School training for the employees of the Tata Works at Jamshedpur was carried. Beniadih School at Giridih used to train workers for the railway workshops. The Industry Department prepared an important scheme for a school of Mines and Geology at Dhanbad during this period. The Tata Iron and Steel Company had already started a metallurgical school, and reorganised the evening and morning classes. Thus with the growth of industries in South Bihar elementary technical education developed on an unprecedented scale. At the same time in North Bihar there was an attempt to establish Technical and Industrial Institute at Muzaffarpur. A Committe was appointed to consider this project.[2]

But the higher technical education could not be started in Bihar during the period under review. Though there was a move to convert the Engineering and Medical schools into colleges, it took a few years after 1921 in achieving this purpose.[3]

---

1. G. E. Owen, **op. cit.**, pp. 135-136
2. **Ibid.**, p. 70
3. The Bihar School of Engineering was converted into college in 1924 and a Medical College replaced Temple Medical School in 1925

The Patna University Committee had recommended that Law should be made an undergraduate subject to be taught on the University campus. This scheme was considered by the Patna University Syndicate and Faculty's of Law in 1918 and it was decided that Law should remain a post-graduate subject as recommended by the Calcutta University Commission, and should continue to be taught in a separate college outside the University campus. Proposals were also made to improve the staff of the Patna Law College. In 1915 the Patna Law College was shifted to the old building of the Patna Training College, but in 1920 it was housed in a large rented building. The total number of students in the Patna Law College in 1921 was 262.[1] On 31 March 1922 the number of students was 272 as against 202 five years before. But the pleadership classes were becoming unpopular, there being only 18 students at one time as against 46 students five years before. The reason was the lengthening of the course from two years to three years in 1920. The pleadership classes at Bhagalpur ceased to exist by 1921-22.[2]

The proposal to have a training college for graduates on the university campus and two institutions for teachers with Intermediate qualifications was postponed with the rest of the scheme for a Central University.[3]

During this period oriental education was encouraged. A Superintendent of Sanskrit Studies was appointed in 1918-19.

The Sanskrit School at Muzaffarpur which had been under Government control was now designated as a 'college'. The *madarsa* at Bankipore was also taken over by the Government. Boards were set-up to conduct examinations in Sanskrit and Islamic studies.[4]

Attempt to improve female education continued against many obstacles. The spread of education among boys had its impact on

---

1. **Report on the Progress of Education in Bihar and Orissa, 1920-21 p.** 10
2. **The Second Quinquennial Review of the Progress of Education in Bihar and Orissa, p.** 48
3. **Ibid., p.** 49
4. **First Decennial Review** (1912-22), p. 230, **Also see J. S. Jha, 'Sanskrit** Education in Bihar' **JBRS,** Vol XLV II parts 1-4

female education. But the sphere of female education remained confined to the primary stage only. The Female Education Committee made further recommendations for the improvement of female education. The Inspectress of Schools suggested that M. P. G. School at Dumraon and the Girls' Upper Primary Schools at Gaya and Muzaffarpur might be raised to the middle vernacular Standard. The Committee also proposed that the number of primary schools for girls was to be doubled in ten years. But the Government could not implement them due to a paucity of funds.[1] The only concrete step they took was to have one female high school in every division so that there could be seven Girls' High schools in the province. Their order regarding opening of I. A. classes at Bankipore did not materialise. The number of public institutions for girls increased from 2,586 to 2,634 in 1917-18. In 1920-21 the primary schools for girls including *maktabs* and *Sanskrit Pathshala* were 2,641 with 61,073 girls students.[2]

Secondary schools for girls in Bihar were two, but there was an addition of one High School for girls in 1917-18. The St. Margaret School at Ranchi was recognised as a High School. The number of girls in the high school of the province (including one school of Orissa) was 719. The number of Middle English Schools fell from 5 to 4 and that of their pupils from 665 to 313, because no other school replaced St. Margaret School of Ranchi.[3] By the end of the period there was an addition of seven new Middle English Schools. Thus the number of such schools in Bihar increased from 4 to 11. These new seven schools were the Bangali schools at Ranchi, the Mokshada Girls School at Bhagalpur, the Chapman Girls' School at Muzaffarpur, the Bangali Girls' School at Hazaribagh, the Lutheran School at Ranchi and the Jamshedpur Girls' School.[4] The increase in the number of Middle English schools indicated a change in future. The number of Middle vern-

1. Educational Proceedings (Govt. of Bihar & Orissa); 1916, nos. 3)-31 p. 9
2. Report on the Progress of Education in Bihar and Orissa, 1920-21 p. 16
3. Report on the Administration of Bihar and Orissa, 1918-19 p. 104
4. The Second Quinquennial Review on the Progress of Education in Bihar and Orissa, 1917-22, p. 103

acular schools remained 11 but there was an increase in the number of students from 1,243 to 1,445.[1]

The majority of Girls' Middle English schools of the province were being run by missionaries. During this period new buildings for the Baptist Mission English School (Middle) were completed. At the same time spacious new premises were acquired for the American Mission Middle School at Muzaffarpur.

There was a great demand for female education which increased due to economic distresses combined with the effect of political agitation. In 1921 over 41 per cent of the girls at school were reading in the boys schools, the great number of them in lower primary schools. There were no female teachers in the boys' school, therefore half of the girl students used to leave the school without getting a proper education.[2] The number of students attached to the Badshah Nawab Razvi Training College was 130 in 1917-18.[3] The Lady Principal of this college reported that the Mohammedan students who passed out this institution were facing a great difficulty in getting employment even though only 0.64 per cent of females in this province were getting educated in 1921.[4] Five such teachers who were discriminated against went to Bengal and four more were about to leave the province in search of service. On the other hand Hindu female teachers of this college were being employed locally.

The number of High Schools for girls remained 3 in Bihar and 1 at Cuttak in Orissa in 1920, but the strength of their students decreased from 719 to 672. The Bankipore Girls' school moved from a rented building to a large Government Bunglow formerly used as a Circuit House on the Bank of the Ganges. Efforts were made to construct the Lady Principal's quarter and a temporary hostel in the school compound. There were 112 girls in the Bankipore school in 1920. Three girls appeared at and passed the Matricula-

---

1. **Ibid.**
2. G. E. Owen, **op. cit.**, p. 112
3. **Report on the Administration of Bihar and Orissa,** 1918-19, pp. 103-05
4. G. E. Owen, **op, cit.** 1. 119

tion examination this year.[1] In 1921 the number of students in Girls' High Schools was slightly increased from 672 to 681.

There was a decline in the number of students in other two girls' school of Bihar. The school at Giridih was run by the Bengali Brahamos of the town. The managing committee of the Giridih High School was reorganised during the year to make it more representative. But when the Sadharan Brahma Samaj lost its control over the school, a number of girls were withdrawn from this school. In 1920 four girls appeared at the Matriculation examination of whom one passed. The third girls' school at Bihar managed by a Mission, St. Margaret's Girls' High School at Ranchi, had 370 students in 1920. One girl appeared at the Matriculation examination from this school but failed in 1920.[2]

The number of students in the Middle English School also increased in 361. However, the number of pupils attending the practising school attached to the Badshah Nawab Razvi Training College fell from 130 to 118. According to Lady Principal the decrease occurred due to the fact that many children discontinued their study on account of the high cost of living in Patna City.[3]

CHAPTER V

COLLEGIATE EDUCATION (1906-1917)

The progress of collegiate education in Bihar continued through the Calcutta University which remained the only university for the whole of Bengal, Bihar and Orissa. The majority of the colleges were situated in Bengal. In 1905-06 the total number of Arts

1. **Report on the Progress of the Education in Bihar and Orissa,** 1919-20 p-15
2. **Ibid.**
3. **Ibid.**

colleges in the Bengal Presidency was 34. Ten among them were under public management and 24 colleges were under private management. Of the ten colleges under public management 8 were Government colleges and 2 were managed by local authorities. Of the 24 colleges under private management 5 were aided and 18 were unaided. Of the 34 colleges as many as 17 were in Calcutta, 4 being Government colleges, 4 aided and 9 unaided colleges.[1]

But the total number of colleges in Bihar remained six, each one of which was established in the later part of the nineteenth century. Bihar had only one Government college viz., Patna college. This college improved considerably during this period : a large area of land in the neighbourhood of the college was acquired in order to make the college premises more compact and to provide rooms for additional building. In 1906-07 arrangements were made for the construction of a hostel for Hindu students to be called the 'Minto Hindu Hostel'. Money for the construction of this hostel was subscribed by the Maharaja of Darbhanga, Giddhour and Sonbarsa, the Raja of Khaira and Maharanis of Bettiah, Dumaraon and Hathua. These donations were made in honour of the visit to Bankipore of the Viceroy in 1905-06[2]

The attendance at Patna College decreased during the years 1902-1907 due to outbreak of plague. In 1904 the number of students was 144, but the average of the last five years was 192, while the number in 1906 was 201.[3] Jackson while commenting on the 'Future working of the Patna College', remarked : "Arrangements are being made for the removal of the collegiate school from the college premises in accordance with the views expressed on the subject by the universities commission and for the construction of new physical and chemical laboratories. Hence there will be no difficulty in providing accommodation for the number proposed.[4]

Charles Russel, the Principal of the Patna College, had the following comment on the progress of the Patna College during

1. **Report on Public Instruction in Bengal**, 1905-06, p. 13
2. **Report on Public Instruction in Bengal**, 1906-06, p. 14
3. **Educational Proceedings** (Govt. of Bengal, 1907, nos. 140-53
4. A. Earle to the Government of Bengal, 19 June 1907.

this period : "It may be claimed for the Patna College that during the past five years it has made some appreciable advance in the direction of what is now universally recognised as the ideal at which one college should aim. It has done much to free itself from the reproach frequently levelled against Indian colleges that they are merely places at which lectures are delivered and certificate of attendance issued. Lecturers have now been supplemented by a system of monthly examinations which has become a very important factor in the work of the college.[1]

But there is no denying the fact that the strength of the college was much below the expectation of the authorities. The officiating Director of Public Instruction, H. R. James, significantly observed : "We have a right to look for very much more than this.......a marked expansion is to be expected in the next five or ten years. ......The Patna College has at present to provide, in great part, for the higher educational needs both of Patna and Tirhut....."[2]

Naturally enough, there was an attempt to develop the Patna College by the Government during this period. In a note on the future working of the Patna College at the beginning of this period (1907-08) Jackson reviewed its prospects as follows :

"When the improvements in the Patna College, which are now being carried out by Government, are completed, this college will be the first Government Arts college in Bengal to possess in anything like a complete form, the essential elements of a residential college-buildings, houses for professors and students, playing fields, gymnasium, common rooms and library, athletic and social organisations. For various reasons it does not appear that any other college will be able to develop, for several years at any rate, these essential, features as fully and completely as the Patna College. This College starts therefore with a great advantage over all others."[3]

1. Quoted in the Proceedings of Education, Government of Bengal, 1908
2. J. N. Sarkar and J. C. Jha, History of Patna College (1863-1963) Patna, 1963, p. 98
3. Educational Proceedings (Govt. of Bengal), December 1907. no. 140, p. 699

A scheme for the improvement of Patna College was at last initiated by the Government authorities. This scheme proposed the construction of a Mohammedan hostel, a Principal's residence, a house for Professors, a Gymnasium and a Laboratory including fittings. The Government of Bengal provided a sum of Rs. 1,00,000 in the budget of 1906-07 for the improvement of the Patna College. The extension scheme thus got underway. The Minto Hostel was completely occupied, the Mohammedan hostel was almost ready for occupation and a gymnasium was provided. There were plans in 1908 for the residential quarters of the Principal and a Professor of the college.[1]

According to the recommendation of Professor Ramsay of the University College, London, the Government decided to start the teaching of physics and chemistry in the Patna College and to have an amalgamated laboratory for the Temple Medical College and the Bihar School of Engineering at the Patna College.[2]

Jackson had rightly said in 1907, that the Patna College was ahead of other Government colleges of Bengal in getting essential elements of a residential college. It maintained its lead in this respect in 1909-10. The scheme of development was not carried with much speed owing to financial considerations. Even so, the progress was not negligible. The Minto Hostel and the Mohammedan Hostel were completed, and these two hostels in the college ground gave it a residential shape.

In extension of this scheme houses for the Principal and one European Professor were also constructed by 1908-09. The collegiate school was removed to some other place so that the Arts classes of the college got more accommodation. The report on public instruction in Bengal mentioned in 1909 that the Patna College, first of the larger Government college was quite single and self-contained. With the severence of the Engineering School, the

---

1. **Report of Public Instruction in Bengal**, 1907-08, p. 10
2. **A. Earle, D. P. I. to the Government of Bengal, 19 June 1907. Jackson however opposed the proposal of amalgamation.**

Patna College became a single homogeneous institution. It was an arts-college—an organic unity and nothing more.[1]

The chief need of the Patna College was an improvement of Laboratories. Plans were made and approved in 1905, but sufficient funds for its execution could not be provided. The Principal reported in 1909 that the accommodation for scientific work was not sufficient. Thus science teaching could not be improved during the period.

All the same, certain distinguishing features of college life were imbibed in the Patna College. There were regular games, and the students common room, and the Archaeological Society were full of life. The students used to stage dramas and contributed articles in college magazines.[2] The colleges other than Patna College were private colleges—both aided and unaided. These colleges in Bihar specially the Bihar National College(1889) at Bankipore and the Tej Narayan Jubilee College (1887) at Bhagalpur were established by private enterprise. They had completed 20 years of their life and were started in response to growing demands for expansion of higher education in this province. Since the opening of these two colleges the progress of higher education in Bihar continued in a remarkable way.

Certain public associations in Bihar were not inactive either. The Bihar Land Holders Association, the Bihar Provincial Association and the Bihar Provincial Muslim League presented joint addresses to Andrew Fraser, the Lt. Governor of Bengal urging to promote higher education. Sri Krishna Sahay, Secretary, Bihar Landholders Association, drew the attention of the Government to the need of grants to the private colleges in Bihar : "The new university regulations have put such a heavy strain upon the resources of private colleges that the public in Bihar have been watching with the gravest anxiety the immediate future of the college. All of them have become more or less mutilated on account of the restriction, and some are almost in the very jaw of death. The

---

1. **Report on Public Instruction in Bengal**, 1908-09, p. 9
2. **Report on Public Instruction in Bengal**, 1907-08, p. 10

cause of higher education in Bihar appears to be seriously threatened and can be saved only if Government be pleased to see that our colleges have a just and proper share of help from the provincial revenues as grants-in-aid.[1]

The total number of students in private colleges in Bengal in 1907 was 4,047 ; of these only 339 belonged to the private colleges in Bihar.[2]

In 1907 out of a total of Rs.60,000 distributed as grants-in-aid, only Rs. 2,000 went to only one college in Bihar, the Bihar National College, Bankipore. Because the grants-in-aid was a recent innovation in 1907, it was confined to very few colleges. The Tej Narayan Jubilee College did not apply that year while the Bihar National College applied for grant of Rs. 300 and received only Rs. 200 a month. The Bhumihar Brahman College, Muzaffarpur, applied for the maintenance grant of Rs. 700, and a building grant of Rs. 26,000. The Director of Public Instruction commented : "The Bhumihar Brahman College was in a very weak state and had been very unfavourably reported on by the University Inspectors. For these reasons no grant could at the time be given.[3] What a strange argument !

The Bihar National College and the Bhumihar Brahman College, however, both made praiseworthy efforts after 1907 to place their institutions on a sound basis. The result was that the Bihar National College received a grant both in 1907-08 and 1908-09. Strenuous efforts were made in Muzaffarpur also and in 1909 it was announced that Rs. 1,61,000 had been subscribed for the support of the Bhumihar Brahman College. With this grant the college was placed on a sound financial basis.[4]

In 1906-07 out of Rs. 2,70,000, Rs. 36,000 were distributed among the colleges in Bihar.[5] These colleges were three in number.

---

1. Krishna Sahay to Government of Bengal, General Dept., 26 March 1909.
2. H.R. James, Offg. D.P.I. of Bengal, to Government of Bengal, 18 August, 1909.
3. Ibid.
4. Ibid.
5. Ibid.

1. Bihar National College	Rs. 14,0C0
2. Tej Narayan Jubilee College	Rs. 19,000
3. Bhumihar Brahman College	Rs. 3,000
Total	Rs. 36,000

In 1908-09 a grant of Rs. 7,000 was recommended to the Bihar National College for the improvement of the library and the Laboratory on condition that the college authorities were prepared to spend Rs. 6,000. Government hoped that the condition would be accepted.[1]

The Diamond Jubilee College at Monghyr could not get financial assistance. It was not thought desirable during the period (1907-08) to recommend a grant for this college, as it appeared uncertain to the authorities that the college would continue to exist for long. On the occasion of his visit to Monghyr the Lt. Governor threw out a suggestion that instead of maintaining the college, the college authorities might consider the propriety of establishing scholarships to enable the students of Monghyr to take admission to some other college in Bihar.[2]

Dubline University Mission College at Hazaribagh established by the Missionaries had been named St. Columba's College. This college applied for a grant of Rs. 25,000 for the construction of college buildings in 1907-08. The construction was estimated to cost at least Rs. 1,00,000 of which the college authorities hoped to raise Rs. 55,000 from private sources. At long last the Syndicate recommended a grant of Rs. 10,000.[3]

The change of outlook on the part of private colleges was hailed by the Director of Public Instruction, Bengal : "A new era has set in with university reform. The colleges which formerly repudiated Government aid now contend for it, and even

1. Govt. of Bengal Education Proceedings (General Dept.), February 1908, nos. 60-62, p. 96
2. Ibid.
3. Ibid., p. 97

claim it as a right. This may be a better tendency and deserving of judicious encouragement."[1]

He emphasised the need of Government encouragement in view of Bihar's backwardness in the matter of education : "Apart from the claims now built up by the efforts of self-help, it may be recognised that the special circumstances and needs of Bihar do constitute a claim on Government which might with advantage be acknowledged in action practically. Education in Bihar does lag behind Bengal, and it is expedient on every ground to help Bihar forward...Bihar was a great home of culture in the past and may be again. For these various reasons Government is already granting liberal support to its own college at Patna"[2]

The following table gives a picture of the number of students in different colleges of Bihar during the period 1906-1908[3]

	1906	1907	1908	1909
1. Patna College	105	178	189	167
2. B. N. College	62	103	110	75
3. Tej Narayan College	183	180	178	118
4. Bhumihar Brahman College	64	57	51	36
5. St. Columba's College	69	—	46	37
6. Diamond Jubilee College	32	16	19	15

On 31 March 1910 the strength of these colleges was 245, 246, 231, 101, 108 and 17[4] respectively.

The seats of higher education in Bihar was, however, limited to only six colleges. But once private colleges began to be opened, the progress was rapid and steady, the number standing at 776 in 1900. The number of students however began to fall after the outbreak of plague in the early years of the twentieth century. The numbers fell every year and the low-water mark was reached in 1906 when the total strength of these colleges stood at 446. The

1. H. R. James to Government of Bengal, 18 August 1909
2. **Ibid.**
3. **Report on Public Instruction in Bengal 1908-09 (Supplement), Table 11, p. 6**
4. **Report on Public Instruction in Bengal (Supplement) 1909-10 p. 6**

new university regulation of 1906 also affected these colleges. As Maulvi Saiyed Muhammad Fakruddin said in course of his budget speech in the Bengal legislative council, under the new university rules the private college faced a crisis. The situation was saved through the Government aid and generous donations from the leading lights of the province. He regretted that the only Government college viz., the Patna College, was not even in a position to provide higher education.[1]

Maharaja Gopal Saran Narayan Singh wondered in the Bengal legislative council if the Government contributions to private college of Bihar were sufficient. The Government had to admit that the aid to Bihar colleges was much less in comparison to their counterparts, in Bengal.[2] By the end of this period however there was an improvement in these colleges. The following table gives name, grade, management and number of pupils of each Arts College in 1911-12 :[3]

Colleges	Grade	Management	No. of Pupils
1. Patna College	Ist	Government	265
2. Bihar National College	Ist	Private	347
3. Tej Narayan Jubilee College	Ist	Private	269
4. Bhumihar Brahman College	Ist	Private	116
5. St. Columba's College	Ist	Missionary	104
6. Diamond Jubilee College	2nd	Private	14

Thus in 1911 there were 6 Arts Colleges with 1115 pupils in Bihar. The total expenditure on these Colleges amounted to Rs. 2,44,803 of which Rs. 1,19,773 was contributed from provincial revenues, Rs. 2,700 from district funds, Rs. 85,211 from fees, and Rs. 30,169 from subscriptions and endowments. The average cost of educating a pupil in an Arts College was Rs. 171.2[4]

1. **The Beharee,** 15 April 1910
2. **Ibid.,** 4 March 1909
3. **Bihar and Orissa Administration Report,** 1911-12 p. 224
4. **Ibid.,** p. 225

Early in 1906 a scheme for establishing a residential Arts college at Ranchi was submitted to the Government of India. This scheme to establish a Model Arts College and a Model School had originated in September 1904. Andrew Fraser, the Lieutenant Governor, had called a conference at Belvedre and addressed the representatives of public opinion who attended it. Originally it was proposed to shift the Presidency College from Calcutta to Ranchi, but after some deliberations the Ranchi scheme was regarded as a new and independent project. The proposal to establish a Model School at Ranchi was also withdrawn in 1906. In its place it was proposed to improve certain zila schools one of which would be the zila school at Ranchi.[1]

The proposal to establish a residential Arts College at Ranchi was a result of long and careful consideration. Opinions were sought and a decision was taken in consultation with the Director of Public Instruction and several officers of the Education Department—as well as with local zamindars, judges and other professional men, both individually and collectively.[2]

Apart from all other considerations, it appeared most desirable that an Arts College should be established at the headquarters of the Chotanagpur division which had a rapidly developing population certain to develop much more rapidly in future owing to the opening of the railways, factories and mines. Since this division had 14 high schools, as against 13 in Orissa; it had better claims to have an Arts College. In fact an attempt to provide Ranchi an Arts College had been made as early as 1875 by the then Lieutenant Governor Richard Temple. But that proposal had been abandoned because then the number of students coming out of schools was not encouraging. But by 1907-08 the picture was different : it was suggested that between 1902 and 1907 about 270 students passed the Matriculation Examination in this division.[3]

---

1. T. W. Richardson, Secretary to the Government of Bengal to the Government of India, Home Department, 10 August, 1906
2. Ibid., 10 February 1907
3. Ibid.

There was a great desire on the part of many influential Zamindars, Indian Government officers, senior Deputy Collectors or subordinate judges, professional men such as barristers, pleaders and doctors practising in interiors, in short the elite, to have a college in healthy surroundings. Sir Andrew Fraser was equally anxious to establish a college at Ranchi to meet the needs of the people of the Chota Nagpur as well as to offer healthy conditions to those who desired them.[1]

All sections of people promised cooperation and a number of gentlemen came forward offering large sums for the provision of hostel accommodation in connection with the proposed college. A sum of over three lakhs of rupees was subscribed. There was also a proposal to construct a hostel for the sons of zamindars. Following persons subscribed for the hostel :

1. Bijoy Chand Mahtab, the Burdwan Maharaj, donated Rs. 40,000 for a hostel after his name.
2. Rameshwar Singh donated Rs. 40,000 for constructing a hostel for Bihari Hindu students.
3. Nawab Khwaja Salimulla's contribution of Rs. 40,000 was for a hostel called 'KHWAJA Alimullah's Hostel'.
4. Raja Durga Pd. Singh of the Jharia Estate donated Rs. 50,000 for the hostel for Hindu students.
5. Maharani Hathwa donated Rs. 40,000 which was meant for the hostel named after Sri Krishna Prasad Sahi Bahadur.[2]

The whole of the money was contemplated to be utilised for the construction of four hostels, and the balance would be reserved for future extension.

The correspondence between local Government and the Government of India continued for five years. But the latter was unable to accept the scheme; for some time it was kept in abeyance In 1909 on 31 July a conference was convened to consider the Ranchi College scheme. The Lieutenant Governor opened the

1. Ibid.
2. Ibid.

proceedings and explained to the meeting that the Government of India had finally refused to give any financial assistance towards the scheme. The local Government had no funds to proceed with the proposed scheme either. Therefore a sum of Rs. 2,90,000 which was contributed for the construction of hostels in connection with the proposed college, was diverted to the construction of residential hostels at the Presidency, Patna and Cuttack colleges.[1] Thus the hope to get a college at Ranchi faded away after much enthusiasm shown by the Bengal Government and the local people. There was a demand by the zamindars for a residential college at a suitble place. The Muhammedans of the province also desired to have an institution on the lines of the Aligarh College. But after much discussion the Government of India refused to assist the scheme on financial ground. Higher education was thus left to private enterprise and Government preferred to remain in the background, trying to improve the institutions on the lines of new regulations.

Teaching of Law in Bihar continued to be imparted in classes attached to Arts colleges for many years. A deputation of representatives of Bihar therefore represented an address to Andrew Fraser in August 1908, demanding a Law College at Patna. The Lieutenant Governor gave a definite assurance and the Director of Public Instruction was accordingly directed to draw up a definite scheme for the establishment of a Law College at Patna from July 1909[2]

The Lt. Governor said that the establishment of a Law College at Patna was "of greatest importance and urgency" and, as such, he strongly supported the proposal.

The need for a teachers' training college was also felt. Therefore a meeting was held at Belvedre on 29 August 1908 to discuss the question of a training college for Bihar. The Lieutenant Governor pointed out in his presidential address the extreme importance of providing some machinery for the training of Bihari teachers.

1. Harold Stuart, to the Govt. of Bengal, General Department, 4 June 1909
2. Report on Public Instruction in Bengal, 1908-09, p. 31

Justice Mookerjee, the Vice-chancellor, Calcutta University said that Bihar urgently required a good Hindu Inspector and also trained Bihari teachers. The Government, therefore, decided to start the college after Puja holidays. Maulvi Muhammad Hashim, resident of Saran district who was working as assistant master, Anglo-Persian department service, Calcutta Madarsa, was selected for the teaching staff of the proposed college and one Thickett was deputed to organise the college.[1]

The Bihar School of Engineering remained under the control of the Principal of the Patna College till 1908. In 1907 the number of students was 151, but it soon increased to 188, the courses included Overseer class, and Amin class. Therefore in 1909 the Engineering Section was removed from the control of the Patna College Principal and it got an independent status. There was a persistent demand to raise the status of the school and convert it into a college. Babu Gajadhar Prasad asked at the meeting of the Bengal Legislative Council whether the Government would consider the expediency of raising the Bihar School of Engineering to the status of a college.[2] Streatfield, Secretary to the Government of Bengal replied that it was hoped to shift the Sibpur Engineering College to Ranchi and therefore it was not possible to have another college.

In fact, Andrew Fraser, who devoted much time to the welfare of Bihar, had suggested as far back as March 1904 to remove the Sibpur Engineering College to a healthier and better site in Ranchi. Fraser, who had made Chhaju Bagh house his residence at Patna, had received several memorials from enlightened Biharis regarding the expansion of education on the basis of which a detailed scheme was prepared for the transfer of this college. But after five years of correspondence the proposal was dropped and the technical education in Bihar remained limited to the Bihar School of Engineering.

---

1. H. C. Steatfield, to the Director of Public Instruction, Bengal, 3 September 1908
2. Interpullation in Bengal Legislative Council, 25 January 1908

The educated men of Bihar, however, were alive to the educational needs of the province during and after the first decade of the present century. Mazharul Haque presiding over the fourth session of Bihar Provincial Conference in 1911 said : "The Bihar School of Engineering and the Temple Medical School are still schools and have not been raised to the status of College. It is idle to blame the people for being apathetic towards technical education.[1]

Attempts were being made by the educated and enlightened persons to create public opinion in favour of technical education. The Bihari students conference passed the following resolution in its session of 28 and 29 September 1907 : "This conference strongly deprecates the tendency among Biharee students to crowd the legal and such other professions and it is of opinion that no true progress will be made in India until technical and industrial education are developed to their fullest extent, and therefore urges its members to take to technical, industrial and commercial lines."[2]

The higher education in agriculture was given at Sibpur College in Bengal. But from November 1908 the agriculture classes at Sibpur college were closed and thus higher education in agriculture closed to be the concern of the education department. Therefore an Agriculture college at Sibpur in Bihar under the control of the Director of Agriculture was established in 1908.[3]

Thus efforts were made for providing technical and scientific education in Bihar—on the eve of its separation from Bengal.

The following table gives a comparative picture of higher education in the province of Bihar and Orissa.[4]

Province	Population	Number of Colleges
Bengal	45,483,077	51
Madras	41,405,404	39
Bombay	19,672,642	15

1. **The Beharee**, 8 December 1911
2. **Ibid.**, 8 October 1907
3. **The Report on Public Instruction in Bengal**, 1909-10 p. 33
4. **Statistical Abstract for British India**, Vol. 1, 1915

United Provinces	47,182,044	49
Punjab	19,974,956	19
Bihar & Orissa	34,490,184	7

A comparison of the proportion of colleges with population reveals that Bihar was very backward. Bihar had only six colleges in all and Orissa had one.

There were two colleges managed by Government in Bihar. The number of students in these colleges increased during the period 1911-1917.[1]

Number of Students.

	1911-12	1915-16	1916-17
Patna College	265	370	382
Greer Bhumihar Brahman College	116	292	270

The Patna College improved during this period a good deal. Considerable improvements were made in its buildings and equipments. Two plots of land on the west of the college were acquired at a cost of Rs. 22,285. A new chemical laboratory and two class rooms were built on this site. The surroundings of the college on the southeast were also greatly improved. Residential Quarters were built for two Professors and a temporary hostel to accommodate 72 students was constructed in 1914-15. The Patna College received special grants amounting in all to Rs. 22,795.[2]

The number of staff was raised from 16 to 23 and the college was capable of teaching 510 students during this period. The maximum number on the rolls in 1915-16 was 455. The college was not full, because students used to apply for admission to more than one college at the same time. Thus all students accepted for admission did not join the college.[3]

Even though the Patna College with both Arts and Science teaching was the chief college of Bihar, it had no real post-gra-

1. **The First Quinquennial Review on the Progress of Education in Bihar and Orissa,** 1912-17, p. 48
2. **Ibid.,** p. 49
3. **Ibid.**

duate classes, though university lectures were delivered in Economics and History. The college library during the period contained 10,974 volumes. The college had three societies attached to the Common Room, the Archaeological Society, the Chanakya Society and the Debating Society.

The Greer Bhumihar Brahman College was taken under the direct Management of the Government in 1915. It was placed under a Governing Body consisting of the Commissioner as President, the Principal as Vice-President and Secretary and four members of whom three were non-officials and one a member of the staff.

A considerable area surrounding the college was acquired in order to provide a site for new building. Pending the permanent construction of buildings, four temporary class rooms were built during 1913-14 at a cost of Rs. 4,803. In 1915-16 again six such rooms were built at a cost of Rs. 4,032 and a temporary hostel for 39 students costing Rs. 10,444 was arranged. These temporary additions marked a great improvement in the college. In 1912 the staff consisted of 11 members, but in 1916-17 there were 16 members.

The three aided colleges in Bihar were St. Columba's College, Hazaribagh, the Tej Narayan College, Bhagalpur and the Bihar National College at Bankipore. The number of students in these colleges, increased during the period 1912-1917.[1]

Colleges	Number of Students		
	1911-12	1915-16	1916-17
Bihar National College :	347	578	588
Tej Narayan Jubilee College :	269	497	621
St. Columba's College	104	164	183
	720	1,239	1,392

Thus the number of students in these colleges increased about two times in five years. It was certainly an encouraging sign of development of higher education in Bihar. The number of colle-

1. Ibid., p. 56

ges remained the same, but the number of students increased with speed. In the beginning of this period the Bihar National College was the largest college.[1] With regards to the number of students, the improvement in accommodation was static. The university committee recommended that the college should be removed to the university area and for this reason improvement in building was suspended. Only when it was decided that one college should be left in Bankipore the construction of additional rooms was taken up. Two such rooms were completed during 1915-16 at a cost of Rs. 8,824. The adjacent female ward of the Bankipore Hospital was acquired by the Government in 1913-14 for the use of the college. Further it was decided in 1912 to erect a hostel in the college grounds, but the site was found to be too cramped for the purpose and in consequence a building was rented elsewhere. In the beginning of 1912-13 the college received a grant of Rs. 400 a month but in 1914-15 the amount was raised to Rs. 1,000 a month.[2]

The Tej Narain Jubilee College was the largest college of Bihar even in 1916-17, as the number of students increased twice during the five years. But the staff increased only from 14 to 19. The college building was not adequate for the number of students and it was decided to construct a new building on a site to the west of the town. Soon the necessary land was acquired for the purpose. The cost of building was estimated by the University Committee at Rs. 6,58,928. The Government gave an assurance for half of the amount and the other half was offered by proprietors of the Banaili estate.[3]

The old Board of Trustees and the Managing Committee of the college were reconstituted. A Board of three Trustees and a Managing Committee of ten members were formed. The Managing Committee consisted of the Commissioner and the District Judge (ex-officio), the three Trustees, the Principal, two Professors and two persons nominated by a senior Member of the Banaili estate.[4]

---

1. **The Patna University Silver Jubilee Souvenir Volume**, p. 86
2. **Ibid.** p. 57
3. **Ibid.**, p. 58. That is why the name of Banaili has been added to name of Tej Narayan Singh.
4. **The First Quinquennial Review of the Progress of Education in Bihar and Orissa**, 1912-1917 p. 56

The St. Columba's College was improving continuously during this period. A new block to accommodate 37 students was added to the hostel with the help of a Government grant of Rs. 30,000. The Government gave another liberal grant of Rs. 50,000 to complete a large science laboratory. There was an active social life in this college. The Athletic Club, the Debating Society, a Common Room and Social Service Guild were the forums for students' activities. The Social Service[1] Guild was established in 1912 by Thomson. It tried to make students familiar with the lives of the people. A large number of students were associated with it. The society opened a small night school in Okni, a suburb of Hazaribagh.[2]

The Diamond Jubilee College was described by the University Committee as a weak institution. This was the only unaided college in Bihar. The number of students was 14 in 1912, increasing to 34 in 1915-16 and 56 in 1916-17. The Patna University Committee thought that in view of its small size this college should be allowed to disappear. This was one of the main points of criticism against the University Bill in the Indian Imperial Legislation Assembly. Consequently the bill was re-drafted, allowing this college to continue.[3] This college was managed through endowments which produced Rs. 1,970 a year.

During the period under review attempts were made to improve female education also. In 1912-13 only 3.4 percent of the girls of the school-going age were at school. The number of high schools remained 2, both receiving a grant of Rs. 350 per mensem from the Government besides an additional Government grant as house rent at Bankipore.[4]

In June 1914 a committee was appointed by the Government to examine the whole question of female education. This com-

---

1. See The Patna University Silver Jubilee Volume, p. 92
2. The First Quinquennial Review on the Education in Bihar and Orissa, 1912-17, p. 57
3. Ibid., p. 61
4. A Report on the Progress of Education in Bihar and Orissa, 1912-13 p. 16

mittee recommended that Intermediate classes for private candidates should be opened in Bankipore Girls' High School. There was a proposal to seek Intermediate affiliation, if the number of private candidates rose to 10. In case there were 20 private candidates a separate women's college might be established. (No body thinks of co-education even in the Patna College in those days : there was no girl student in the Patna College). The number of girls, attending the High schools increased from 286 to 300 in the province (including the Cuttack School). The Bankipore Girls' High School was taken under direct Government management. This school had 97 pupils in 1917. The Girls' High School at Giridih had 41 girls in High schools out of a total on the rolls.[1]

The number of Middle English schools for girls in Bihar was five during this period. The number of girls increased from 408 to 679 in these schools. The old schools were the Baptist Mission school at Bankipore, the American Mission school at Muzaffarpur and S. P. G, Mission school at Ranchi. Deoghar was raised to the Middle English status in 1913-14 and the practising school attached to the Badshah Nawab Razvi Training College for women became a Middle English school. The S. P. G. School at Ranchi was the largest with 367 girls on the rolls in 1917. The practising school attached to the Training College for women was developing steadily[2].

Thus the *parda* stricken Bihar was slowly receiving female education. The enlightened population and missionaries were trying to attract Bihari girl students. The Middle Vernacular schools increased from 10 to 11 during this period; the number of their students raising to 1,243 from 654. The sanctioned number of Government primary schools for girls was 59 but it was only 33 in 1912[3].

The leading newspaper of Bihar *The Beharee* tried to focus attention of the Government and people on the necessity for Wo-

---

1. The First Quinquennial Review on the Progress of Education in Bihar and Orissa, 1912-17, p. 95
2. Ibid.
3. Idib., pp. 97-98

men's College in Bihar. On 15th July 1916 it commented that it was lamentable that there was no one to come forward to help the cause.[1]

The Patna Training College since its establishment in 1908 had no building worth the name. The new buildings for the college in the compound of the old lunatic's asylum were completed and occupied and the number of the students raised during this period. The Bachelor of Teaching class in addition to the existing licentiate in teaching class was opened, and the teaching staff was proportionately strengthened. In addition to the new and spacious buildings for the Patna Collegiate School which was the practising school of the Training College was opened. There were 5 first grade (including one at Cuttack) training schools in which there were 280 students[2].

The law classes continued to be popular in Bihar. The figures in law classes show an increase of five times in the Patna Law College. The rapid development in the number of students necessitated two additional appointments of lecturers. The staff of the Law College consisted of a whole-time Principal and six part-time teachers[3]. The profession of law was most popular in Bihar and the educated middle class monopolised and patronised this branch.

Teaching of law continued to attract students in Bihar. The increase in this branch was seen in all the institutions of Law in the province. It was indeed a very encouraging sign. The variations in the number of students in these institutions during this period were the following[4].

	1911-12	1915-16	1916-17
Patna Law College (B. L.)	41	139	202
Patna Law College (Pleadership Class)	30	35	46
Bhagalpur Pleadership Class	20	21	30

1. Report on the Vernacular Newspaper of Bihar and Orissa, no. 26, 1916 p. 181
2. A Report on the Progress of Education in Bihar and Orissa 1915-16 p-11
3. The First Quinquennial Review on the Progress of Education in Bihar and Orissa, 1912-1917, p. 63
4. Ibid., p. 62

The other professional college in Bihar was the Patna Training College, which had only 6 students in 1911-12. But in 1915-16 the number rose to 40. During the next session, however, there was a decline in the number of students again. In fact this college had been started on an experimental basis in 1908, but in 1912 the formation of the new province made its permanent retention necessary. In August 1912 a scheme was prepared to develop the college and provide it with a new building. But with the appointment of the Patna University Committee, this scheme was abandoned. Now the development of this institution was linked up with the establishment of the Patna University[1].

The session 1915-16 proved to be the most eventful in the history of Bihar : it was during this period that the Imperial Agricultural Research Institute which was situated at Pusa and a provincial Agricultural College situated at Sabour and managed by the Department of Agriculture came into prominence. The Temple Medical School was also under the Health Department of the Government of Bihar.

In 1917 the Medical School of the province at Bankipore had 130 students : in 1912 it has only 118 students. There was no hope of establishing a medical college in Bihar[2]. Commenting on the opening of another Medical College in Bengal *The Express* of Bankipore regretted on 8th July 1916 that the necessity for a Medical College in Bihar and Orissa was not yet keenly felt by the people and no effort worth the name had yet been made by the local elite to raise the Temple Medical School to a College. The Medical College of Calcutta was beyond the reach of the majority of Bihari graduates and undergraduates who desired to have a scientific training in medicine. This paper further expressed the hope that with the inauguration of the Patna University there might be an attempt to raise the school to the status of a College.[3]

There were only 3 Bihari Hindu doctors (L. M. S.) and not a single engineer (B. E.) during this period.

1. A Report on the Progress of Education in Bihar (1913-14), p. 11
2. Report on the Progress of Education in Bihar and Orissa, 1917-18 p. 12
3. Report on the Vernacular Newspapers of Bihar and Orissa, no. 26 1916 p. 178

There were 10 seats reserved for Bihari students in the Calcutta Medical College, but it was seldom availed of. There was a strong prejudice among Bihari Hindus against medical education. The Bihari Mohammaden students were free from such a prejudice. Therefore there were 10 Mohammaden students in the Medical College during this period. But there was only one Bihari Hindu in it. In 76 years of its existence the Medical College of Bengal produced only 3 Bihari L.M.S. and the Sibpur Engineering College could not produce a single Bihari engineer. Therefore, a scholarship, Fraser Memorial Scholarship Fund, was established for the encouragement of technical education. It was hoped that this fund would solve the difficulty of aspiring youths.[1]

The Beharee commented : "Educated young men are very loath to take technical and industrial education. The bar is already overcrowded and our youngmen should turn their attention to adopt technical and commercial pursuits. But we have to regretfully admit that the facilities offered to the Biharee students to take education other than purely literary, are not attractive enough".[2]

The creation of the new province gave the Bihar School of Engineering a new impetus. In the year 1913 a committee was appointed to consider in what direction it should be developed. But this committee could not favour its conversion into a college. The number of students was 159 in 1911-12 and 166 in 1916-17.[3]

The First World War and its Impact :

The creation of Bihar as a separate province had aroused high hopes in the hearts of educated men of the province. This gave a great impetus to the advancement of education. There was a talk of making the new province self-contained. The material condition of the people was expected to improve, as new opportunities were sure to be opened. But very soon the First World

1. The Beharee, 26 May 1912
2. The Beharee, 12 July 1912
3. The First Quinquennial Review on the Progress of Education in Bihar and Orissa, 1912-17, pp. 91-92

War began and its impact was felt on social and educational life of the people. The development was retarded due to the diversion of the Government's attention to war preparation.

During those years the material condition of the people was affected in various ways by the war. Owing to the practical stoppage of imports and unscrupulous profiteering the prices of such indispensable commodities as salt, kerosine oil, cloth, etc. rose abnormally and all classes of the population suffered in consequence. Wages increased on account of the increasing demand of labourers. It helped the labouring class of the province to some extent. But the people who suffered most, were the middle classes and persons on small fixed incomes. The lack of railway facilities rendered the marketing of agricultural products difficult, the prices of which except for wheat, were lower. Cultivators were short of cash for the payment of rent and for other necessary expenditure. Merchants also generally suffered from the shortage of wagons.[1]

The economic condition of the people was unfavourable due to the war. All classes of people, specially low-income group, agriculturists and merchants were in trouble. This naturally affected the field of education.

There were high hopes when Bihar was separated in 1912 and specially when a separate university, the Patna University, was established in 1917. But the period of first World War (1914-1918) brought indecision and stagnation in educational matters. Nothing concrete could be done during this period due to war. Of course, the Patna University was established as a result of the University Committee's report. But many ambitious suggestions of the Patna University could not be included in it. According to the scheme of the committee, the university to be established was to get three new colleges besides the existing colleges. The committee recommended to establish King's College, Mission College and Sanskrit College simultaneously at Patna. But the new university was started only with the existing institutions. It could not be possible to start the construction of the building of the new university.

---

1. **Report on the Administration of Bihar and Orissa**, 1917-18, p-5, Para 30

The impact of the war was felt on the development plans of the Patna College. The accommodation of the Patna College could not be improved. There was a lot of agitation in the mind of the teachers and students of the college because of the vagaries of the Calcutta authorities in neglecting the accommodation problem of the college.[1] But the establishment of the university at Patna had made the people bolder. They expected many developments.

But perhaps due to the war and its aftermath nothing tangible could be done. The only change in the period was the removal of the I. A. classes from the Patna College. This led to the addition of a new college in the province. It was only when the period of war was over that attempts were made to improve the Patna College. Many distinguished teachers of the Patna College left the college and joined the emergency service in the war.[2] This gave a set back to the teaching work in the Patna College. All the construction work of the college and the expansion of educational institutions were suspended during this period.

The war had social impact as well. Large number of Biharis joined the war as soldiers and they had to cross seas as they were sent to distant places to fight in war. Many of them came back to their villages. But they returned with a changed outlook. There was no opposition in taking them back to their respective castes. This helped a good deal in removing the restriction on sea-voyage. The period after the war witnessed a continuous stream of visitors to foreign lands.

According to the Census Reports, Bihar and Orissa supplied 7,270 men to the combatant and 21,621 men to the non-combatant forces during the war. Of the combatants the greater number came from Shahabad (3,352) and Saran (1,603), the districts which in the old days used to be regular recruiting grounds for the Rajput regiments. Of the non-combatants who served in various labour corps the greatest number came from the Santhal Parganas and Ranchi. No difficulty was experienced with regard to rein-

---

1. J. N. Sarkar and J. C. Jha, op. cit., 1-116
2. Principal Russel of the Patna College died fighting in the Middle East.

statement into castes after the voyage across the ocean and generally the men seem to have returned to their old pursuits as if they had never been abroad.[1] In short, the Bihari soldiers on their return home were easily absorbed in the society, pursuing their old professions with dignity.

CHAPTER VI

CONSCIOUSNESS FOR HIGHER EDUCATION

Creation of Bihar :

Among the enlightened people of Bihar the educational development created social and political consciousness with a growing awareness of the government's discriminatory policy against the Biharis. The problem of the employment of the educated Biharis in the Public Service became more acute, and they became more and more organised as well as dedicated to the cause of the separation of Bihar from Bengal.[2] They began to question the motive behind every move of the Calcutta authorities directed towards Bihar.

The grievances of educated Biharis, were usually expressed in *The Beharee* : "Unfortunately, for Bihar and her students the M.A. classes have been abolished even from the Patna College, the only state college in our province and the university has also not thought fit to appoint university lecturers for reasons best known to Government and the Senate.[3]

This newspaper expressed alarming surprise at the news that the services of the only Bihari Professor, Kalika Sinha of the Patna

---

1. **Census Report of India**, 1921 Vol. VII, Bihar and Orissa, pp. 237-38
2. V. C. P. Chaudhary, **The Creation of Modern Bihar** p. 82
3. **The Beharee**, 27 January, 1911

College was going to be dispensed with from the end of the first week of February. Since this had caused great consternation among the people of Bihar and the newspaper invited the pointed attention of the Government to the act of injustice.[1]

Educated Biharis naturally began to think that the separation of Bihar was the panacea of all ills, and they started demanding the separation of the province as a prelude to the setting up of a separate High Court and University.

The first consciousness of this state of affairs came with the spread of education. The few persons who received education felt the sting of discrimination in the matters of services, and it made them think over the whole process. The consciousness gradually took the form of a movement, though weak and fitful in initial stages. It was natural that the leadership should go to the persons of educated middle class, whose interests were at cross-purposes with those of their counterparts in Bengal.[2]

The prominent among the educated men of Bihar were Sachchidanand Sinha and Mahesh Narayan. They jointly wrote a book in 1906 *The Partition of Bengal or the Separation of Bihar.* In this book they advanced their argument in favour of the creation of Bihar as a separate province. They justified that on cultural, historical, geographical, sociological and ethnological grounds Bihar had been separate and distinct. It was suggested that if Bihar was separated from Bengal, it would have numerous advantages both of local and imperial nature. In any case, a separate and local Government of Bihar would be more solicitous of the welfare of the Biharis than any administrator in Calcutta.[3]

This would be a stepping stone for having an Engineering College and a Medical College ; the creation of Bihar would enable Biharis to be medical and engineering graduates in large numbers. There was not a single Bihari engineering graduate at the moment. It was further pointed out that with the advent of

---

1. Ibid
2. V. C. P. Chaudhary, op. cit., p. 196
3. Ibid. p. 96.

the local Government of their own, the competition for the Provincial Civil Service would be naturally confined to the children of the soil, the large ministrial departments—mostly monopolised by Bengalis—would be thrown open to the Biharis, the revenues raised in the province would be mostly spent for the benefit of Bihar itself, a healthy stimulus would be imparted to local talent in general, a greater consideration to the special needs and requirements of the province would be given. They said further "we go further and hold that the separation of Bihar, which being absolutely necessary for the progress of the province itself, will at the same time help in the general progress of the whole country.[1]

The movement for the separation of Bihar was carried by the Hindus and Muslims jointly. Educated Muslims like Ali Imam, Hasan Imam[2] and Muhammad Fakhruddin were closely associated with the movement. The first session of the Bihar Provincial

---

1. Sachchidanand Sinha and Mahesh Narayan, **The Partition of Bengal or the Separation of Bihar**, p. 4

2. **Ali Imam : (1869-1932) :**

Born in 1869 at Neora in the Patna district ; (matriculated in 1887 ; went to England in September 1887 ; was called to Bar in June 1890 ; returned to India and enrolled in November 1890 as an advocate of the Calcutta High Court ; began his practice at the Patna Bar ; soon) became a leading figure of the legal world of Bihar ; (was appointed in 1909 a standing counsel to the Government of India in the Calcutta High Court); was appointed a Law Member of the Government in 1910); was associated with the Despatch of Lord Harding's Government to the Secretary of State for India, recommending the separation of Bihar and Orissa from Bengal ; (visited England on retirement ; returned to resume his practice in 1916 ; accepted a permanent judgeship in 1917 ; was appointed as successor to Syed Sharfuddin, after his retirement from the Executive Council of the Governor of Bihar and Orissa ; but soon was called in by the Nizam of Hyderabad to work as his chief minister).

Presided over the first session of the Bihar Provincial Conference at Patna in 1908. Presided over the famous session of the Muslim League at Amritsar.

Syed Hasan Imam (1871-1933) :

Born in August 1871 in the Patna District ; in 1918 was elected to preside over the special session of the Congress ; represented British India at the 1923 session of the League of Nations at Geneva. died in April 1933.

Conference was held at Patna in April 1908, under the presidentship of Ali Imam in which Muhammad Fakhruddin moved a resolution on the separation of Bihar from Bengal, and its constitution as a province.[1]

On 14 August 1908, a joint memorial was submitted to the Governor. A deputation also waited upon the Governor to submit the memorandum. The deputation had been organised by the three leading public associations in Bihar, acting in concert and co-operation with one another viz., the Bihar Landholders Association, the Bihar Provincial Association and the Bihar Provincial Muslim League.[2]

The Bihari leaders adopted method of submitting petitions and tried to show loyalty to the British Government. They made loyalty the main plank of their stand. The real test of loyalty was presented to Bihar on the issue of partition of Bengal. There was upsurge of nationalism in Bengal and the whole country was swayed by it. But the Bihari leaders refused to be drawn into it. They realised that only by convincing the Government of their loyalty could they hope to get their demand conceded.[3] The educated Biharis were mainly interested in their political and economic emancipation. They hoped to get better opportunities in services, better educational facilities and chances for all round development following the creation of Bihar.

The Government of India later realised the urgency of creating a separate province in Bihar and wrote to the Secretary of State : "The cry of Bihar for the Biharis has frequently been raised in connexion with the conferment of appointments, an excessive number of offices in Bihar having been held by Bengalis. The Biharis are a sturdy, loyal people and it is matter of common knowledge that, although they have long desired separation from Bengal, they refrained at the time of partition from asking, for it, because they did not wish to join the Bengalis in opposition to

---

1. **The Behar Herald** 18 April, 1908
2. Ibid, 22 August, 1908
3. V. C. P. Choudhary, op. cit., p. 199

Government. There has been a very marked awakening in Bihar in recent years, and a strong belief has grown up among Biharis that Bihar will never develop until it is dissociated from Bengal. The belief will, unless a remedy be found, give rise to agitation in the near future, and the present is an admirable opportunity to carry out on our own initiative, a thoroughly sound and much desired change."[1]

The Secretary of State supported the proposal and informed the Government of India that at the time of His Imperial Majesty's visit the announcement for the creation of Bihar would be made. Consequently at Delhi Durbar on 12 December 1911 the Emperor announced a series of far reaching administrative changes, which included the creation of Bihar as a separate province under a Lieutenant Governor in Council.[2]

The new province came into existence on 1 April 1912 and Sir Charles Bayley was appointed the first Lieutenant Governor of Bihar and Orissa. This date was a landmark in the history of Bihar, to bring as it did Bihar on the map of India. New hopes were entertained about the cause of education getting new dimensions and larger funds being arranged for its expansion. A separate province for Biharis necessitated the need for establishing a new university for Bihar.

Agitation for a New University and Establishment of the Patna University.

The creation of Bihar as a separate province opened a new chapter in the history of educational development in Bihar. This new province needed certain important institutions such as the University, the High Court etc. It had been an ardent desire of the educated people of Bihar to make their province a self-contained unit of administration. For that it was necessary to furnish it with two institutions in particular, viz., a High Court and a University.

---

1. Government of India to the Secretary of State for India, 25 August, 1911
2. The Historical Records of the Imperial Visit to India, 1911, p. 175

On the formation of Bihar and Orissa as a separate province, educated Biharis became more vocal in their demand for a separate University. They pleaded that their dependence on a University outside the province did not cater to their educational needs. The chief organ of educated men of Bihar, *The Beharee* which had worked strenuously for the creation of a separate province carried a similar campaign for the establishment of a university in Bihar. In a series of editorial comments and articles by many prominent public figures it emphasised the need of establishing a university in Bihar. It put very convincing arguments in favour of a university: "We have materials for our University at hand. We have 84 High Schools and 6 Colleges already at work. We have 811 students actually passing through them with university certificates and degrees each year. What we want is to incorporate them into a body distinct from the Calcutta University in which they are swamped and merged beyond all recognition."[1]

In the new province of Bihar and Orissa, 1,989 candidates appeared for the Matriculation examination, 98 for the Intermediate and 68 for the B. A. examination in 1912. These numbers at different stages of examination were sufficient feeders for a new university.

Public opinion in Bihar was unanimous in demanding the establishment of a separate university for the province. The educated men sorely felt the need of a separate university. There was a strong desire among them to build up modern Bihar, and for the advancement of the new province, the educational progress was absolutely necessary. Therefore the demand of a university was made with great vehemence.

A large and representative meeting of the citizens of Patna was held on February 1912. In this meeting, Mazharul Haque proposed that the new province of Bihar and Orissa should have a separate university of its own as soon as practicable and that in the meantime there should be a proportionately adequate representation of the people of Bihar in the Senate and the Syndicate

1. The Beharee, 25 April, 1912

of the Calcutta University. Purnendu Narayan Sinha seconded this resolution.[1]

The agitation for the establishment of a University spread throughout Bihar. The residents of Saran district assembled in a public meeting, under the presidentship of Durga Prasad Vakil on 26 June 1912 and passed a resolution demanding a university for the new province.[2] Another crowded public meeting under the presidentship of Giddhour Maharaja was held on 19 July 1912 at Monghyr. This meeting was attended by the leading zamindars, traders, merchants and pleaders of the district. Deep Narayan Singh moved a resolution for the establishment of a university at Patna which was adopted with great enthusiasm.[3] Such meetings were held in other towns as well.

An extraordinary session of the Bihar Provincial Conference held on 19 February 1912 under the presidentship of the Tekari Maharaja advanced the following arguments for establishing a University at Patna : "In ancient times Nalanda, which is not far from Patna was probably the most famous seat of learning in all India. It is needless to refer to the great fame of Mithila for learning. In more recent times, under Mohammedan rule, Patna was a famous centre to which students used to come from distant quarters to learn the various branches of learning prevalent in those times. Why should not Patna then be once again the centre of learning that it used to be ?"

The practical advantage of having a university in Bihar could not be doubted. Such a university would develop Bihar's education a great deal more than a university situated at a considerable distance from the province and subject to influence which did not respond to Bihar's wants and wish.[4] Many speakers including Purnendu Narayan Sinha, Kedarnath of Gaya and Dwarkanath of Muzaffarpur pointed out that the establishment of a University was the crying need of Bihar.

1. **Ibid.**, 9 February, 1912
2. **Ibid.**, 30 June, 1912
3. **Ibid.**, 25 July, 1912
4. **Ibid.**, 23 February, 1912

According to *The Beharee* a university, specially adapted to the requirements of Bihar would usher in a new era in the history of education, helping the recruitment of the public service "from the sons of the soil and the dissimination of knowledge among the masses". The creation of a university at Bankipore was not an intellectual but a social and moral lever for the people."[1] This newspaper pointed out to the public as well as to the Government the absolute necessity of expediating the establishment of the Patna University. Besides the Press, other forums were also utilised for putting weight to the demand.

In 1912 Sachchidanand Sinha raised the issue of establishing a university at Patna in the Imperial Legislative Council. Harcourt Butler replied that Government was aware of the necessity of providing a university to the new province, but the opinion of the local Government in the matter was awaited.

Bihar's Lt. Governor-in-Council was convinced that there was a strong and growing demand for a separate university for the province. He agreed that time had come for a thorough examination of the case. He proposed to constitute a representative committee with a view to the formulation of a definite scheme. The committee's report would be examined and submitted for the consideration of the Government of India.[2]

The Government of India approved of the proposal to appoint a committee to consider the question of establishing a University at Patna. On 19 May 1913 the Government of Bihar announced the following resolution : "The Government of India have, on several occasions, explained the necessity which has arisen for circumscribing the limits of Universities in India and the desirability of the teaching and residential system of university life may be enjoyed." With the growing demand for a separate University, the local Government proposed to constitute a representative committee with a view to formulate a definite scheme. The

---

1. Ibid., 16 February, 1912
2. H. Lemurier, Chief Secretary to the Government of Bihar & Orissa to the Government of India, Education Department, 6 November, 1912.

Lt. Governor announced at the meeting of the Legislative Council held on 12 February 1913, that a committee would be appointed to enquire into and report on the whole subject. This announcement was received most favourably, and a cordial desire to co-operate in the execution of the project was expressed on all sides.

The resolution of the Lieutenant Governor-in-Council constituted the Patna University Committee to frame a scheme for the establishment of a University at Patna. The following gentlemen were appointed members of this committee.[1]

1. R. Nathan —President
2. J. G. Jennings —Principal of Muir College, Allahabad, Officiating Director of Public Instruction.
3. A. G. Wright —Director of Public Instruction Central Province.
4. W. A. J. Archbold —Principal, Dacca College
5. C. Russel —Officiating Principal of Patna College
6. R. W. F. Shaw —Principal of Rovenshaw College, Cuttack.
7. S. L. Thompson —Principal, St. Columba's College, Hazaribagh
8. D. N. Sen —Principal, Bihar National College, Bankipore
9. V. H. Jackson —Professor of Physics, Patna College
10. K. S. Caldwell —Professor of Chemistry, Patna College
11. Rajendra Narayan Bhanj Deo of Kanika, Orissa
12. Sheo Shankar Sahay Bahadur
13. Madhu Sudan Das, M. A., B. L.
14. Saiyid Muhammad Fakhruddin, B. A., B. L.
15. Dwarka Nath, B. A., LL. B.
16. Saiyid Nurul Huda, M. A., LL. M., Barrister-at-Law

---

1. Report of the Patna University Committee also called Nathan Committee.

17. Sachchidanand Sinha, Barrister-at-Law
18. P. C. Tallents was appointed to act as Secretary of the proposed Committee.

This committee consisted of 9 Europeans and 8 Indians.

The Lt. Governor desired to leave the committee unfettered in the execution of the important task entrusted to it. But he made a few observation for general guidance, which fixed the nature of the scheme. The following conditions were laid down.[1]

1. The University being intended for the benefit of the whole province, the needs of all parts of the country and of all sections of the people should receive careful attention.

2. Provision should be made for a University at Patna or at some convenient place in its neighbourhood, of the teaching and residential type, and for the affiliation to this central institution of college situated in other places.

3. The scheme should not involve any such additional cost to the students as would discourage them from taking full advantage of the facilities to be offered.

It was decided that the report of the committee would be published and circulated for comment and advice before any definite action was taken.

Rajendra Prasad who was then practising at Calcutta wrote a long letter in *The Beharee* on this occasion : "The question of the proposed University of Patna is naturally engaging the attention of all the thoughtful people of our province. Various rumours are afloat, and some of them at any rate are of a very disquieting nature. On an occasion like this it is absolutely necessary that the people of the province should express their opinion, so that the Government as well as the non-official members of the University committee may be in a position to gauge the public feeling...... I venture to think that if there was any time in the history of Bihar under the British regime when a conference was needed to give

---

1. Proceedings, Government of Bihar and Orissa, Education Department, 19 May 1913, no. 28, pp, 15-16

expression to the public feeling on any important topic, the present is such a time."[1]

The committee met at Bankipore from 16 to 23 July 1913 to settle the main outlines of the project. The report of the Dacca University Committee served as a basis for discussion. The President and several members of the committee visited Muzaffarpur, Bhagalpur and Cuttack, where schemes for local colleges were prepared with the aid of local advice. The committee held its last meeting on 15 and 16 December and outlined its final report.[2]

The committee submitted its report in March 1914. The Government of Bihar and Orissa resolved on 19 March 1914 that the report of the committee which had been received and published should be circulated for comment and advice. Copies of the report were forwarded to newspapers, the leading associations of the province and interested persons. Comments were solicited by 31 May 1914.[3]

The committee's scheme envisaged a central institution at Patna which would undertake the higher branches of instruction, conduct the examinations, supervise the general life and training of the students, and regulate the teaching and organization of a number of incorporated colleges. Some of these colleges would be in the university area, and others would be situated in different parts of the province. In the central university, laboratories, lecture halls, and seminars, a library and a museum, and other similar facilities would be provided for the common use, while ample accommodation and opportunities would be afforded for all kinds of games, and for the various associations and social amenities which a University should encourage.[4]

Commenting on the object of this scheme, it said : "The aim of a University should be in the first place to discover students of

---

1. The Beharee, 10 August, 1913
2. Report of the Patna University Committee, p. 10
3. Proceeding of the Government of Bihar and Orissa, Education Department, May 1914, no. 6, p. 5
4. Report of the Patna University Committee, p. 13

merit, and the net must be cast as widely as possible. From this point of view the existence of the various local colleges is all to the good, as they will connect all parts of the province with the Central University. Once attracted to a college a clever boy will have a clear path, and there is no reason why he should not gradually qualify himself for the duties of a teacher and for a work of an original kind. Such a student would join the Central University after the Intermediate Examination. The passing from the local college to the central university, or, even if that does not happen, the connection with the larger institution cannot fail to have a broadening effect upon the character."[1]

The committee recommended that the University of Patna should contain departments of Arts, Science, Sanskrit Studies and Law, and a department for the training of teachers. The central University and the external colleges would share between them the work of the department of Arts and Science. The more advanced studies were suggested to be concentrated in the central university and the department of Sanskrit Studies, Law and teaching would be also attached to the Central University.[2]

According to the scheme the proposed University was to include the following colleges as Central Institutions.

Name of Institution :	**No. of Students**
1. Patna College	450
2. Bisheshwar (Bihar National) College	300
3. King's College	300
4. Mission College	200
5. Non-collegiate Department	300
6 Sanskrit College	200
7. Training College for Teachers	32
Total	1,782

The students of the first five institutions were divided between the departments of Arts, Science and Law; in Arts 950, in science 410 and in Law 190; total 1,550 students in these departments.

1. **Ibid.**, pp. 14-15
2. **Ibid.**, p. 19

The following colleges were proposed as the external colleges of the new university.[1]

Name of Institution	No. of students.
1. Greer Bhumihar Brahman College, Muzaffarpur	400
2. Tej Narayan College, Bhagalpur (aided)	500
3. St. Columba's College, Hazaribagh (aided Mission)	170
4. Ravenshaw College, Cuttack (Government)	650

The committee suggested ordinarily to accommodate 400 students in colleges, but made provision of the 50 extras in Patna College for the members of a proposed special residential hall. Two of the external colleges also exceeded the limit of students recommended. This was unavoidable, because none of the divisions, except that of Patna could support more than one college. It was laid down as a general principle that no college of the University ought to accommodate more than 600 students. In case of further accommodation a new college should be established.[2]

All the existing colleges were taken in the scheme of university, except the Diamond Jubilee College at Monghyr. The committee considered it weak institution and observed that it could not flourish. So this college was not recommended in the new university scheme.

The committee outlined the scheme as follows :[3]

The Central Colleges would be residential so that the students might be well cared for : every opportunity to enjoy a happy and useful University career would be afforded. Non-collegiate students who came from the city and neighbouring places would have separate accommodation and a separate organization adapted to their special requirements. A college would also be provided in each of the divisions—Tirhut, Bhagalpur, Chotanagpur and Orissa. These outlying colleges would be based on existing institutions, enlarged, reorganised and thoroughly well-fitted for the residential system.

---

1. **Report of the Patna University Committee, p. 24**
2. **Ibid.**, p. 30
3. **The first Quinquennial Review of the Progress of Education in Bihar and Orissa** (1912-1917), p. 43

A site was selected west of the new capital and it was proposed to transfer to it the existing colleges at Bankipore, namely the Patna College and the Bihar National College. The Law College was to cease to exist, students of law being accommodated in the ordinary colleges and being given a special course after passing the Intermediate standard. The training college was to be split up into two branches, a college for graduates being included in the university area and the existing college being reserved for undergraduates who were henceforth to be eligible only for a departmental diploma or certificate.[1]

The sum required for the central institution at Patna was estimated at Rs. 77,40,030 for capital charges, while the recurring cost was to amount to an additional net sum of Rs. 6,35,000 a year.[2]

The cost of the scheme of external colleges was estimated at Rs. 15,06,847 for capital charges and Rs. 1,30,205 for recurring expenditure, the grand total being Rs. 92,46,877 and Rs. 7,65,205 respectively.[3]

The management of the university was to rest with a Chancellor, a paid whole-time Vice-chancellor, a Convocation of 160 members and a Council of not less than 24. The Chancellor, who was to be the Lt. Governor of the province, was to nominate 50 college or university teachers and 31 other members of the Convocation and 6 of the Council and the election of other members was to be subject to his confirmation. He was to appoint the external members of the governing bodies of the colleges to select professors and assistant professors from amongst the members of the staff and to confirm proposals for the grant of honorary degrees. The Vice-Chancellor, as the Deputy of the Chancellor and the Head of the Executive, would preside over the council and more important Boards and Committees and be the principal visiting and inspecting officer of the university for both external and internal colleges.[4]

---

1. Ibid.
2. Report on the Patna University Committee, p. 117
3. Ibid., p. 118
4. Ibid, p. 103

All important executive matters were to come before him and he was to be responsible for the general working of the University. The Convocation was to consist of 16 ex-officio members besides all Principals of the college, senior Professors and Professors, so senior lecturers and 31 other persons nominated by the Chancellor and 25 elected graduates. It was to deal with legislative matters and questions of principle only and to have no power to revise the executive matters of the council. It was to be open to the Convocation to initiate legislation, development or reform. Such resolutions, if carried, were to be forwarded to the council and the latter was to be required to inform the Convocation in due course of the action taken.[1]

If the Convocation was not satisfied it was at liberty to address the local Government on the subject. The council was to be the supreme executive authority of the University, responsible for its general and financial administrations. It was to consist of 3 'ex-officio' members all Principals of colleges and the Dean of the non-collegiate students, 6 teachers appointed by the Chancellor and 7 Fellows elected by the Convocation.[2] In the words of the committee the Government of new University was to be entrusted mainly to its Principals and teachers but the graduates were also to be given a share in its management and a sufficiently strong outside element was to be introduced to ensure due weight to popular opinion and sentiment.[3]

The report of the Committee was published in the local Government Gazette followed by criticisms which centered mainly on the following points.[4]

1. The amount of Government control.
2. The proposed position and duties of the Vice Chancellor.
3. The constitution and relative functions of the Convocation and Council.

---

1. **Ibid., p. 104**
2. **Ibid., p. 105**
3. **Ibid., p. 114**
4. **The first quinquennial Review on the Progress of Education in Bihar and Orissa (1912-1917), p. 43**

4. The omission of courses in medicine and engineering and other professional subjects.
5. The omission of a department of Islamic studies.
6. The proposed Mission College.
7. The proposal to move the University out of Bankipore to the New Capital.
8. The limitation of the courses of study in external colleges.
9. The absence of any provision for the opening of external colleges other than the four already in existence.
10. The insistence on residence in the case of so large a proportion of students.

The local Government considered the criticisms and submitted its reports to the Government of India on 28 May 1915. The local Government desired to provide the province a University as soon as possible because the eagerness of the people of Bihar to have its own University had increased much.

The new conditions made heavy expenditure postponment inevitable. So when the draft bill was prepared, it incorporated into the university only the colleges already in existence.

The Patna University Bill was introduced in the Imperial Legislative Council by C. Sankaran Nair, Member of Education in the Viceroy's Executive Council on the 27th September 1916, after the due examination of the scheme by the education department of the Government of India and the Secretary of State in-Council.

In the Bill the Chancellor was empowered to nominate 4 out of 16 members of the Syndicate. Of the ordinary Fellows 12 were to be elected and the remainder (40 to 60) nominated by the Chancellor. The Vice-Chancellor was to be the principal executive officer of the university.[1]

The Council was replaced by a Syndicate of 16 members of whom 3 were to be appointed 'ex-officio' while the remainder 9 were to be elected by the Senate and 4 to be nominated by the Chancellor. The Syndicate was to have the entire management of

1. Proceeding of Imperial Legislative Council, Sept. 1916, pp. 86-87

and superintendence over the affairs and property of the university. The convocation was replaced by a smaller Senate which was to be constituted on the lines of Act VIII of 1904 and to include 8 'ex-officio' Fellows besides 40 to 60 ordinary Fellows. The Senate was only a deliberative body : its resolution would not be binding on the Syndicate. The new Senate thus differed from the one constituted under the Universities Act of 1904.[1]

The bill laid down that no college should be affiliated except five approved existing centres, namely one in each division. The Diamond Jubilee College was left out. The select committee had added a provision that intermediate colleges might be opened without restriction.[2]

Many members participated in the debate on the Patna University Bill in the Imperial Legislative Council. Sri Krishna Sahay, a member from Bihar expressed his sincere gratitude on behalf of the people of Bihar. He refrained from making any observations on the Bill. Pandit Madan Mohan Malviya speaking on the Bill welcomed the creation of this university. But he considered the proposal to make the Syndicate practically independent of Senate, retrograde and objectionable. C. H. Setalvad also pinpointed the retrograde character of the Bill, which would turn the university into a department of the Government. Dr. Tej Bahadur Sapru condemned its retrograde character and called it most backward.

Mazharul Haque, Bihar's representative, expressed satisfaction at the fulfilment of Bihar's demand : "It was the long cherished desire of the people of Bihar to have a University of their own, and that desire is on the point of fulfilment now." He did not like some of the provisions of the Bill which were elucidated by the education-member in the council. However, he observed that the time for a detailed criticism would come after some time at Delhi. He was not prepared to call it a retrograde measure and reserved his criticism for a future occasion.[1]

---

1. Ibid., p. 88
2. Ibid., pp. 89-98
3. Educational Proceedings (Govt. of Bengal), 1917, no. 35, p. 151

Thus many of the provisions of the Bill were criticised as 'retrograde and reactionary' on the day it was introduced. In fact, this became the most controversial Bill in the legislative council. The newspapers and journals, not only of Bihar but of the whole country commented on it. The Bihar Provincial Association[1] took a very active part in educating public opinion on this Bill. It published pamphalets and collected comments. Rajendra Prasad, the Joint Secretary of Bihar Provincial Association, published two pamphalets, which were called the 'Bihar Provincial Association' Tracts. The object of these pamphalets was to provide those interested, the views expressed in different parts of the country. The Bihar Provincial Association tried to place the text of the Bill and comments on it within easy reach of the public. The two Bihar representatives in the Imperial Council issued a letter to some persons in the Province asking their opinions and suggestions. Brajkishore Prasad was actively organising public opinion against the retrograde provisions of the Bill.

Caste organisations also opposed the bill tooth and nail. The Bhumihar Brahman Sabha, for example, described most of the provisions of the bill as 'unsatisfactory.'[2] It passed into an Act, it imagined, it "would prove highly injurious to the case of education."[3] An ideal university of Bihar, it thought, should have an adequate representation of educated people from every community in the different university bodies. Moreover, there should be a provision for starting and fostering of a network of colleges and schools all over the province.

The Bihar Provincial Muslim League also described the bill as "a highly retrograde measure", aiming at preventing the spread of education by restricting the opening of external colleges and of lowering the quality of education in the external colleges.[4]

Similarly the Orissa Association of Cuttack opposed the bill

1. **Ibid.** It unanimously adopted a resolution protesting against the bill
2. **Ibid.**, no. 36, p. 155
3. **Ibid.**
4. Educational Proceedings (Govt. of Bengal), 1917, no. 37, p. 157

on the ground that the Ravenshaw College without proper equipments, would gain nothing from the change in jurisdiction.[1]

Citizens of some towns also passed resolutions condemning the new bill. For example, the citizens of Muzaffarpur criticised the principle underlying the bill, demanding the modification of its "stringent and retrograde provisions."[2]

The Leader of Allahabad considered the Patna University Bill retrograde. Its proposal not to allow honours and postgraduate instruction at any centre outside Patna was not commendable. This newspaper advocated that doors for future development in education should be kept open.[3]

Special attention was paid to the comments of the *Times of India* of Bombay which was one of the foremost organs of Anglo-Indian public opinion. This paper was as strong in its condemnation of the Patna University Bill as any of its Indian counterparts. It commented : "The powers to be conferred on the Chancellor, to begin with are unprecedented in the annals of Indian Universities Legislation...The Bill, as it is drafted, is far from satisfactory. We have worked up in India to a certain standard of independence and public spirit in University administration. Nothing can be more detrimental to the growth of higher education in this country than that any thing should be done to debase that standard."[4]

The Express of Bankipore regretted the exclusion of the Diamond Jubilee College of Monghyr from the pale of the University. It was indeed a matter of surprise. Monghyr was one of the most important districts of the province and the college had been supplying the educational needs of a large number of youngmen of Bihar. If it was badly managed and badly equipped it should have been the duty of the university authorities to make it as efficient as other colleges. It further criticised the restriction that colleges would not be recognised if they were not located either in Muzaffarpur, Bhagal-

---

1. **Ibid.**, no. 41, **p.** 167
2. **Ibid.**
3. **The Leader, 20 September 1916**
4. **The Times of India,** quoted in **B. P. A. T. II, p.** 15

pur, Cuttack, Hazaribagh or within one mile of the Senate House. But there were other towns which needed a college. There were four H. E. Schools in the town of Gaya and five in its sub-divisions, including those lately established. Thus Gaya urgently required a college. There was a demand for it. The district of Chapra had ten H. E. Schools, and it required a college. The effect of the Act would surely be to check the growth of educational institutions in the province.[1]

A very lengthy article published in *The Modern Review* of Calcutta analysed the draft bill in detail, and put forward its own opinion on the needs of Bihar. It was pointed out that a province like Bihar should equip itself with technical institutions, but the Bill had ignored this requirement. The number of colleges provided in it was inadequate for a big province comprising Bihar and Orissa. The omission of a college for women was most regrettable. The most astonishing feature of the Bill was that it practically made university education stationary in the province. It quoted Professor Jadunath Sarkar's presidential address at the Bihari Students' Conference, saying the Bihar had been 50 years behind the other provinces in taking to English education, and must make more exertion than they to come to the front line and take her legitimate place in the march of national life.[2] The article in *The Modern Review* concluded with the following comment : "We have written at some length on the Patna University Bill, as we think the educational interests of not only the Province of Bihar and Orissa but of the whole of India may be prejudicially affected by it...The cause of high education in India would suffer most seriously if the existing Universities were fashioned after the model of the Patna University"[3]

The Bengalee of Calcutta regretted that the proposed Patna University would not be an improvement on the existing universities in India. *The Amrit Bazar Patrika* thought it impossible to

1. **The Express**, quoted in B. P. A. T. II, p. 20
2. The Modern Review, November 1916.
3. **Ibid.**, pp. 551-560

conceive of a more retrograde and reactionary measure. In fact, no journal published in any part of the country shirked from commenting on the proposed Bill : the Patna University Bill became an all Indian topic. *The Hindu* and the *Indian Patriot* from Madras, the *Punjabi* from Lahore, the *Marhatta* from Poona and *The Indian Social Reformer* from Bombay joined in condemning the provisions of the Bill.

The Bihar Provincial Conference held a special session to examine the provisions of the Bill under the presidentship of Purnendu Narayan Sinha. A note on the Bill specially prepared by a committee was laid before the conference. It was resoluvd that unless timely measures were taken to remove the retrograde character of its provision, the university would not serve the cause of education in Bihar. The Congress Session of 1916 held at Lucknow also sharply reacted to the restrictions provided in the Patna University Bill. Ambika Charan Majumdar, the President of the Congress, said in his address : "The Patna University Bill, which empowers the Chancellor to deal with any matter connected with the University in any manner 'that may seem to him to be fit and proper' places the university education in a large province entirely under the authority of the Lieutenant-Governor of Bihar and it makes the spread of high education impossible by practically prohibiting the establishment of new college."[1]

Principal R. P. Paranjapey of Bombay moved that, "this Congress places on record its emphatic protest against the highly retrograde character of the Patna University Bill, and strongly urges that it should be so amended as to make it a thoroughly liberal and progressive measure."[2]

Sachchidanand Sinha who subsequently rose to be the Vice-Chancellor of Patna University, said that Bihar was opposed to the unprogressive and reactionary measure embodied in the Patna University Bill.

---

1. B. B. Majumdar and B. P. Mazumdar : **Congress & Congressmen**, p. 194
2. **Ibid.**, pp. 194-195

The Beharee which had led movement for the creation of Bihar as a separate province and demanded a university by publishing many articles, now took up the cause of educating the people of Bihar on the draft Bill. It had the following comment: "We will be failing in our duty if we do not give vent in unmistakable terms, to the great disappointment that the Bill has caused in the province and already many amongst our countrymen are wondering if it would not be better to continue the old regime rather than enter the new one which seems certainly to usher in an era of a more or less officialised university. We know with what lively interest the ruler of our province has been working for the realization of our wish for a university of our own; and we now look up to him to intercede on our behalf and guarantee that the Bill in its present form would not be passed, and shall be thoroughly liberalised before it becomes Act."[1]

Thus the objections raised against the Patna University Bill were mainly with regard to the undue power vested in the local Government, to the peculiar and unlimited powers given to the Vice-Chancellor and to the Constitution of the Syndicate and the Senate.

The Bill was modified in certain respects in response to public criticism. But it is note-worthy that for more than twenty years after the passing of the Act, Orissa had to be satisfied with only one college, Chotanagpur with one first grade and one second grade college, the Bhagalpur and Tirhut division with one college each and the Patna division with only three—one first grade and two second grade institutions.[2]

The Patna University Bill was referred to a select committee which modified the draft, especially in the direction of increasing popular control in the Senate. On September 23, 1917 the Bill as amended by the Select Committee, was passed unanimously by the Imperial Legislative Council. Thus Patna University Act came into force on 1 October, 1917.[3]

---

1. **The Beharee,** quoted in B. P. A. T. II, p. 106
2. B. B. Majumdar and B. P. Mazumdar, **op. cit.**, p. 196
3. **Patna University Silver Jubilee Souvenier Volume,** p. 30

The regulations of the new university were drafted on the lines of those in force in Calcutta, but were substantially modified from time to time. Two important changes were the abolition of the age limit for matriculation and the institution of a system of Supplementary Examination.[2]

University Education

The number of universities in India upto 1916 remained five. After three universities at the Presidencies, two more universities were established at Lahore (1882) and Allahabad (1887) respectively.[3] From 1887 to 1916 the growing demand for university education was met by increasing the number and size of affiliated colleges, not by founding new universities. Thus in 1917 there were only five universities. The following figures show the distribution of students in these five universites :[4]

Name of University	Number of Students
1. Madras University	8,080
2. Bombay University	6,188
3. Allahabad University	7,625
4. Calcutta University (Covering Bengal, Bihar and Orissa)	21,118
5. Punjab University	4,318

The Government of India's Resolution of 1913 had expressed the desirability of smaller universities which would be residential and teaching and possibly based on linguistic divisions.[5]

So far as higher education in Bihar was concerned the province still remained under the jurisdiction of the Calcutta University. The University of Calcutta was imparting higher education to the whole of Bengal, Bihar and Orissa. The number of students in the Calcutta University was many times more than that of other univer-

1. **Ibid.**, p. 24
2. **First Decennial Review** (1912-22) Bihar & Orissa, p. 220
3. T. N. Siqueria, **The Education in India** p. 89. Also see **Radhakrishnan Committee Report** p. 20
4. **Statistical Abstract of British India,** Vol. 5. 1913-14
5. T. N. Siqueria, **op. cit.,** p. 89

sities. The Calcutta University had outgrown its proper dimensions. The Universities were established as a result of the increase in the number of students in the nineteenth century. In 1885 there were only 47 English schools in the whole of Bengal, Bihar and Orissa and in 1871 there were 133 High schools but by 1882 the number of High schools had risen to 209. This number went up to 535 in 1902.[1]

In Bihar the response to English education began slowly, but the number of students had increased in the first two decades of this century. Formerly the educational needs of Bihar were subordinated to those of Bengal. But with the creation of Bihar as a separate province, a ray of hope was seen. Both Government and the people of Bihar set themselves to make the new province self-contained in education. At the same time reducing the size of the Calcutta University was realised by the authorities. One of the objects of the projected Dacca University was to reduce the number of students under the jurisdiction of the Calcutta University. As regards the proposals of the Patna University, the last paragraph of the Bill for establishing the Patna University was the following :

> The constitution of the new university will enable the province of Bihar and Orissa to attain a university of its own, and will effect some reduction in the large number of students under the jurisdiction of the Calcutta University.'[2]

University education in Bihar began with the establishment of the Patna University in October 1917. There was a proposal to construct buildings for the new university. But it could not be possible to start the construction in 1917-18. The land was acquired and the Government architect was engaged on the preparation of plans. A draft of the regulations was prepared and finally sanctioned in February 1918. The first examinations were held between February and April that year. The figures of the results of examinations of 1917 and 1918 show that with the inauguration of Patna's own university, the result became more satisfactory ;

---

2. **Report of the Calcutta University Commission, p. 94**
1. **The Patna University Bill**

more particularly on the science side, 16 out of 18 came out successful at B.Sc. (6 with Honours and 6 with Distinction), a Patna College student heading the list in Chemistry Honours. In Mathematics Honours two secured first class. The inauguration of the new university added equally to the enthusiasm of the students and teachers.[1]

The expenditure on the university from provincial revenues was Rs. 1,18,527 for the acquisition of land and Rs. 33,009 for recurring charges.[2]

There were seven Arts Colleges in the province of Bihar and Orissa. Three colleges of the Patna University were managed by the Government, viz., the Patna College, Greer Bhumihar Brahman College and the Ravenshaw College of Cuttack (Orissa). The three other colleges were chracterised as aided institutions. These were the Bihar National College, the Tej Narayan Jubilee College and the St. Columba's College, Hazaribagh. The college at Monghyr, the Diamond Jubilee College was also included in the new university. A temporary grant in-aid was made to the Dimond Jubilee College. The total number of students in all the colleges increased from 2, 575 to 2,811 in 1917-18. The direct expenditure declined: it came down to Rs. 3,91,193 from Rs. 3,99,090. The expenditure from the provincial revenues also fell from Rs. 2,44, 510 to Rs. 2,27,089. This curtailment was felt due to the beginning of the first world War.[3]

Even so, the creation of Bihar and subsequent inauguration of a separate university for Bihar and Orissa gave an impetus to higher education. All colleges except the Diamond Jubilee College made a steady progress. This college still remained weak : Its working was not satisfactory in the year 1917-18. A new science block at St. Columba's College was opened by the Lt. Governor in November 1917.[4]

---

2. J. N. Sarkar and J. C. Jha, op. cit., p. 127
1. **Report on the Administration of Bihar & Orissa**, 1917-18, p. 100
2. **Ibid.**
1. **Ibid.**, p. 101

The Patna College was the premier college of the new University. This college naturally contained the cream of the new province even though it felt the impact of war. The war deprived the college of the services of some distinguished teachers, such as Moore, Armour and others. Some of them returned to resume their duties, but others met their death. Professor Armour of the English Department, for example, returned but Charles Russel, the Principal was killed in action in 1917. The *Time's Educational Supplement* described him as a great scholar of Sanskrit and a most energetic Professor and Principal, doing his utmost to improve the physique of the students by encouraging athletics and stimulating and personally assisting in original research, more particularly in the domain of Economics. He was solely responsible for the many wholesome reforms in the Patna College, the fruits of which were enjoyed by generations of students. Several college societies, e. g., the Chanakya and the Archaeological, and the College Magazine owed their establishment to his initiative.[1]

During the war period very few changes were possible in the staff of the Patna College. In 1916, Armour went over as the Principal of the Patna Training College, while Ouston Smith left the college on promotion to the Principalship of the Muzaffarpur College. The staff of the Patna College was weakened by the transfer of Professor J. N. Sarkar to the Banaras Hindu University in 1917. He was not only a successful teacher and a great scholar, but there was hardly any form of college activities with which he did not thoroughly identify himself.[2] At one time he taught all the papers of History, besides English, Economics, etc.

To fill in the vacancy of J. N. Sarkar, W. Ouston Smith was recalled from the G. B. B. College, Muzaffarpur. But he took a long leave to join the post of the Principal of the Holkar College, Indore. The college in general and the History Department in particular, suffered another terrible loss when Professor W. Ouston Smith left the college.[3]

1. J. N. Sarkar & J. C. Jha, op. cit., p. 122
2. Ibid., p. 121
3. Ibid.

As the new university settled down to work the number of students increased year by year. The total number of students was 457 in 1918 against 382 in 1917.[1] Next year the students'number increased to 468.[2] In 1919 a new Intermediate College was established at Patna under the Patna University. The early part of the year 1919 witnessed the transfer of the I. A. classes from the Patna College which reduced the number of students in the college. The number of students fell from 468 to 276, which included 20 students of the post-graduate classes.[3]

The number of students in the Patna College had been steadily increasing since the establishment of the Patna University. It reached its peak in 1918-19. The removal of I. A. classes from the Patna College reduced the strength. But the creation of the University opened the door for post-graduate education. There was not much enthusiasm among Bihari population for post-graduate education before this. Few cared to attend the post-graduate classes held in the Patna College. The educated middle class was mostly inclined to a law degree after their graduation. There was a comment in *The Beharee* : "the majority of our Beharee graduates do not pursue their university career to the degree of the Master of Arts or Science..... unfortunately, for Behar, and her students the M. A. classes have been abolished even from the Patna College, the only state college in our province and university has also not thought fit to appoint university lecturers for reasons best known to the Government and the Senate."[4]

A scheme for improving the post-graduate classes in History and Economics and for opening other subjects at the Patna College was submitted to the Government in 1918. Soon after the establishment of the Patna University post-graduate classes were started in English, History, Persian, Mathematics, Physics and Chemistry in 1919. There were no formal post-graduate classes before this, but

1. **Report on the Administration of Bihar and Orissa**, 1917-18, p. 101
2. **Ibid.** 1918-19, p. 102.
3. **Ibid.**, 1919-20, p. 90
4. **The Beharee**, 27 January 1911

lectures were delivered to post-graduate students by recognised university lecturers.[1]

The post-graduate classes in Persian were sanctioned but in the absence of students wishing to take the subject, these classes were not opened. M. Sc. classes in Chemistry and Physics could not be started for want of adequate arrangements in the laboratories. These schemes necessitated five posts in the Indian Educational service, six in the Provincial Education Service and one in the Subordinate Education Service, created at the Patna College. The New College at Patna also got two Provincial and four sub-ordinate Educational Service.[2]

The Patna College was developing a corporate life of the university during this period. A new element was introduced in the college life—the boys were given freedom to manage their own activities. Attempts were made to associate them with the college activities. This became more evident after 1917, when the Patna University was established. The Common Room and the different Societies of the Patna College aimed at all round development of the personality of the students through the various activities in the social and cultural life of the college.

But the removal of the I. A. classes from the Patna College, as mentioned earlier reduced the number of students in this institution. The Principal of the Patna College reported that the corporate life of the college had suffered much, but this loss might be compensated with the increase of students in the post-graduate classes.[3]

The various departments on the Arts side in the Patna College were made self-contained as far as possible. A block of rooms consisting of a class room, a library, a tutorial room and a senior Professor's room for each of the subjects, English, History, Economics and Mathematics were provided. The accommodation was improved, though it was not sufficient for the growing institution.

---

1. J. N. Sarkar & J. C. Jha, *op. cit.*, p. 128
2. **Report on Administration of Bihar & Orissa**, 1919-20, p. 90
3. **Report on the Progress of Education in Bihar & Orissa**, 1919-20 p. 5

There was a considerable fall in the number of students in the colleges of Bihar in 1919-20 : students reduced this year from 2,914 to 2,591. This was partly due to the severe outbreak of influenza. There was an outbreak of local epidemics like plague and small-pox as well. But the economic reasons appeared to be more important factor for depression in institutions because the fall was felt most in private colleges. There was a loss of 288 students in private colleges, where students were drawn from the less well-to-do classes.[1]

The external colleges of Bihar also felt the impact of the new university. The G. B. B. College was admitted upto the I. Sc. class in Chemistry and Physics after the foundation of the University. There was no change in the number of students : in 1919 it remained 297. Therefore the Principal pressed for further admission in the B. A. course in Philosophy and in the B. A (Honours) course in History in order to attract more students. The college possessed an instrument in the astronomical observatory, which was carefully regulated and adjusted. The construction of the new building was in progress : in fact by 1919-20 a large portion of the new hostel was completed. There was a marked improvement in the social life of the college.[2]

The decrease of students was felt at the St. Columba's College : the number of its students decreased from 173 to 160 in 1919-20. The Rev. H. G. S. Kennedy was in charge of the college, when he left the college in September 1919, his place was taken by Rev. F. W. H. Kerr. The college was admitted in Physics upto the I. Sc. standard on the University's recommendation. The building was improved, as a new office and the Principal's quarters were completed. The establishment of the University and the missionary background of the college accounted for an active social life among the students. This college established a social service guild, which enthused students to social work. They conducted a night school and during cholera epidemics they did valuable works. There was a co-operative store in the college, which deserves mention.[3]

---

1. **Report on the Progress of Education in Bihar & Orissa' 1919-20 p. 10**
2. **Ibid., p. 6**
3. **Ibid., pp. 6-7**

The fall in the number of students was more severe in the Bihar National College than in any other college. The strength of its students was 682 which came down to 639. The establishment of the university attracted more attention of the Government to this institution than before. The post of the Principal was included in the cadre of the Indian Educational Service. Valuable apparatus was added to the Psychological laboratory. A building was acquired for the hostel, which soon became full. But the college faced serious financial troubles and more funds were demanded by the college authorities.[1]

The wave of decrease in the external colleges of Bihar during 1919-20, reduced the number in the Tej Narayan Jubilee College from 620 to 536. However, the construction of the building made a very good progress during 1919-20 and the teaching of English Honours at the B. A. stage was started in 1919.[2]

The Diamond Jubilee College also had a decrease in the number of students from 73 to 55. But the general condition of this college was improving : the old building was replaced by a new building lent by the Government in July 1919. The college received a recurring grant from the Government and a considerable capital grant for the improvement of the buildings, surroundings and furnitures was also sanctioned. The teaching staff underwent a considerable improvement. Two hostels, one for the Hindus and the other for Mohammedans, were provided.[3]

There was a further decline in the colleges of Bihar. In 1920-21 the wave of non-cooperation movement affected the strength of students in the colleges at Muzaffarpur, Bankipore (B.N. College), Bhagalpur, and Monghyr. Even the Patna College, a Government institution, lost some good students. The fall was as follows:—from 297 to 265 in the G. B. B. College; from 639 to 405 in the B.N. College; from 536 to 487 in the T. N. J. College ; from 66 to 51 in D.J. College.[4]

1. **Ibid., p. 7**
2. **Ibid.**
3. **Ibid., p. 7**
4. **Report on the Progress of Education in Bihar & Orissa**, 1920-21 p. 8

The Bihar National College was perhaps the worst sufferer. The new regulations were no less responsible for this decline than the non-cooperation movement. Efforts were made in 1920 by the B. N. College Council to get this college provincialised, but the Government shirked its responsibility.[1] The situation in the Patna College was not so bad : even though fortynine students left it owing to the non-cooperation movement, the opening of the post-graduate classes in Physics and Chemistry compensated the loss. Thus there was an increase of one student in the Patna College, as there were 277 students as against 276 one year before.[2] There was slight increase in the number of students of St. Columba's College : 166 from 160.

Towards the end of the period under review there was a sharp decline in the strength of students in all the colleges of Bihar. The decline was due to political upheaval in 1921. The following table gives a picture of the decline in the colleges of Bihar:[3]

Name of College	1916-17	1921-22
1. Patna College	382	355 (including 85 post-graduates)
2. G. B. B. College	270	240
3. T. N. J. College	621	346
4. B. N. College	588	390
5. St. Columba's College	183	116
6. D. J. College	56	37
7. New College (at Patna)	—	178
8. Nalanda College	—	31
Total	2,100	1,693

1. Educational Proceedings (Govt. of Bengal), January 1921, no. 1: The Council resolved that subject to any limitation imposed by the deed of trust, it would hand over to the Government all the assets of the college including buildings and lands provided the Government fully undertook the financial responsibility
2. Ibid.
3. The Second Quinquennial Review of the Progress of Education in Bihar and Orissa, 1917-22, p. 37-48

Already in 1919 the Calcutta University Commission had published its report and the Patna University was now compelled to consider how far the recommendations were applicable to it. The Senate of the Patna University appointed a Committee on 27 March 1920 to consider the report of the Calcutta University Commission. This led to the adoption of many resolutions of which the one about the discontinuation of the Intermediate classes from the Central University was the most important. It recommended that the Intermediate classes should be included in the external colleges. The Senate also decided that the encouragement should be given to the establishment of institutions of the new type combining the Intermediate and higher classes.[1]

This led to the advent of a New College at Patna in 1919. This New College came into existence on 9 August 1919 after the abolition of classes V to VIII from the Patna Collegiate School and the addition of I.A. classes transferred from the Patna College. It was the first institution of its kind in the province. But soon a second college of this type, the Nalanda College at Biharsharif was founded in 1919.[2] The Nalanda College, Biharsharif, was established by the generous endowment of Rs. 8,000 a year from the Trust properties donated by one Edal Singh. There were 31 pupils on the rolls in 1921. The future of the college was not certain as it was started just before the non-cooperation movement. In fact its impact was felt and the number of boys remained static.[3]

These new colleges marked the beginning of the expansion of higher education in Bihar. The number of students in the I.A. classes of the New College at Patna was 190. Four of the classrooms of the former school building were converted into two lecture rooms suitably furnished. The transfer of the I.A. classes to the college was accompanied by the addition of two posts in the Provincial Educational Service and four in the Sub-ordinate Service.

---

1. **Patna University Minutes of the Senate, Syndicate and Faculties;** 1920-21 p. 81.
2. **Report on the Progress of Education on Bihar & Orissa,** 1919-20 p. 7
3. **The Second Quinquennial Review of the Progress of Education in Bihar and Orissa,** p. 47

D. Auchterlonie was appointed to officiate as Principal of the New College on 27 September 1919. It was primarily due to his sincere efforts that the initial difficulties in the college were overcome.[1] But soon the wave of non-cooperation movement reduced the number of students from 190 to 130 in 1921.[2]

The scheme to establish the Central University remained pending for three years after the establishment of the Patna University. In 1920 the Government of India refused to make any further contribution towards the establishment of a Central University. This announcement came when education was transferred to the state from the Central Government. It necessitated the consideration of the whole scheme. The Director of Public Instruction proposed that the university should be located in the neighbourhood of the Patna College in place of the site beyond the new city which was originally chosen. The Government of Bihar began to consider this proposal, announcing that the public opinion would also be taken into account.[3]

During the first three years of the university the work of development of the Patna College suffered, owing to the delay in getting a green signal from the Central University scheme. On the other hand external colleges at Muzaffarpur, Hazaribagh and Bhagalpur were greatly improved. New buildings for Bhagalpur and Muzaffarpur were completed, and a substantial portion of Hazaribagh was also constructed.

But these years were also years of serious decline in the number of students in Arts Colleges, the statistics of fall being the following : from 2,914 in 1918-19 to 2,591 in 1919-20, and from 2,591 in 1919-20 to 2,269 in 1920-21.[4] The fall of more than 22 percent in three years was probably due to various causes. The economic conditions of the province during these three years remained unfavourable. The impression that the standard in the Calcutta University

1. Ibid.
2. Report on the Progress of Education in Bihar and Orissa, 1920-21, p. 9
3. G. E. Owen, Bihar and Orissa, 1921, p. 121
4. The figures include the number of students in Ravenshaw College at Cuttack in Orissa also.

was lower encouraged the migration of students. But the most important cause of the decrease in the number of students was the effect of non-cooperation movement.[1]

The fluctuation in the number of students in the colleges during this period presented a peculiar situation. The number of students went up with the establishment of the university. It came down partly due to the effect of economic depression and epidemics, but it met its lowest ebb during the non-cooperation movement. This decreasing tendency, which was seen in all the colleges was temporary. This trend was arrested, and soon there was a marked improvement.

Though the number of students who joined the college after passing the Matriculation Examination was still far from being satisfactory, it was not less than half of the number of successful candidates.[2]

An outstanding feature of the Patna University scheme was the construction at Patna of a group of University buildings in order to give it the shape of residential University where the teaching would be of a very high standard. The students would live in a real university atmosphere with all the amenities enjoyed by the students at the great western universities like Oxford and Cambridge. It was expected that the Government of India would provide necessary funds for the execution of the university scheme. The funds for the construction of the university were not provided when the province was separated : only a temporary financial settlement, which would be revised after five years when the needs of the province could be fully ascertained, was effected. With the establishment of a university in the province the final shape of the scheme appeared. Unfortunately, owing to the war the desired thing could not materialise. Meanwhile, the situation changed as a result of the Montagu-Chelmsford reforms. To complete the scheme of financial decentralisation the imperial revenues and the provincial revenues were completely separated. The Government

1. G. E. Owen, op. cit., p. 112
2. Convocation address of Vice-chancellor, Patna University, 20 November 1920

of India now decided not to grant for provincial schemes. All these developments greatly influenced the scheme of the university at Patna. A teaching university could not be established in such circumstances. The Patna University therefore decided to improve the post-graduate classes started in 1919.

The Patna University Senate decided that, as a temporary measure, pending the establishment of a teaching university, M.A. or M.Sc. classes should be held in the Patna College campus. This arrangement was meant for eight branches of advanced study in which classes were already running.[1]

In 1917 nine students were attending the M.A. classes in economics and twentythree in history, while two students were doing practical work in the chemical and physical laboratories to get the M.Sc. degree.[2] There were seven postgraduate scholarships of Rs. 30 each a month tenable for two years and awarded every year to students graduating with Honours or with distinction in order to enable them to prosecute postgraduate studies. Gradually, the standard of higher education improved, the number of postgraduate students, especially in English, History and Mathematics began to increase and there were 63 Fifth year and 37 Sixth year students in 1921-22 as against 56 and 17 respectively a year ago.[3]

The university was getting prepared to become the vanguard of higher education during this period. Raja Kalanand Sinha and Raja Kirtyanand of the Banaili Raj contributed for the endowment of a University Readership in Indian Economics. They also donated Rs.5,000 for the purchase of books for the Economics Section of the University library. Kumar Madhava Swarindra Sahi of Manjha donated Rs. 5,000 to encourage the study of Sanskrit. The number of University Readers recommended by the Senate was four. It increased to five in 1921. In Anthropology and the Mughal

1. Patna University Minutes of the Senate, Syndicate & Faculties, 1921-22 P. 8
2. Educational Proceedings (Govt. of Bengal), 1917, no. 18
3. Patna University Minutes of the Senate, Syndicate & Faculties, 1921-22 P. 8

period of Indian History Readership continued by the Government grant.[1]

Sarat Chandra Roy moved in the Bihar Legislative Council on 18 July 1921 that a college should be established at Ranchi within two years. He said that there were 37,000 aboriginals in schools and a massive demonstration was held at Ranchi by the Mundas for pressing the demand for a college at Ranchi. One could well imagine how violent these demonstrations could become. Mr. Roy therefore argued that Ranchi had an improved road and railway communication and it was easily accessible to the students of Singhbhum, Manbhum and Palamau. Moreover, there were eight high schools to feed a college. The Education Minister replying to the debate said that the Government were themselves anxious to have new colleges but paucity of funds was a serious obstacle in the way.[2] In short, the attempt to establish a college in this underdeveloped tribal region ended in smoke.

Constitutional Reforms : Their Impact on Bihar

The war situation in Europe had become very grave and England was anxious to secure more help from India. The national movement in India continued since the last century had developed into a mass agitation. The people in India were ready to help but they wanted better treatment and a definite promise of *Swaraj* in the near future. In 1917 Bal Gangadhar Tilak and Mrs. Annie Besant had intensified their agitation for Home Rule. The British Cabinet set to work in drafting a new declaration of policy for India in spite of its pre-occupation in war.[3] On 20 August 1917 the Secretary of State for India made the following announcement in the House of Commons : "The policy of His Majesty's Government, with which the Government of India are in complete accord is that of the increasing association of Indians in every branch of the administration and the gradual development of self governing

---

1. **Patna University Minutes of Senate, Syndicate & Faculties**, 1920-21, p. 10
2. Proceedings of the Legislative Council of Bihar and Orissa, 1921, Vol. II, p. 56 Also see **The Searchlight**, 21 July 1921. The college at Ranchi was established in 1924 with affiliation of Intermediate classes in Ranchi Zila School.
3. See, C. H. Philips (ed.), **op. cit.**, p. 91

institutions with a view to the progressive realisation of responsible Government in India as an integral part of the British Empire...... I would add that progress in this policy can only be achieved by successive stages. The British Government and the Government of India, on whom the responsibility lies for the welfare and advancement of the Indian peoples, must be judges of the time and measure of each advance, and they must be guided by the co-operation received from those upon whom new opportunities of service will thus be conferred and by the extent to which it is found that confidence can be reposed in their sense of responsibility."[1]

The Secretary of State announced at the same time the decision of His Majesty's Government to send him to India almost immediately for purposes of consultation and enquiry. On 10 November 1917 Montagu, the Secretary for India, arrived in India and began consultation and enquiry, as a result of which a joint scheme of reforms was put forward by the Secretary of State and the Viceroy. The report on Indian Constitutional Reforms was published on 8 July 1918. This report touched all aspects of Indian life under British rule and suggested administrative reforms. It discussed educational problems and social factors also. It examined the progress of education in retrospect, pointing out the defects of the existing systems. It recommended, "We contemplate that the direction of Indian education should be increasingly transferred to Indian hands. Only, so we believe, can the stimulus be forthcoming which will enable the necessary money to be found...Educational extension and reform must inevitably play an important part in the political progress of the country. We have already made clear our conviction that political capacity can come only through the exercise of political responsibility, and that mere education without opportunities must result in serious mischief. But there is another important element. Progress must depend on the growth of electorate and the intelligent exercise of their powers ; and men will be immensely helped to become competent electors by acquiring such education as will enable them to judge of candidates for their votes, and of the business done in Council.'[2]

1. **Report on Indian Constitutional Reforms**, 1918, p. 1
2. **Report on Indian Constitutional Reforms**, 1918, p. 122

On the basis of these recommendations the Government of India Bill, 1919 was drafted. It became the Government of India Act in December 1919 after the royal assent. The Government of India published the rules framed under this Act on 20 July 1920. Elections to the reformed Legislatives were held in November and reforms were introduced in India on January 1, 1921.[1]

The constitutional reforms of 1919 had a direct impact on Bihar. As a result of constitutional changes, the status of Bihar was raised and it was made a Governor's province. On 29 December 1920, Satyendra Prasanna Sinha was appointed Governor of Bihar and Orissa. He was the first Indian Governor of an Indian province under the British Crown. The dyarchy with a limited representative Government under the Montagu-Chelmsford scheme was started in Bihar with great zeal and enthusiasm. Both the 'reserved' and the 'transferred' halves of the Government of Bihar and Orissa began to function with high hopes. The two ministers Fakhruddin and Ganesh Datta, taken from the elected Members of the Legislative Council represented the newly emerged educationaly developed and socially conscious class of Bihar. They were in charge of Education, Local Self-Government, Health etc.[2]

The results of the constitutional changes were felt greatly in the sphere of education. In the Legislative Council thirteen resolutions were moved and discussed. The debate in the Council contained a definite attack on the Government's policy and many constructive suggestions were put forward. There was not only an attack on waste and suggestion to limit building and inspection charges, but a definite attempt to define the relative importance of primary and secondary education was made. Improved curricula, the introduction of a new religious, agricultural and vocational training, to increase the grants of scholarships to aborigines, and the development of Government control over Middle English schools were suggested.[3]

---

1. G. N. Singh, **Landmarks in Indian Constitutional and National Development**, p. 288
2. **Indian Statutory Commission Report**, Vol. I, p. 148. Also see, R. C. Aggrawala, **Constitutional History of India**, p. 170
3. G. E. Owen, op. cit., p. 28

Some of these resolutions were withdrawn or lost because they were found to be impracticable by the Government, but others were carried. New scholarships and free studentships were created for the aborigines of Chotanagpur.[1] An Education Committee was formed to examine the various educational problems. In the university affairs the reduction of the age limit for the Matriculation examination was a change of great imporatance. There was a long debate on the question of a honorary Vice-chancellor for the Patna University, reflecting the popular interest created in University affairs in the province. The legislature served as a veritable barometer to gauge public opinion regarding social and educational developments from time to time. Only four years later a bill was introduced in the Legislative Council to amend the Patna University Act and was passed after a long debate.

The question of female education now received much attention as a result of constitutional changes. A committee was formed to discuss this problem in 1921 when the legislative council met after the new constitution was enforced.

Non-cooperation Movement : Its Effect on Education

In 1920-21 Mahatma Gandhi started the Non-cooperation movement. The impact of this movement was felt most in Bihar as this province had been under the spell of Gandhian methods of *Satyagraha* since the days of the Champaran Movement. Its effect on the educational progress was very significant : the progress of English education received a serious set back, but attempts were made to establish 'national' schools. As mentioned earlier, the effects of this movement were first seriously felt in November-December 1920 though outside Patna and Tirhut there was not much withdrawal from schools and colleges. But there was a serious strike at the Bihar school of Engineering.[2] Moreover, a few national schools were opened to give a new type of education to students.

By the end of 1920 several students of the colleges and schools, including no less than 110 students of the Bihar School of Engin-

1. Proceedings of the Legislative Council, Bihar and Orissa, 1921 p. 956
2. G. E. Owen, op cit, pp. 122-123

eering left their respective institutions. The students of the Bihar School of Engineering and other institutions who left their institutions were accommodated in the *Sadaquat Ashram* near Digha in the Patna district under the charge of Mazharul Haque. Mazharul Haque marched to that site with all these young students after leaving his magnificent building called the Sikandar Manzil on the Frazer Road.[1]

In the Tirhut division, the Chapra Collegiate School developed into a national school and there was considerable unrest in the Bhumihar Collegiate School at Muzaffarpur. After Mahatma Gandhi's visit to Muzaffarpur, about thirty students left the G. B. B. College. The non-cooperation movement also affected the schools of some of the Mufassil areas of the Tirhut division. Among others, the Head Master of Bagaha M. E. School in Champaran took a prominent part in the movement, while one teacher and 34 students left the Hajipur High School. The Watson School at Madhubani was also affected to some extent. In Bhagalpur about 40 students withdrew from the T. N. J. College. Rajendra Prasad, a prominent public figure, resigned from both the Senate and the Syndicate of the Patna University.[2]

In January 1821 the wave of non-cooperation movement swept the whole of Bihar. By the end of February some 6 precent college students withdrew from their institutions and joined the movement. The effect of this movement was felt mostly in colleges and in secondary schools. These educational institutions lost a good number of students as a result of the boycott of students. The decrease of students in the secondary schools by the end of March 1921 was 11,831. In the Middle English School there was 9 percent decline of the strength of students.[3]

The decline in the number of students was almost entirely due to political crisis. But the non-cooperation movement was comparatively less virulent in Chotangpur. It was most marked in

1. K. K. Datta, **History of Freedom Movement in Bihar**, Vol. I, p. 133
2. K. K. Datta, op. cit., p. 3.4
3. G. E, Owen, op. cit., p. 213

Tirhut, Patna and Bhagalpur where the withdrawals amounted to roughly 7,000 : 3,800 and 1,000 respectively. Five High Schools were nationalised and a number of 'national' schools were established. In the colleges the number of students which had increased from 2,905 in March 1920 to 3,265 on 1 November 1920, fell by the end of March 1921 to 2,548. There were 2,610 students in the colleges by November 1921 : it was a very slow recovery as it was less by 655 or 20 percent than the total of a year before.[1]

The primary schools of Bihar also felt the impact to some extent. In primary schools there was a loss of 1,700 students by the end of March 1921. It was 1.6 percent less than the previous year. In the case of primary schools the decrease occurred entirely in unaided schools and in lower primary schools.

Another factor responsible for the loss of students was the Khilafat Movement which brought a loss of 6, 368 Mohammedan students in the Government aided primary schools. At the same time Mohammedan students in private institutions gained, as there was a small increase from 9,820 to 10,253.[2]

The Bihar students conference at Patna had made a vigorous appeal to the students to boycott the Government schools and colleges. There was an attempt to establish 'national' schools to train those students. When Mahatma Gandhi toured Bihar in December 1920 and in the beginning of 1921, some 'national' schools were started.[3] And some existing schools were converted into' national' schools on the pattern of Bihar Vidyapith which served as a model.[4]

Thus the non-cooperation movement had a tremendous impact on the educational development of Bihar on 'national' or indigenous lines. It gave a courage of conviction and a new confidence both to the students and teachers; a large number of whom left their schools or colleges and to the new education in the' national'

---

1. **Ibid.**
2. **Ibid.**, p. 123
3. Rajendra Prasad, **Mahatma Gandhi in Bihar**, p. 43
4. **Report of the Bihar Vidyapith**, 1921-26, p. 45

institution. By June 1922, there were 41 such high schools spread all over the province, teaching 4,500 students and there were were about 600 primary and middle schools teaching 17,000 students.[1]

CHAPTER VII

SOCIAL REFORM MOVEMENT

MAIN-CURRENTS OF REFORMS MOVEMENTS

(a) Brahma Samaj :

The spread of education in India brought a stimulating process of social reform in the nineteenth century. With the introduction of English education many Indians came to realise the need of social renovation.

Of all the religious movements of the nineteenth century the Brahma Samaj was the most influential. Ram Mohan Roy, the founder of Brahma Samaj was the pioneer of all advance, religious, social and educational, in the Hindu community during the nineteenth century.[2] The Brahma Samaj, however, remained confined to Bengal. At the census of 1921 only 6,388 persons of the 320 million inhabitants of the Indian continent returned themselves as Brahmo. In Bihar and Orissa the number of Brahmos in 1911 was only 585 and in 1921 the number had risen to 794. Of these 25 percent were those who had contacts with Bengal.[3] The appeal of the Samaj was limited to the intellectual classes. This movement however had never taken deep root in this province. But in the realm of ideas, the contribution of the Brahma Samaj was much more important than what these figures suggest. It was the first

1. K. K. Dutta, op. cit., p. 310
2. J. N. Farquhar, **Modern Religious Movements**, p. 21
3. **Census of India** (Bihar & Orissa), 1911, Part I, p. 122

important intellectual movement which spread the ideas of nationalism and enlightenment in modern India.[1]

The most important centres of the Brahma Samaj in Bihar were Bhagalpur, Monghyr, Patna, Muzaffarpur and Ranchi and Giridih. There were good number of Bengalis in Government services and other professions working in different towns of Bihar, many of whom settled in Bihar and made it their permanent homeland. In Bihar the Brahma Samaj movement, confined mostly to these settlers, began in the sixties of the nineteenth century.[2] Many important leaders and missionaries of the movement toured the different parts of the province. Devendra Nath Tagore, Keshava Chandra Sen, Rabindra Nath Tagore and Jagadish Chandra Bose, one of the greatest scientists of India, were some of the prominent leaders of Brahma Samaj who visited Bihar. Besides them, there were the Brahmo missionaries like Trailokya Nath Sanyal, Nagendra Nath Chatterjee, Gurudas Chakravarti, Braj Gopal Neogi and other who visited most of its districts.[3] Bhagalpur, having the largest number of Bengali population among the districts of Bihar, was the first to receive the Brahmo influence. Since a number of educated and influential Bengalis settled here a Samaj was established at this place as early as 1863. One Niharan Chandra Mukherjee became a pillar of strength to this movement. There were other two Bengali gentlemen, Dr. Nakul Chandra Banerjee, a medical practitioner, and Bama Charan Ghose who were equally devoted to the cause of Brahmo Movement. When Harisundar Bose also joined them this progressive movement was carried with great success. There used to be a regular weekly meeting of the local college students, in which these leaders spoke on aims and objects of ths Brahmo Samaj.[4]

Next to Bhagalpur a Brahmo centre was established at Monghyr in 1867. A pretty large number of educated Bengalis were employed in Railway office at Jamalpur. Some of them started the Brahmo Samaj Movement. In 1868 Keshava Chandra Sen's

1. K. P. Karunakaran, op. cit., p. 50
2. Sivanath Sastri, **History of the Brahmo Samaj**, Vol. 11, 1912, p. 530
3. R. R. Diwakar (ed.), op. cit., p. 677
4. Sivanath Sastri, op. cit., p. 531

visit to Monghyr gave a great impetus to this Movement. Of course when the number of Bengali settlers became less this movement received a set back. But when one Dwarkanath Bagchi settled there after his retirement a new life came to the movement.[1]

At Patna the Brahma Samaj was founded in 1866. In the beginning two Bengali pleaders of the local Bar, Harisunder Bose and Govind Chandra Rakshit were related with Brahma Samaj. But the real man behind Brahma Samaj at Patna was Sri Prakash Chandra Roy, backed by his wife Aghore Kamini, who was a remarkable lady. Prakash Chandra was the life and soul of Bankipore Brahma Samaj. He devoted all the time and energy to the work of Samaj, the more so after his rettirement. His wife worked among the women of Patna bringing a new outlook in the women of Patna.[2]

The Brahma Samaj of Patna was the pioneer of female education in Bihar : the first Girls' High School in Bihar was opened by the Brahma Samaj. As Bihar had been much backward in female education, the opening of a High School for girls in Bihar was a significant event pregnant with weighty consequences. It was through the initiative and exertion of the Brahma Samaj that the Bankipore Girls' School was established. It remained the only institution for girls' secondary education for many years. A girls boarding house was also opened, and the eldest daughter of Prakash Chandra dedicated herself for this school and its boarding house. Aghore Kamini was so earnestly moved to work for female education in Bihar that she detached herself from her husband and children. She went to Lucknow and got herself trained for running public institutions. Unfortunately her career was cut short by her premature death. But a good beginning had been made by the Brahmos of Patna towards female education in Bihar. After the death of his wife and his retirement from service, Prakash Chandra gave himself to the mission work. He passed away on 7 December 1190, but his work was continued by his friends and admirers.[3]

---

1. Ibid., p. 533
2. Ibid., p. 536
3. Sivanath Sastri, oprcit., p. 536

Fortunately, the Brahma Samaj Movement secured adherence of a few Bihari workers, who brought strength to the cause. In this connection the name of Brahmadeva Narayan, an influential Bihari judicial officer, deserves special mention. He along with Dr. Prakashnath Chatterji, a medical practitioner of Patna gave a helping hand to Prakash Chandra. Another Bengali medical practitioner, Chandranath Chatterjee, made Gaya an active centre of Brahmoism where it was established in 1866.[1]

There was another group of workers at Patna, who belonged to the Sadharan Samaj sect of Brahmos. They had established Ram Mohan Roy Seminary, a secondary school for boys at Patna. Satish Chandra Chakravarti was the leading figure of this group. He was the Headmaster of this school and also the Minister of this branch of the Sadharan Samaj. He had behind him a number of learned men and women, who carried the work of Samaj. The Ram Mohan Roy Seminary was daily growing into a vigorous and useful institution. It became a source of positive moral influence amongst the rising generation of Bihar.[2]

Though the Brahmo Samaj exerted little influence on the Biharis the intellectual life of the province was definitely stirred. The personality of men like Prakash Chandra drew into the Brahmo fold a few earnest Bihari minds. Bajarangbihari was the first Bihari who became a whole-time missionary of the Brahma Samaj. He came into contact with S. N. Agnihotri, a missionary of the Sadharan Brahmo Samaj, and left a comfortable post at Hazaribagh. His son Srirang-Vihari carried on the Brahma Samaj work in his native town Sitamarhi in North Bihar. He gathered a number of earnest men, in his native village, Bishanpur and tried to establish an Ashrama.[3]

Besides Brahmadeo Narayan, Baldeo Narayan at Patna and Bhai Baldeo at Gaya were other Biharis who joined the Brahma Samaj. Bhai Baldeo was drawn to it mainly through the preachings of Keshava Chandra Sen at Gaya in 1879. He remained an earnest

1. Ibid.
2. Ibid., p. 537
3. Ibid., p. 538

devotee and took a wandering life of missionary. The examples of these Biharis encouraged the Brahmo movement in Bihar. A few more Biharis joined the team of missionaries to work at the various branches of the Brahma Samaj.[1]

In South Bihar the Brahma Samaj was established at Deoghar, Hazaribagh, Giridih and Ranchi, during the seventies of the nineteenth century. These places being health resorts, many Brahmo families acquired land, built homes and settled down as permanent residents at these healthy spots. Their presence at these places became a source of inspiration and to the Samaj workers. Perhaps the Brahma Samaj at Giridih was doing the most useful work : it ran a girls' boarding school[2] the second in Bihar, a ladies' society—both pioneering efforts.

(b) Arya Samaj :

The second most important social reform movement was the Arya Samaj, started by Swami Dayanand Saraswati. Its impact on the life of the Hindus in Bihar was felt from the very beginning.[3]

The Arya Samaj was in position to influence a larger number of people than the Brahma Samaj. It had a far wider audience than the Brahma Samaj. For Bihar, nay for the whole of North India (save Bengal where the Brahma Samaj was a dominant force) Dayanand could be considered the father of modern progress. The Arya Samaj had been directly or indirectly, the motive force in bringing about a social awakening and even the political consciousness among the masses. Dayanand's main aim was to effect a reform in the religious life of the Hindus. But its influence was comprehensive, steadily reaching every aspect of social and individual life.[4] The educational activity of the Arya Samaj, for

---

1. **Ibid** , p. 539
2. **Ibid.**, p. 530. The other girls schools in Bihar were those of Bankipore and a mission school at Ranchi.
3. R. R. Diwakar, op. cit., p. 678
4. Har Bilas Sharda, **Life of Dayanand Saraswati**, p. 255

example initiated a condemnation of the rigid caste-system, untouchability, inferiority of women and the custom of *parda*.

In Bihar the Arya Samaj was established in April 1878 at Dinapur for the first time. As Janakdhari Lal, Madholal and some others of that place had lost faiths in the Hindu worship, they established a society, called *Hindu Satya Sabha*. They came in contact with Dayanand after reading his Introduction to the Vedas. They were advised by Dayanand to establish a branch of the Arya Samaj.[1] The Arya Samaj at Dinapur became the nucleus of the Arya Samaj Movement in Bihar.

The Arya Samaj Movement made a great headway in Bihar. The census reports record a fair number of Arya Samajists in this province : 4,085 in 1911 and 4,578 in 1921.[2] The majority of the Aryas in Bihar belonged to the lower castes, e.g., the Kurmi, Kahar, Goala, etc. Contrary to this, the Arya Samajists in the United Provinces were recruited from the educated upper classes. In Patna 826 of the Arya Samajists were from the Goala caste, 545 from Kurmi and 514 from Kahar in 1921.[3] The Arya Samaj raised their social status to the chogrin of the upper caste.[4]

The Arya Samaj at Dinapur extended its activities to Patna and to the villages in the interior. The Arya Samaj established some schools and the 'Dayanand Orphanage' at Dinapur. The influence of the Arya Samaj in the Phulwari Thana of Patna was so great that about 2,575 Aryas were recorded in the census of 1911. The lower castes of the Patna district responded most enthusiastically to this new movement because the theory of the submergence of caste in the Arya community appealed very much to the lower castes. They regarded Dayanand as their saviour and his system as aiming at improving their position and bringing them on a par with the upper classes. Moreover, the custom of widow re-marriage was already an established custom with many of the lower

1. **Ibid.**, p. 230
2. **Census Report of India**, 1921, Vol. VII, Part I, p. 123
3. **Census Report of India**, 1921, p. 123
4. One of the slogans to the Arya Samajists was to stop the feeding of the Brahmans on the occasion of **Sradha**.

castes of Bihar. They were naturally attracted towards the Samaj which sanctioned this practice.[1]

The spread of the Arya Samaj Movement in the nineteenth century owed its origin to Dayanand himself. He came to Bihar on his way to Calcutta in 1872. Touring Dumraon and Arrah in connection with his campaign against idol worship, he arrived at Patna on 6 September 1872. At Patna he converted P. Ramjiwan of Patna College, a non-believer in idol-worship. Then he went to Monghyr and Bhagalpur where he had a discourse (Shastrarth) with the orthodox Hindus. He also gave public lecture, preaching against idolatory and challenging the orthodox Brahmans to have Shastrarth (discourse) with him.

While coming back from Bengal in early 1873, he stopped again at Bhagalpur and Patna and delivered speeches condemning idols, *shraddha* and *puranas*. He arrived at Chapra on 25 May 1873 and was cordially received by Rai Shivagulam Sah. The orthodox Brahmans of Chapra brought one Pandit Jagannath to have a discourse with Dayanand. He was badly defeated by Dayanand which infuriated the orthodox Brahmans. *The Bihar Darpan* for May 1873 contained an interesting note on this incident.[2]

Makhan Lal and Shyamlal of Dinapur went to Mirzapur to invite Dayanand in 1879. They brought him to Dinapur on 30 October and Dayanand Saraswati camped in the bungalow of Jones, a merchant. Dayanand, while campaigning for the Arya Samaj ideals at Dinapur, converted many persons to his fold. He delivered lectures daily from 2 to 16 November except 13th. Saudagar Singh, Subedar Singh and Jairam Singh once saved Dayanand's life, when he was entrapped in a conspiracy by some orthodox Hindus. Eventually they all joined the Arya Samaj and became devoted Arya Samajists.[3] The very presence of Dayanand at Dinapur turned the place into a stronghold of Arya Samaj in Bihar. It has

---

1. **Census Report of India**, 1911, Vol. V, Part-I, p. 211. Also see Har Bilas Sharda, op. cit. pp. 81-82
2. Har Bilas Sharda, op. cit., p. 96
3. Ibid., pp. 236-37

continued to occupy a central place for the Samaj activities since then.

Dinapur as the headquarters in the Arya Samaj movement for the whole of eastern India turned into a place of pilgrim for the Arya Samajists in the early years of the present century. After sometime its branches were established at Patna, Patna city, Arrah, Chapra, Siwan, Monghyr, Ranchi, Bhagalpur, Muzaffarpur, Motihari and several other places.

In 1901 when the 24th anniversary of the Dinapur branch was celebrated, a proposal for organising a 'Prantiya Pratinidhi Sabha' was discussed. There were 16 Arya Samajas in Bihar at that time, but on 5 October 1904 the 'Arya Pratinidhi Sabha' for Bihar and Bengal was established with headquarters at Patna. Balkrishna Sahaya, a Vakil of Ranchi, and Mithila Sharan Singh, a Vakil at Patna, were elected President and Secretary respectively.

After the death of Balkrishna Sahaya, who had the distinction of becoming one of the Vice-Presidents of the All India Arya Samaj in 1911, Shyam Krishna Sahaya, was elected the Secretary for Bihar. He remained the Secretary till 1918 when Ranchi became the headquarters of the Samaj—an important centre of Arya Samaj activity in Bihar. Eventually when Shankarnath and Hargovind Gupta of Calcutta became the chief office bearers, the office was transferred to Calcutta.

At the Gaya session of the Indian National Congress in 1922 the Arya Samaj opened its camp and the Youth Aryas of Bihar organised a big rally.[1] On this occasion the Arya Kumar Parishad with Baidyanath Prasad as head and Mahadeo Sharan as Secretary was established. Baidyanath Prasad was mainly associated with the educational activities of the Arya Samaj. He was instrumental in the establishment of several Arya Samaj schools and orphanages in the province.[2] In Dinapur a school named Ved Ratna Vidya-

1. History of 'Arya Pratinidhi Sabha' of Bihar has been based on the manuscript of the book under publication written by Ram Narayan Shastri.

2. Baidyanath Prasad established the D. A. V. College at Siwan in Saran district in 1937

laya was established in 1915. The most important educational institution of Arya Samaj in Bihar was 'Gurukul Mahavidyalaya' at Deoghar, established by the efforts of one Lakshmipati who became the Secretary of the Dinapur Arya Samaj after the death of his father Madhava Lal. This Gurukul was initiated by Lakshmipati who dedicated his whole life for the Arya Samaj on his return from England.

A meeting of the Arya Pratinidhi Sabha was held on 30 June 1913 at Dinapur for establishing the *Gurukul.* Lakshmipati proposed the resolution of a Gurukul in Bihar which was enthusiastically supported by Ramchandra Dwivedi. A sub-committee was formed which collected funds and finalised its establishment at Deoghar. Lakshmipati's death in 1915 gave a setback to the *Gurukul* project. In 1918, however, it was opened on a temporary basis in Mustafapur School, Dinapur. Later it was shifted to Deoghar. It had an unique history of imparting Vedic education in Bihar. There were nearly 40 Arya Samajas in Bihar during this period which worked for the propagation of Dayanand's ideals. Indeed, in Bihar, the Arya Samaj spread very fast, making it necessary to separate it from Bengal. There were four smallar *Gurukuls*, three orphanages and many Sanskrit Pathashalas run by the Arya Samaj. Swami Muniswaranand was a famous leader of Arya Samaj during this period. His lectures produced tremendous impact on common men. He made Patna his headquarters.[1]

Many important leaders in different walks of life in Bihar in spite of their low caste owe their elevation to Arya Samaj. They got their education through Arya Samaj and raised their social status through it. Around 1911 the Arya Samaj movement in North India seems to have made a strong appeal to low castes. The Samaj founded Suddhi movement to prevent low castes from conversion to other religion and to reclaim those who had already been converted. In Bihar it had a strong appeal for low castes such as Kurmis, Goalas and Mushahars.[2]

---

1. Indra Vidyavachaspati, **Arya Samaj Ka Itihas**, Vol. 2, pp. 225-226
2. M. N. Srinivas, **Social Changes in Modern India**, p. 101

The Arya Samaj, for the first time, focussed attention on the deplorable condition of the untouchables. In a press-note of 1915 we find the complaint that contact with western civilization and English education had not successfully combated the old ideas about untouchability.[1] The Arya Samaj, therefore, started a crusade against untouchability so that so-called untouchables were accepted on equal terms with other members of the society. In 1918 it held a big meeting of the Chamars at Dinapur. It was also attended by some representatives of Chamars of the United Province. It was decided that Chamars should join the Arya Samaj and should refrain from eating cow's flesh. A large number of Chamars attended and accepted the decision. Those who did not accept the decision were condemned by the rest.[2]

The Bihar Theosophical Federation was established in 1900; it held its annual session regularly.

The successful sessions of the Society were a new phenomenon in the towns of Bihar. The first attempt to organise all sections of educated classes was initiated by the Theosophical Society. The tenth Bihar Theosophical Federation was held at Chapra on 27 and 28 August 1910 which collected a good number of educated men together. Purnendu Narayan Sinha, one of the most prominent theosophists and a great promoter of education in Bihar presided. This conference was attended by leading lights of the theosophist movement in India. Purnendu Narayan Sinha described in brief the activities of the Theosophical Society. Arundale of Banaras Central Hindu College strongly condemned the system of prostitutes. This conference also collected some money for the Central Hindu College.[3]

Annie Besant had a very close contact with Bihar : she frequently visited the province. Many of the lodges of the Theosophical Society were inaugurated by Annie Besant herself. The Patna

---

1. G. S. Ghurye, **Caste and Class in India**, p. 166
2. **Bihar and Orissa Police Abstract of Intelligence**, Vol. VIII p. 18, para 88
3. **The Beharee**, 2 September 1910

Theosophical Lodge was an important centre of cultural activity. In January 1910, Annie Besant gave a very impressive lecture on the value of theosophy in India at Patna. She said that theosophy meant divine wisdom and it viewed all religions as having a common federation. It was a progressive cult. She said that theosophists had taken the lead in every important movement of the time. The Central Hindu College had been trying to discourage early marriage of students. The Hindu Collegiate School put a restriction on the admission of married students.[1] This rule was quoted by many social reform organisations as suitable means to check early marriage.

The Theosophical Society appealed as a panacea for several evils to a large section of Indian people at a time when the religious future of India was in the melting pot and there were hesitation and doubt. With an unprecedented public backing its efforts were crowned with success. There appeared a letter in the leading newspaper of Bihar, *The Beharee* eulogising the contributions of the Society. But at the same time it said that the Theosophical Society would not make a lasting impact on the Society. It criticised the Society's undue emphasis on religion. The surrounding of mystery around the society was also disapproved.[2]

The importance which this society had in Bihar in the early period was naturally decreasing with the growing activity of educated men in other spheres. Many associations had emerged, monopolising the attention of educated men. But Theosophical Society in Bihar had some staunch followers. The enthusiasm of the delegates present in the 17th session of the Bihar Theosophical Federation on 17 and 18 November 1918, second session at Purnea was unprecedented. It was presided over by the General Secretary of the Theosophy Society (Indian Section). Delegates from Patna, Chapra, Gaya, Madhubani and Banaras attended the session. The President pointed out that theosophy taught that men need not believe in dogmas and need not rest content with mere faith.

1. **Ibid.**, 20 January 1910
2. **Ibid.**, 13 January 1913

The enthusiasm prevailing in Purnea on this occasion was unique as this town was notorious for inactivity, apathy and indifference.[1]

Monghyr was another important centre of theosophical activities. Chhedi Prasad Choudhary and Hari Mohan Mishra were important leaders of Theosophical Society.[2]

(d) Ram Krishna Mission :

The Ram Krishna Mission was one of the main currents of social reform movement along with the Brahma Samaj, the Arya Samaj and the Theosophical Society.

Though the Ram Krishna Mission was founded towards the end of the nineteenth century, it began its work in the twentieth century. The Ram Krishna Math and Mission finally established by 1897 and legally registered in 1909, had the dual purpose of contemplation and social action. In its first aspect it was inspired by the tradition of mysticism and devotion, in the second by Western philanthropy and Social Welfare Work.[3] In Bihar the Ram Krishna Mission could not make any headway during the period under review. There might have been indivldual followers of this cult in Bihar, specially among Bengali population, but this movement was not properly organised before 1920. However, there was one Ram Krishna Ashram at Kunda in Santhal Parganas as early as 1911.[4]

The Bengali Community working at the Steel City of Jamshedpur organised a Vivekanand Society in 1920. The year 1922 was remarkable for the Ram Krishna Mission in Bihar, as three branches were established simultaneously. The Ram Krishna Ashram, Patna and a Vidyapith at Deoghar were opened this year. The Ram Krishna Vivekanand Cave at Gaya was also established

---

1. **The Searchlight**, 5 December 1918
2. Srikrishna Abhinandan Granth (Hindi), p. 113
3. Charles H. Heimsath, **op. cit**, pp. 44-45
4. **Report on the Ram Krishna Math and Mission Convention**, 1926 Appendix, p. 293

in 1922.[1] Thus organised activities of the Ram Krishna Mission in Bihar began. Its branches rendered a unique service to the people of Bihar during distress and calamities.[2]

Deoghar Vidyapith of Ram Krishna Mission was a residential school for boys upto the Matriculation stage. This school aimed at imparting an all round education with a view to bringing about a harmonious development of mind and physique. It was an ideal institution which is still flourishing. In course of time more branches of Ram Krishna Mission were established in different towns of Bihar.

The Ram Krishna Mission Ashram, Patna, was started in June 1922 and since then it has been trying in its own way to serve the people. Its activities are mainly educational, medical and religious. The medical activities of the Ram Krishna Ashram cover dispensaries, in which large number of people are treated free of cost. The Ashram at Patna runs Students' Home, for poor and deserving school and college students. The students live in them as a member of a homogeneous family, taking part in the prayers, gardening and other activities of the Ashram.

INDIAN NATIONAL SOCIAL CONFERENCE

There was an all-Indian Organisation exclusively concerned with social reforms. When the Indian National Congress was founded in Bombay in 1885, its organisers felt that along with political topic, a place should be given to the discussion of social topics. Hence it was Diwan Bahadur R. Raghunath Rao and Mahadevo Govind Ranade who addressed the congress on the subjects related to social reforms. On a second consideration, however, the organizers of the congress felt that the congress platform should be devoted to political topics alone. As those interested in

1. Ibid., p. 294
2. The Relief works organised by the Ram Krishna Mission in Bihar deserve special mention. Famine, flood and drought were a common feature of Bihar and the hardships felt by poor sections of population were sometimes unbearable. It was at such moments when the cup of sorrows of the people was full to the brim that the Ram Krishna Mission came forward to their secure.

social reform also felt the need for it, it was decided to inaugurate it as a separate movement. Its first conference was held in Madras in 1887. The leaders of the new organisation were Ranade and Raghunath Rao.[1]

The subjects that were included in its programme covered a wide range, for example, social evils like infant marriages, extravagant ceremonies, prohibition of widow marriage, polygamy, prohibition of inter-marriage, disfigurement and other discomforts to which widows are subjected, money consideration for which girls were given in marriages, seclusion of women, etc.[2]

The object of the National Social Conference was to stimulate and to strengthen the forces of reform by bringing together every year in mutual consultation representatives of various associations and movements scattered all over India, which were struggling against the social evils.[3] There were many local associations and caste associations working for social reform. Now the National Conference tried to coordinate all of them. True, the Indian circumstances needed local action, on the part of different organizations in different parts of country, but the National Social Conference had a very important role to play. It did not supersede the local association, but it tried to strengthen their local efforts. It focussed attention on the whole country paying particular attention to the works of social reform by local associations. Thus it stimulated mutual cooperation by extending sympathy and help.[4]

Unfortunately, at the outset there was no branch of social conference in Bihar, even though there were many social evils in Bihar which attracted the attention of the educated men of the province. Later, there was an attempt to create public opinion against these social evils. The resolution passed at local associations and caste-conferences included social reforms. However, what was needed was an organisation exclusively devoted to social re-

---

1. C.Y. Chintamani (ed.) **Indian Social Reform**, p. 32
2. Ibid., p. 146
3. James Kellock, **Mahadeva Govind Ranade**, p. 89
4. K.P. Karunakaran, **op. cit.**, p.28

from in Bihar. As *The Beharee* commented on the eve of the third Bihar Provincial Conference in April 1910, "In these days when the need of social reform has fortunately come to engage so much public attention, the necessity of a social conference as a prominent feature of our public activities, does not require to be emphasised in so many words." In all other provinces, it pointed out a social conference invariably followed the session of the political conference, but in spite of many social evils in Bihar, as elsewhere, such an effective organisation could not be organised. The education of public opinion was an essential preliminary step to the effectual remedy of social abuses. Under such circumstances the need of social conference was self-evident.[1]

The demand for the expansion of the programme by having a social conference in addition to the provincial conference continued. A proposal to start a Bihari Social Conference came in newspapers in 1911. But in Bihar attempts to remove social evils continued mainly through caste organisations. The proposed Bihari Social Conference was limited to the improvement of the social status of Bihari Kayasthas only. This conference was proposed to be held at Gaya under the presidentship of Nand Kishore Lal.[2]

The session of the Indian National Social Conference held at Bankipore in 1913 under the presidentship of Ramavatar Sharma[3] was remarkable. In course of his presidential address, Sri Sharma pointed out that social evils were retarding the progress of Bihar. He said that *parda*, indolence, early marriage, caste rigidity, toleration of immorality and mendicancy, celebacy under the compulsion of any adult member of the society were the stigmas which cast a beneful influence on society. He, therefore, gave a clarion call to the *pandits* of the society to remove them.[4]

---

1. **The Beharee**, 9 April 1910
2. **Ibid**, March 1911
3. Ramavatar Sharma was born in 1877 in the district of Saran. He was a great scholar of Sanskrit. He worked as a professer in the Banaras Central Hindu College, later came to the Patna College. He died in 23 April, 1929
4. **The Beharee**, 5 January 1913

The resolutions passed at the conference covered the relaxation of the rigour of the *parda* system with a view to its final abolition, raising the marriageable age for girls to 16 and of men to 25, elevating the status of the depressed classes, admitting back into castes those who undertook sea-voyage, appealing to the leaders to permit remarriage of the young widows, supporting the principles of Dadabhoy Naoroji's bill for the protection of minor girls, urging the promotion of elementary and higher education.[1]

Ramavatar Sharma was not a born reformer, but he had realised the evils of orthodoxy by his experience. He condemned these social evils and tried to show that they had no 'shastric' sanction. Ganganath Jha was another scholar who boldly supported social reforms. Conservation was so strong in Mithila that Maithil Conference could not support sea-voyage.[2] But Ganganath Jha,[3] even though a Maithil Pandit, boldly came out in support of sea-voyage.

CHAPTER VIII

SOCIAL DEVELOPMENT

BEGINNING OF A NEW TREND IN BIHAR'S SOCIAL LIFE

Social progress is indicated by the level of intellectual development of each person in it. Educational backwardness is the main

1. Ibid.
2. Even Maharaja Kameshwar Singh was once excommunicated by a large section of Brahmans for his visit to the U.K. in the round table conference.
3. Ganganath Jha was born in 1871 in the district of Darbhanga. He was a brilliant student. He served Darbhanga Raj for several years and worked as professer of Sanskrit in Muir Central College. He was elected thrice Vice-Chancellor of Allahabad University from 1923 to 1932. He died in 1943.

factor of social degradation. The role of new education introduced by the English in bringing social changes in the nineteenth century cannot be denied. The object of some of the British officials behind the move for the spread of education in India might not have been purely humanitarian : the British introduced and encouraged education to get a better class of subordinate staff for administration. But no one can deny that it unfolded before the Indian youths the vista of a new world and sowed in their minds the seeds of an intellectual revolution pregnant with weighty consequences. In Bengal Raja Ram Mohan Roy, with the support of a section of the society pleaded for English education so that he took a lead in English education in the nineteenth century. Thus the demand for English education also came from Indians themselves.

But in Bihar the case was quite different : here the desire to learn English could be found 'in fewer instances than in Bengal districts.'[1] English education in Bihar was in fact misconstrued as an attempt on the part of the Government to convert the province to Christianity. A rumour was spread that those who took to English education would be departed to *Mouritious* and other British colonies and employed there as slaves. It was suspected that the introduction of the 1854 plan had something to do with the outbreak of the mutiny of 1857 in Bihar.[2]

The Government had established zila schools at district headquarters. The period which followed the mutiny saw the emergence of secondary schools. The Patna College after initial struggles came to be established in 1863. In the beginning the Biharis were more averse to higher collegiate education. But the history of early years of the Patna College shows a gradual change in their attitude. With the growing appreciation of the advantage of higher education by Biharis, a new orientation of their general outlook appeared. The figures for this period reveal a gradual increase in the number of Bihari students. In 1899 there were 85 Bengalis as compared to 150 Biharis in the Patna College.[3]

---

1. B.B. Misra, op. cit., p. 154
2. Ibid., p. 54
3. Edn. Proceedings, 1900, nos. 28-29, p. 41

The number of Bihari students in the zila schools of Bihar and in the only college at Patna remained less than Bengali students for many years. Considerable difficulties were experienced by different administrators posted in districts and subdivisions, in the educational administration. Most of the districts were in a very backward condition. Difficulties were experienced even in the extension of primary education owing to the prejudices of the people. The Assistant Magistrate of Bettiah reported that he had great difficulty in inducing the people to send their children to new schools and in obtaining qualified teachers. People did not view with favour the new education but passively resisted it as much as possible.[1]

The *Patwari* class opposed the new-system of extending primary education because they feared that an extended system of education would afford too great facilities to aspirants for the particular business. The zamindar class also failed to give an assistance to the educational development. There were very few intelligent members of this class who could understand the utility of an extended system of education among the masses; and so they did not take an active interest in the promotion of education at any level.[2]

But, gradually, there came about a change in the attitude of the higher classes in society towards education. By the end of the nineteenth century the Government zila schools were filled entirely with Bihari students.[3] There were some gentlemen of the nobility who took interest in the welfare of the Patna College. Among the students in 1863-64 were a son and protege of Rajah Bhoop Singh, a son of Wilayat Ali Khan, a son of Roy Hari Kissen, a wealthy zamindar, a son and nephew of Nawab Soorat Jung, the sons of Zainuddin and of Surya Kumar Mukherjee, the Deputy Collectors, besides some children of certain other respectable people, Indian and European.

There was no public activity in Bihar. In social matters Bihar was like a pool of stagnant water and even the whirlwind

1. P.C. Roychoudhary, (ed.) B.R.D.G. Champaran, p. 446
2. Ibid., p. 444
3. The Behar Times, 12 February 1897

of reform in the East and the West of the province had failed to cause the faintest ripple in the sea of social life. The only political association in the province, the Bihar Landholders Association was inactive. But the birth of the Bhagalpur National Improvement Association marked a radical change in the social life of Bihar.[1]

A meeting of the enlightened persons of Bihar held at Bhagalpur under the presidentship of Harballabh Narayan of Sonbarsa discussed the need of public life in Bihar. This Association was started in 1897 for the regeneration of Bihar. It commenced a career of active and many-sided usefulness.[2]

The introduction of steam ships and of railways as well as the establishment of courts, these two were the greatest factors in bringing a change in educational and social life of Bihar. Public interest began to develop in higher education—partly as a result of the introduction of English in the chief appellate courts, and partly due to the expansion of new means of communications.

By the extension of railways the economic side of agriculture in India changed, and the cultivator was brought into contact with the commercial world. The cultivator was involved in a transaction in which an illiterate man was at a great disadvantage. The census of 1971 supplied statistics on various aspects of life in Bihar. The miserable state of affairs in the matter of education attracted the attention of Government officials in 1870-73. The Commissioner of Patna in his report on the state of education in Bihar pointed out that Patna division was educationally backward, and that there was very little desire amongst the people for this education. To improve the condition it was suggested that encouragement should be given to education reserving a certain number of appointments exclusively for Biharis.[3]

A public meeting was held at Chapra on 10 July 1870 to consider the resolution of the Government of India which annou-

---

1. **The Behar Times**, 5 January 1900
2. **Ibid.**, 25 February 1897
3. V.C.P. Choudhary, **The Creation of Modern Bihar**, p. 29

nced reversal of the educational policy.[2] This was a unique gathering in which, besides the ordinary members of the Chapra Association, 400 persons were present. The memorial prepared here and submitted to the Secretary of State for India said : "The withdrawal of state from English education, would be a great misfortune to the people of this country. Apart from the intellectual, social, and moral advantages which flow from it, it has a direct economic value to the Government, which can hardly be exaggerated......English education, for the people of this country is a state necessity, and is therefore the duty and interest of the British India Government to appropriate a portion of the public revenues to its advancements."[1]

The memorialists emphasised that the improvement of the country depended on the education of both the vernacular and English languages It pointed out that the expenditure on English education also helped the growth of vernacular education. This memorial signed by nearly two thousand persons urged the Government to continue its aid to English education.

These measures induced the Biharis to receive education. By 1875 they were overcoming their distrust of English education, beginning to avail themselves freely of its advantages. The upper classes were now no longer keeping aloof from schools or from colleges. The D.P.I. while commenting on the progress of the Patna College expressed satisfaction and indicated an increasing appreciation of the advantages conferred by education. He hoped that in a few years this college would stand in the foremost rank of mufussil colleges.

In the last decades of the nineteenth century big zamindars of the province came forward to champion and promote higher education in Bihar. Four colleges out of five, which were establi-

1. The Government of India, Finance Department. had announced in its resolution no. 2296 dated 31 March 1870 to withdrew State aid from English education.
2. The Memorial of the inhabitants of Saran to the Secretary of State for India, Tracts, Indian Education, pp. 5-6

shed in this period came through the liberal donations of landed magnates. The Tej Narayan Jubilee College was established by Tej Narayan Singh of Bhagalpur with the cooperation of the Banaili Raj, while the Bihar National College was founded by Bisheshwar Singh, the zamindar of Kulharia. It was established with the object of a wider diffusion of high English education among the people of Bihar and of bringing it within the reach of men not in affluent circumstances. Bisheshwar Singh and his brother Babu Saligram Singh and their friend Govind Charan were the political trio of Bihar; the first and the last were Vakils of Patna Bar, and the second was a Vakil of the Calcutta High Court.

The Bhumihar Brahman College of Muzaffarpur was established by a liberal donation of public spirited zamindar Langat Singh. The Monghyr College also received help from the fostering care of a noble class of the district.

These attempts led to the emergence of a group of educated persons, who were eager to adopt the modern way of life. The growth of education brought new ideas to this group of men. Some of them tried to act against social-evils and broke prejudices. Thus there came about a new trend in Bihar's social life. There existed a strong prejudice against sea-voyage (specially among the Hindus) in the nineteenth century and it continued for many years in the twentieth century. But there came an educated Bihari Hindu during the last years of the nineteenth century who acted against it. Sachchidanand Sinha was the first Bihari Hindu who took courage and crossed the seas in 1889 and went to England for higher studies. On his return in 1893 he had to face a serious opposition from the communtiy but still he remained firm.

The English-educated Bihari middle class became the most vocal element in the society. A look at its composition explains its motivations. It was wholly upper caste, and predominantly upper class. The scions of the landed aristocracy or the Kayastha community contributed to its numbers. It now spearheaded the revolt against conservatism in religious beliefs and social practices.

Thus the onslaught against social prejudice began. Educated persons among both Hindus and Muslims began to raise their voice against ritualism, evils of dowry system and unnecessary pomp. Some of them also supported the widow remarriage. Several local associations were formed by enthusiastic young men. Mention may be made of the Muzaffarpur Dharma Samaj Sabha which brought out two magazines to preach against the dowry system and other social evils.

The upper castes of Bihar suffered from many social inhibitions. There was no marriage between different sub-sections of the castes. Thus Sachchidanand Sinha took a step forward in this direction. His wife belonged to a different section of the Kayastha community.

The educated and resourceful men of Bihar tried to begin Bihar organs in English and Hindi to propagate new ideas. The two brothers, Bisheshwar Singh and Saligram Singh, founders of the B. N. College, started the first Bihar organ in English under the name of '*The Indian Chronicle*' with one Chick of Calcutta as editor. Eventually, Govind Charan edited the paper and galvanized lifeless Bihar ; he was the first Bihari M. A. in English. His mantle fell upon his brother Mahesh Narayan who conducted the paper with conspicuous ability and when it languished for want of support, started a paper of his own under the name of '*The Bihar Times.*' Sachchidanand Sinha, who had commenced his practice at Allahabad, now settled down at Bankipore. He joined Mahesh Narayan and Krishna Sahay, who subsequently rose to be a member of Bihar and Orissa executive council. Nand Kishore Lal, Ali Imam and Hasan Imam were other prominent figures among that educated group of men, who dominated the social and political life of Bihar for many years. They began their work towards the end of the last century.

Besides the English journals many vernacular journals in Hindi, Urdu were started in this period. A periodical in Hindi, '*Bihar Bandhu*' came out first. It was first established in 1874 but towards the end of the 19th century it was closed. It appeared again and continued for many years. It played a very important part in propagating Hindi and creating public opinion against social evils. It campaigned for social reforms among the common masses of Bihar.[1]

The growth of literacy led to the rise of the press, both English and vernacular, which helped to accelerate the pace of social reforms and national consciousness. Though the first daily newspaper was not published till the first decade of the twentieth century, yet periodicals both in English and vernacular were printed and various pamphlets were in circulation from time to time.

Social Consciousness :

The beginning of the twentieth century saw the continuation of the trend started in the second half of the nineteenth century. The foundation of English education in Bihar had been laid with the establishment of zila schools and Government college at Patna. Eventually, secondary schools and a few private colleges came into existence. A group of educated men emerged who showed leanings towards new ideas. Naturally enough, attempts were made by a few enlightened persons of Bihar to encourage this education. Educational institutions received support from rich persons also.

Educational endowments to promote education in different castes were a common phenomenon during this period. Perhaps the endowment by Muhammad Husain Khan was the earliest educational endowment in Bihar. It was established through the Government notification no. 748 of 12 February 1901.[2]

In the beginning a demand for education in English arose amongst those castes, which were accustomed to take Government service. They desired to learn English because it was not only the language of the administration but also of the law courts. The Muslim nobility had a background of administration during the Moghal period. The Kayasthas among the Hindu were scribes by

1. Kamla Prasad Verma, **Bhulti Bhagati Yaden** (Hindi) p. 170
2. Proceedings of Government of Bengal, General Department Education, February 1901, no. 49-50 p. 137.

profession and their social status had risen during the Moghal period and during the Company period they were the first to avail of the advantages of new education. Naturally enough, in the beginning of the twentieth century almost all the leaders of educational development belonged to these classes. In fact the educated group of Bihar was mainly constituted by members of these castes. The branches of All-India Kayasthas Conference and the Mohammedan Association were established in Bihar during this period and they did a pioneering work in the field of education. In 1901 out of 17 barristers practising at Patna, 12 were Mohammedans. Prominent among them were Syed Ali Imam, Syed Hasan Imam and Syed Mazharul Haque.[1] All the 12 vakils of the High Court were Hindus mostly Kayasthas. In short, the Kayasthas outnumbered other castes in all spheres of educational field.

During this period the Government was approached by various private agencies to help education. The Lt. Governor of Bengal Andrew Fraser was presented an address by the Patna branch of the Calcutta Central Mohammedan Association. The Lt. Governor gave the following reply : "It is a great pleasure to me to find that the Address of the Patna Branch of Calcutta Central Mohammed an Association is occupied mainly with propasals for the improvement and advancement of female education. I am glad to hear that one of your most prominent and liberal citizens is prepared to help a suitable female education scheme financially ; and others have been inspired with interest in the matter, so that there is some reasonable hope that progress may be made. I am informed that the attention of the Hindu community is also earnestly devoted to this question. Efforts are being made to secure good teachers for schools and *zenanas* alike and to give a great impulse to this cause...."[2]

He further said : "In regard to education, I find that there are several other matters, which engage the attention of the enlight-

---

1. B. B. Misra, op. cit.,
2. Proceedings of the Government of Bengal, General Department (Education)' April 1906, nos. 6-7, pp. 59-60

ened leaders of the people. Here the feeling is apparently strong that a great effort should be made to push forward education in Bihar."[1]

The educational development, naturally, led to the removal of many social evils and inhibitions. The subject of the removal of brothel houses from the vicinity of the Patna College stirred the social life of Bihar's metropolis during this period. The Principal of the Patna College initiated the removal of houses of illfame from the surroundings of the Patna College. The District Magistrate of Patna consulted the Principals of the Patna College and B.N. College. The leading citizens of Patna like Purnendu Narayan Sinha, Government Pleader and Guru Das Chakravarti, enthusiastically supported this move. They all agreed that the Bengal Municipal Act, 1884, should be amended in such a way that these houses might be removed from their existing places.[2] This created a stir throughout Bihar and people began to press for the removal of brothels from the vicinity of educational institutions.

Chaturbhuja Sahai, a pleader of Arrah Bar and a member of the Bengal Council, and Shiv Saran Lal, Manager, Dumraon Raj, agreed with the proposed amendments. The Vice-chairman of the Chapra Municipality was strongly in favour of the amendment. At Muzaffarpur Vishwanath Prasad Mehta, Vice-Chairman of the municipality as well as Shib Chandra Chatterjee, Government Pleader, and Shiva Nandan Lal, Senior Magistrate, were equally enthusiastic about the proposed measure. In fact, this matter was considered at a meeting of the Municipal Commissioners of Motihari and the object was considered praiseworthy.[3] Eventually, this favourable public opinion led to the amendment of the Bengal Municipal Act, 1884 and the brothel-houses were removed to distant places from the surroundings of the Patna College and possibly from other such institutions.

---

1. Ibid., p. 59
2. C. R. Marriot, Offg. Commissioner, Patna Division, to Bengal Government, 9 September 1904
3. Ibid.

Many local associations were formed at district headquarters by educated people of the place. The establishment of the Bhagalpur National Improvement Association was a major step forward in the path of social development. Bankipore and Purnea also formed associations on the Bhagalpur pattern. At Muzaffarpur similar association came up, with the removal of social evils as their main task. The Bhagalpur National Improvement Association took positive steps to remove the backwardness of the Biharis and offered a scholarship of sixteen rupees per mensem to any qualified Bihari for prosecuting studies in Calcutta in a Medical or Engineering College. This step was highly appreciated by the people in Bihar who wanted other associations and rich Biharis in general to follow suit by awarding such scholarships to Bihari students.

At Muzaffarpur the first College of North Bihar had been established towards the end of the nineteenth century. This college was fortunate in enlisting the sympathy and support of a number of public-spirited gentlemen of the Tirhut division, who submitted to the Calcutta University syndicate a registered trust deed for Rs. 50,000 executed by Chowdhury Mahanth Raghunath Das, Zamindar of Jaitpur, Rai Parmeshwar Narain Mehta Bahadur, Banker, Jageshwar Prasad Singh, Pleader and Langat Singh, a philanthropist Zamindar.[1]

Many private scholarships were started to encourage education in Bihar. The Patna District Board and Patna Municipality also established a few scholarships for Bihar students reading in the Bihar School of Engineering. In the Patna College scholarships to the tune of Rs. 1,152 were awarded annually, most of these derived from Kazi Saiyid Reza Hussain endowment. In the B. N. College there were three scholarships of a total value of Rs. 408 awarded annually.[2]

Several enlightened Zamindars of Bihar had helped higher education in Bihar towards the end of the nineteenth century. Many of them responded enthusiastically to the proposal of Lt.

---

1. P. C. Roychoudhury, (ed.) B. D. G. Muzaffarpur, p. 81
2. L. S. S. O' Malley, (ed.) B. D. G. Patna, 172.

Governor Andrew Fraser in 1904 to open a college at Ranchi. A subscription of Rs. 3,12,897 for the proposed college was promised of which Rs. 2,48,897 were deposited by the leading Zamindars of Bihar.[1]

The Bengalis, by and large, were much advanced in education and the Bengali dominance in educational and social life of Bihar was apparent for quite some time. The educated Middle class was much inclined to legal profession as avenues in other spheres were closed. In the beginning of this century leaders on educational and social front generally belonged to this profession. In the beginning all the lawyers of Bihar came from migrated or domiciled Bengali families. In the later part of the nineteenth century Guru Prasad Sen was the most dominant personality and an acknowledged leader of the Patna Bar. In 1893 he had started *Behar Herald*, the first English Journal in Bihar. The only Bihari, who might have become (had his life been spared) a leader was Harbans Sahaya of Arrah, a distinguished lawyer. He was the first Bihari to be nominated in 1882 to the Legislative Council of Bengal.[2] Biharis were not inclined to join Medical or Engineering professions either. So doctors and engineers were also imported.

Fortunately a change was visible in the attitude of the Biharis during the early years of this century. A group of educated middle class emerged, who came to assert Bihar's interests. Most of them belonged to those castes, which first took the initiative to take to new education. Khuda Bux (1842-1908), Bisheshwar Singh (1849-99) and Shaligram Singh (1852-1905), Sachchidanand Sinha (1871-1950), Mahesh Narayan (1859-1907), Shiva Shankar Sahay (1863-1914), Mazharul Haque (1866-1930), Nand Kishore Lall (1866-1918), Parmeshwar Lall (1874-1919), Sir Ali Imam (1869-1932), Syed Hasan Imam (1871-1933) and Sir Ganesh Dutta Singh[3] were prominent among the educated Biharis. They constituted an *elite*, the vanguard of social and political movements in Bihar. They began their

---

1. Proceedings, Government of Bengal. General Department (Education) May 1906 no. 7, p. 98
2. Sachchidanand Sinha, Some Eminent Behar Contemporaries, p. 88
3. See Appendix-A

work during this very period They acted against social taboos and many of them went to England for higher studies. Parmeshwar Lal undertook a sea-voyage, which greatly influenced the contemporary social life of Bihar. He was elected Vice-President of the London Union Society, which had as its President Dadabhai Naeroji.[1]

The publication of journals in Bihar also helped in bringing about a new outlook. The Kayastha Samachar which was started towards the end of the nineteenth century by Sachchidanand Sinha took up the cause of educational and social development. A few Bihari educated and enlightened men had got a chance to preside over all-India Kayastha Conference. The branch of this association in Bihar started a campaign for educational development and social changes. The publication of the *Behar Times* was started in 1894 under the editorship of Mahesh Narayan. With its birth may be said to have begun the period of renaissance in Bihar.[2] By the end of the first year the paper was fairly well-established, and was recognised as the accredited exponent of Bihari public opinion. This was largely possible due to the great personality of its editor, Mahesh Narayan, who was well-versed in Indian politics.[3]

The vernacular journals were also developing, among which *Bihar Bandhu* was prominent. *The Bihar Times* hailed the publication of this vernacular journal. It was the oldest journal of Bihar and was redolent of a train and association of ideas connected with the awakening of a national and public life in Bihar. *The Behar Times* commented : 'the progress of vernacular journalism is the sure index of the progress of people.'

Structure of Society :

In Bihar there had been a preponderance of Hindu population, though there are areas of Muslim dominance and small pockets of Christian influence. Chotanagpur in South Bihar is dominated by animists. The Census Report of 1911 says that Hindus form an

1. Sachchidanand Sinha, op. cit, Intr., V.
2. Ibid.. XI-XII
3. Ibid.

overwhelming majority, representing 82.6 per cent of the total population and then 'Longo intervallo', the Musalmans with 9.6 percent and animist with 7 per cent.[1] Christians account for over a quarter of a million. This figure did not change and in 1921 we get the same proportion of population.

The structure of society continued to be based on caste system. The basic principles of this system are endogamy and heredity. A man must marry a woman of the same caste as himself; their son is born of the same caste as his parents, and all his life must remain a member of it. According to Risley a caste is "a collection of families or groups of families bearing a common name; claiming common descent from a mythical ancestor, human or divine; professing to follow the same hereditary calling, and regarded by those who are competent to give an opinion as forming a single homogeneous community." The name generally denotes or is associated with a specific occupation. A caste is almost invariably endogamous in the sense that a member of the large circle denoted by the common name may not marry outside that circle each of which is also endogamous. Thus it is not enough to say that a Brahman at the present day cannot marry one who is not a Brahman; his wife must not only be a Brahman, she must also belong to the same endogamous division of the Brahman caste.[2]

Caste appears to be an institution of highly complex origin, so complex indeed that by its very nature it must be limited to a single area; and that is why it is only found in India. For although social institutions that resemble caste in one respect or another are not difficult to find elsewhere, and some of them, undoubtedly, have some association with caste in their ultimate origin, yet caste in their fullest sense, as we know it, is an exclusively Indian phenomenon.[3]

---

1. Census of India, 1911, vol. V, p. 199 (Bengal, Bihar & Orissa Part-I).
2. Herbert Risley, The People of India, p. 68
   Also see S. V. Ketkar, History of Caste in India, p. 15 and N. K. Dutta, Origin and Growth of Caste in India, p. 3
3. J. H. Hutton, Caste in India, p. 46

There were two main varieties of caste, tribal and functional.[1] The original tribe is an aggregation of persons who are, or believe themselves to be united by blood, by common political interests, and by the need for mutual defence. There were often subsidiary bonds of union—common deities, common worship, common taboos and totems. Tribal castes sprang from those tribes which, both in pre-historic and historic times, have come in close contact whih Hinduism, have gradually accepted its social ordinances, and have finally merged in the Hindu social system.[2]

The functional castes are numerous and their characteristics are so prominent that the function of the community is regarded essential in the evolution of the caste. But thc proportion of a caste that actually follows the traditional occupation varies greatly; during the period under review 80 percent of Ahirs in Bihar, traditional herdsmen, were engaged in agriculture, while only 8 percent of Bihar Brahmans were engaged in religious functions.[3] Hutton says that apart from Rajputs, 'the caste which probably stand next to Brahmans and are in some ways allied to them are babhans (Bhumihar Brahmanas). The Bhumihar Brahmans are land holders particularly associated with Bihar and claim to be Brahmans who have given up the priestly function for a life of agriculture.[4] The greatest cultivating caste of Bihar, however, has been Kurmi, a caste equivalent in status to the Kunbi, of the Maratha community. Equally numerous in the 19th century was the caste or tribe known as Bhar who had sunk to the class of labourers and small cultivators, but who seemed at one time to have been the ruling people of Bihar. Kalwars who distilled spirit from molasses or from the flowers of the 'Mahua' tree had a status as low as the Bhars, not because they represented a conquered and dispossessed tribe, but on account of their occupation. An occupation again was in part

1. There are other minor varieties, which need not be mentioned. See Risley's **People of India** 1915, pp. 75-95 and Blunt's **Caste System of Northern India**, pp. 2-3
2. For example, See Risley, op. cit., pp. 75-76
3. Herbert Risley, op. cit., pp. 76-77
4. J. H. Hutton, **Caste in India**, 1951, p. 33

at any rate the reason for the low standing of the Pasi who taps toddy palm, the dhobi—a washerman, khatik-butcher or the chamars who worked in leather. Below all these were scavengers the various grades of Bhangi or sweeper and the numerous castes of Dom.[1]

The higher castes of Bihar, such as Brahmans, Bhumihar Brahmans, Rajputs and Kayasthas had no organisation for the detection and punishment of breaches of caste rules. But most of the lower castes of Bihar had an organised system of caste government which had certain common features, though the procedure and the names of the office-bearer vary in different parts and among different castes.[2]

The people of Bihar have been described by O'Malley as assiduous and industrious cultivators. He found them conservative, and 'they have neither the mental versatility nor the education of the Bengalis, though an exception must be made of the writer caste of Kayasthas, whose shrewdness and acumen are proverbial. On the whole, they are men of slow thoughts but long memories, vigorous and disciplined traits."[3]

According to the census Report of 1921 the caste system was the steel frame of the Hindu society. In Bihar there was no sign of caste system breaking down or ceasing to be the dominant influence that it had always been. The most important aspect of caste was the system of restrictions on marriage which it imposed and the neglect of caste distinctions in this matter in Bihar was unheard of. However, relaxations started in respect of marriages among the sub-castes within the limits of the same caste, especially among the Kayastha. The Ahirs also, in an effort to improve their social position tried to neglect sub-caste in marriages. These were attempts to adjust the caste system to modern conditions.[4]

---

1. Ibid., p. 34
2. **Census of India,** 1911, vol. V, Part I, Report, p. 461 (Bengal, Bihar & Orissa)
3. L. S. S. O' Malley **Bengal, Bihar and Orissa,** 1917, p. 181
4. Census of India, 1921, vol. VII, Part I, p. 334 (Bihar and Orissa)

The attitude of people towards caste restrictions on food and drink showed signs of change. In places like Jamshedpur where work was done under modern conditions, men of all castes and races worked side by side. In the matter of untouchability, the railways, the steamers and moter-bus produced some effect. But conservatism in this matter still prevailed. The children of the untouchable classes attending one of the zila schools in Bihar were made to sit in the verandah.[1]

Education in Different Castes :

As already seen in Chapter I, there was a monopoly of Brahmans and Kayasthas in the educational field in the 19th century and that the demand for new education arose amongst those very classes and castes that were connected with education and governmental service. And by the second half of the nineteenth century, there was a veritable race between the various communities aspiring to enter the government service. This was started with the parts which had felt the need first. The desire for schools, colleges, saminaries, academies etc., began to sweep the country. Organisations were formed by members of the leading communities for spreading English or Anglo-vernacular schools and colleges throughout the country. Bihar was slow to get the impact of this trend in the beginning, but with the opening of the 20th century the situation changed. Those very castes who were dominating the educational field in the last century, now took the lead.

In education Bihar was far behind Bengal in 1911, only 11 millions or 4 per cent of the population were literate.[2]

The number of literate persons in Bihar and Orissa was 1,439,000 males and 76,000 females in 1911; which increased to 1,591,1754 males and 109,735 females in 1921.[3]

The most educated caste in Bihar around 1920 was that of the kayasthas, among whom one in every three could read and write. The second place was shared by Karans, the writer caste of Orissa

---

1. Ibid., p. 234
2. **Census of India**, 1911, vol. V, Part I, p. 361
3. **Census of India**, 1921, vol. VIII, p. 196

and North Bihar and those keen traders, the Agrawalas, the propotrion among them being one in four. They were followed by the Saiyads (Muslims) and the Brahman, the percentage of literates among them being 17. The only other castes with 10 per cent literacy were Bhumihar Brahmans and Kalwars. Next came the Rajputs and Baniyas. The abysm of ignorance was found among the animists among whom the average number of literates varied from 1 to 7 per mile. The latter figure was for the Hos, who might be regarded as the least ignorant of the animist tribes.[1]

So far the literacy in English in Bihar was concerned, Kayasthas were the first among the individual castes, the second being held by the Saiyads (Muslims).[2] Education was more widely diffused among the Muslims in every division of Bihar, except North Bihar, even though they numbered as much as 21 millions or two fifths of the Musalman population of Bihar. The most advanced Musalman community was found in Patna, where 17 per cent of males and 2 per cent of the females could read and write.[3]

Patna was far ahead in all spheres of educational development. Among the districts of Bihar, it stood first in literacy both among males and females. The prominence of Patna in female literacy was not a new thing : it had always stood ahead of other districts in this sphere as the proportion of persons living in the towns of this district had been from time immemorial far higher than elsewhere and the life in towns was much more conducive to the spread of education. The Muslim aristocracy had shaken off the sea-voyage taboos much earlier, and there had been regular departure of Musalmans to England for higher studies.

The percentage of literates among Anglo-Indians was 87. Patna had 1 per cent of its population (males) acquainted with English, but that too due to the presence of a British regiment at Dinapur. Elsewhere the average was very low. In other districts also, the areas which had a high proportion of literates and which

---

1. Census of India, 1911, vol. V, p. 363
2. Ibid., p. 363
3. Ibid., p. 263

rose above the higher proportion of literates could be attributed to Anglo-Indian colonies or European Missionaries employed in coal mines, iron-works and other industrial works.[1]

Role of Caste Organisations :

The British brought with them a casteless culture and a literature full of thoughts on individual liberty. With the introduction of English education many of the intelligent minds of the country came in closer contact with the religion of the rulers, some of them being outstanding personalities. As a result Raja Ram Mohan Roy and others started movements of reforms.

In Northern India local social reform movements were organised. In Bihar the main currents of social reform movements assumed a relatively minor place. The cause of social reform movement was carried under the auspices of different caste organizations. These caste organizations played a progressive role in championing the cause of social change.

The leaders of the National Social Conference acknowledged the caste association as Social Reform Societies, and several caste leaders became prominent in conference proceedings.[2] Most of the caste organisations which were established in the 19th century drew their leadership from western educated caste members, men who were aware of the social reform movement and for whom advancement of their caste implied adoption of modern social ideals.[3]

Thus the practice of holding caste conferences became common, many of them showing progressive leanings. Interest in practical social reform began to grow. All over the country efforts

---

1. **Census of India**, 1911, Vol. V. p. 262 (Bengal, & Orissa, Part-I). The Census Report of 1921 informs that the proportion of literates in towns was naturally much higher than rural areas. The cities are the centres of social, intellectual and commercial life. They contain the principal law courts and some of them are headquarters of Governments. They are better provided than the villages with schools and they contain most of the higher educational institutions.
2. Charles H. Heimsath, **Indian Nationalism and Hindu Social Reform** 1964, p. 279
3. *Ibid.*, p. 280

were being made in different directions and as a result a gradual change in ideas began to come over the community as a whole.[1]

Due to the impact of education even caste in the Hindu society developed a tendency to form its association comprising all members of the caste. The function of these new organizations were (1) to further the general interests of the caste and particularly to guard its social status in the hierarchy from actual or potential attacks of other castes; (2) to start funds to provide studentship for the needy and deserving students of the caste; (3) to help poor people of the caste and (4) sometimes to try to regulate certain customs of the caste by resolutions passed at the annual meetings of the members of the caste.[2]

The meetings of both Brahmans and Kayasthas in Bihar were almost entirely confined to the consideration of the following offences: (1) sea-voyage and the eating of forbidden food, (2) intermarriage between sub-castes, (3) widow-marriage and (4) immorality on the part of females.[3]

The caste sabhas were a form of caste organizations which came into existence during the last part of the 19th century. Their main object was to improve the social condition of the caste, and their organization was modelled upon European associations or companies. The capital of the sabha was to be spent for promoting education amongst the caste and for improving their religious social and moral condition.[4]

The model for many caste organizations in Bihar was the Kayastha Conference established in 1887 at Lucknow. Munshi Kali Prasad had founded the Kayastha Pathshala at Allahabad in 1873. The Kayastha Conference gave considerable attention to the strengthening of the Pathshala as major means of training young Kayasthas and thereby improving the level of the community in general.[5] It

1. S. Natarajan, **A Century of Social Reform in India**, p. 98
2. G. S. Ghurye, **Caste and Class in India**, p. 191
3. **Census of India** 1911, p. 482
4. Ibid., p. 348
5. Charles H. Heimsath' op. cit., p. 282

was an all India organization established to promote social development of the Kayastha community. Its third session was held for the first time in Bihar at Patna in 1889. This organization was very active in Bihar in the beginning of this century. It had district branches throughout the province. On 26 December 1899 its session was held at Monghyr under the Chairmanship of B. Kedar Nath, A Vakil of Gaya. In this session the Education Committee of the Kayastha Sadar Sabha opened three literary clubs at Bhagalpur, Monghyr and Bankipore respectively.[1] This organisation discussed at its sessions questions of child marriage, female education and widow-marriages. There was much enthusiasm and sympathy among educated Kayasthas of Bihar for this organisation. The sessions of this conference were regularly held in different parts of Bihar during the first decade of this century.

In December 1904, the Kayastha Conference adopted a resolution that the best way of propagating the ideals of the conference among the Mufassil Kayasthas would be to appoint an *updeshak* for each province. The Dinapur Kayastha Local Sabha at its anniversary on 1 October 1905 proposed to give a practical effect to this resolution. As a result *updeshaks* were appointed for the areas where they were needed most. They toured the different parts of the province and lectured on the problems of social reform among the Kayasthas.[2]

The 18th session of the Kayastha Conference met at Dumraon on 24 and 25 December 1906. The President of the session, Baldeo Prasad a pleader of Bareilly, said that the education of 'our boys and girls should form the chief item in the conference propaganda'. He called on the Kayasthas to marry sub-castes and deprecated early marriages.[3]

The 6th resolution of this session moved by Gajadhar Prasad of Patna proposed the setting up of a sub-committee of selected men of position and influence in Bihar to enforce the abolition of 'mone-

1. The Kayastha Samachar, February 1900
2. The Hindustan Review, September 1905
3. Ibid., January 1907

tary stipulation in marriages maintaining a complete record of all the marriages performed within their circle, and to report the names of those who observe the conference rules, for being read and applauded in the conference hall.

This sub-committee for Bihar consisted of Makoond Lal of Arrah, Mahabir Sahay of Patna, Brajkishore Prasad of Darbhanga, Deokinandan of Gaya and Gajadhar Prasad of Bankipore with power to increase their number.[1]

There was a strong prejudice against sea-voyage among the Bihari Hindus. The Kayastha Conference faced a difficult situation when Sachchidanand Sinha attended its Lucknow session in 1901. On this occasion a great deal of time of the conference was devoted to a discussion on how to advise effective means for getting rid of him.[2]

The reason was that a good number of Bihar Kayasthas were against the admission of Europe-return Kayasthas into the conference. The Kayastha Samachar wrote the following :

> "In view of the fact that other caste conferences which do not claim to be so educated and enlightened as we do, have practically solved the problem of sea-voyage by taking back into caste England-returned members of their community, it is a matter of shame and regret that notwithstanding the fact of our being more liberal in some social matters than these castes, we should have yet been behind them in finding a practical and workable solution for the sea-voyage question."[3]

In the 16th Kayastha Conference at Gorakhpur, from 26th to 28 December 1904, a resolution was passed, allowing sea-voyage. However, according to the same resolution, those who returned from abroad had to perform certain *dwijdharmi* rites before they were allowed to join their community again. But this question did not reach the stage of final settlement in Bihar during early years

---

1. Ibid.,
2. Sachchidanand Sinha, A Selection from the Speeches and Writing, p. 726
3. The Kayastha Samachar, April 1910

of this century. Progressive members of the Kayastha community started sending their sons to England for higher studies, but the orthodox among them still opposed it vehemently.

The sea-voyage question was raised at Chapra in 1904. The occasion was an attempt to retain Ganesh Prasad in caste who had returned from England. Brajkishore Prasad had organised a group of progressive educated Kayasthas in favour of Ganesh Prasad. Rajendra Prasad and his elder brother Mahendra Prasad attended dinner with Ganesh Prasad in support of retaining him in caste. The opponents were equally organised and had good number of supporters.[1] The question of sea-voyage assumed a new dimension in Bihar, when Parmeshwar Lal returned from England after three years' stay. There was tremendous enthusiasm among the progressive sections of the Kayasthas. The *Beharee* wrote :

> "The 6 October will be remembered as a red letter day in the social history of Bihar. Parmeshwar Lal reached Gaya in the early morning of that day."[2]

Meetings were held at many places and resolutions passed in favour of taking Mr.Lal into caste. The supporters of sea-voyage arranged *Prayaschitt*-ceremony with great pomp and show. A dinner was arranged at Gaya attended by over hundred representatives of Kayasthas from different parts of Bihar. Many letters were published in newspapers in defence of sea-voyage.

On the other hand, meetings at Gaya and Patna were held to outcaste Parmeshwar Lal.[3] While meetings, both in favour of and against the retention of Parmeshwar Lal were attended by his castemen, the incident echoed throughout the country eliciting adverse comments from several newspapers. *The Indian Mirror* commented :

> "It seems that the sea-voyage question has yet to be solved in some parts of India......From the manner in which Parmeshwar Lal is being prosecuted by his orthodox castemen, it would seem that Bihar is still half-century behind."[4]

1. Rajendra Prasad, **Autobiography**, 1957, p. 34
2. **The Beharee**, 11 October 1907
3. **Ibid**, 1 November 1907
4. **The Hindustan Review**, December 1907

The Advocate of Lucknow wrote :

> "The sea-voyage question in Bihar—one has a right to expect better things from the Kayasthas of Bihar, whom we considered hitherto to be more advanced than their fellow castemen, but they appeared very backward in matter of social reforms."[1]

The advocates of social reform, however, were on the side of Parmeshwar Lal and they carried on an organised campaign to create public opinion in favour of sea-voyage. At a meeting of the influential citizens of Patna in 1907, ninety students of the local schools and colleges submitted a representation appealing to open the way to visit foreign countries.

The 19th Kayastha Conference at Aligarh adopted the following resolution in support of sea-voyage.

> "That this conference rejoices on the returning home of those young men of the community who have obtained splendid success in foreign countries in various branches of learning, and hopes that the number of such young men will be ever on the increase. This conference also thanks those who heartily espoused the cause of Mr. Parmeshwar Lal's retention into caste, and deplores the conduct of those who started an opposition and declares the proceedings of the latter to be invalid."[2]

The Kayastha Conference promoted marriages among sub-castes, and successfully arranged many dinners of sub-castes. There was a growing demand among the youths to solve 'intermarriage problem'. In *the Beharee* there appeared a letter which runs as follows :—

> "Some of the leading Kayasthas have set a good example by boldly solving the difficult problem of sea-voyage to a greater extent. To make a request on behalf of the younger generation, to make a second move in other directions, viz., to solve the 'intermarriage problem'. It is a

1. Ibid., November 1907
2. The Hindustan Review, January 1908

problem of mass......we hope that as they have solved the question of sea-voyage they also solve the problem in their own families."[1]

In Bihar the leading educated Kayasthas established an organisation to help needy students. It was 'The Kayastha Sishu Hitkari Sabha'. This organisation collected funds and provided financial help to the poor Kayastha students. A meeting of this organisation was held in the Bihar National College with the leading Kayastha gentlemen of Bankipore. It was pointed out that education was the main factor in the elevation of the country. The noble and philanthropic object of this sabha was to educate poor Kayastha boys by means of stipends and scholarships. In 1909 it met the cost of five Kayastha students reading in the Bihar School of Engineering, Temple Medical School and other schools. This organisation started in 1908 carried its work for many years.[2]

At the time of the census various castes saw chances of raising their status. They invited conferences of their members, and formed councils to take steps to see that their status was recorded in the way they thought honourable to them.[3] There was great commotion when the census operation of 1911 started. Hundreds of petitions were filed, the applicants requesting that they might be known by new names, be placed higher in the order of precedence, be recognised as Kshattriyas, Vaisya......etc. All the castes other than Brahmans and Rajputs thought it a suitable opportunity to advance new claims.

The Bhumihars were a large and very influential caste in Bihar. They claimed that they should be regarded as Brahmans.[4] This caste in Bihar had within its fold many a big landed aristocracy, who were very resourceful. It felt the impact of a new wave. The Bhumihar Brahman Mahasabha was established in the later

1. The Beharee, January 27, 1911
2. The Beharee, 15 October 1909
3. G. S. Ghurye, op. cit., p. 170
4. Census of India, 1911, vol. V, Part I, p. 44

parts (probably in 1896) of the nineteenth century. Many big zamindars of Bihar and United Province became its patrons. There were already many lawyers in this caste, who took interest in educational matters of their community.

The Calcutta University was established in 1857. For 42 years after its establishment there was no other institution for higher education to the North of the Ganga between Dacca and Gorakhpur. In March 1899 a meeting of Bhumihar Brahman Mahasabha at Muzaffarpur resolved to establish a college at that place. A second grade college established three months later in July 1899 was raised to the status of a first grade college within a year. Thus the credit for establishing the first college in North Bihar goes to the Bhumihar Brahman Mahasabha. A subscription of nearly a lakh was raised from the members of the Bhumihar Brahman community. It was maintained by the Mahasabha upto June 1908 without any help from outsiders.

But this college was not meant for the Bhumihars only. It was to impart education to youths without any distinction of caste, creed and colour. Many non-Bhumihars were associated with this institution prominent among them being Parmeshwar Narayen Mehta and Muhammad Yusuf, pleaders. Thus the Bhumihar Mahasabha through their initiative fulfilled a distinct need of the people of North Bihar.

The 13th session of the Bhumihar Brahman Mahasabha was held at Motihari in January 1909. Maharaj Kumar Sivapratap Sahi presided and many leading men of the community particip-ated. The Sabha succeeded in establishing schools in many villages. Resolutions were passed reiterating its aims as the spread of education in the community, the establishment of boarding houses and schools and preaching simple living and high thinking.[1]

A public meeting of the Bhumihar Brahman Mahasabha was held on 7 July 1909, under the presidentship of Chandreshwar Prasad Sinha, Raja of Muksudpur. It was attended by the leading men of the community of all the districts of the province. The

---

1. The Beharee, February 5, 1909

object of the meeting was to spread education among the members of the community and to remove social evils by preventing early marriage, etc.[1]

On 21 January 1910 the Bhumihar Brahman Mahasabha held its meeting under the presidentship of the Maharaja of Banaras. A resolution condemning money stipulation and extravagance in marriage was passed. The president laid great stress upon the urgent need of reform and a resolution was moved from the chair to the effect that praise worthy action of those observing the resolution should be suitably recognised and those violating it should be socially punished by the Sabha.[2]

The foundation stone of the proposed college building was laid at Muzaffarpur. Greer, the commissioner of the Tirhut division thanked the Maharaja for his princely donation of Rs. 50,000 and the monthly subscription of Rs. 200.[3]

The second day's session of the Mahasabha, attended by about ten thousand people, was presided over by Maharaja Kumar Vishnu Prakash Narayan Singh of Madhuban. The audience showed a keen interest symbolising the new awakening among the masses. Resolutions advocating the spread of education, prevention of early marriage and help to widows and orphans were passed. The Sabha remained active all through the year in different spheres. Volunteers were recruited to propagate the ideals of the Sabha.[4]

The Sabha adopted another resolution advocating female education on national lines, popularisation of Sanskrit study, the promotion of Brahmacharya (celibacy), simple living, village sanitation and organisation of local Sabhas.[5]

Langat Singh appealed for a scholarship fund of rupees two lakhs, himself making a princely donation of Rs. 10,000. The

---

1. The Beharee, July 1909
2. Ibid., 28 January 1910
3. Ibid.
4. The Beharee, 28 January 1910
5. Ibid.

response was favourable, and several leading men promised to contribute liberally. Mention may be made of Maharaja Kumar Vishnu Prakash Narayan Sinha of Madhuban, who promised a substantial amount.[1]

The controversy over the name of Muzaffarpur College was ended by a compromise to add the name of Greer with Bhumihar Brahman College. Bhumihar Mahasabha had protested against the attempt to change the name of the college.

The 17th annual session of the Bhumihar Brahman Sabha held at Bankipore on 23 February 1913 under the presidentship of Seoraj Nandan Sinha passed the usual resolutions covering the programme of the spread of education, foundation of schools and pathshalas. This was a unique session in as much as it discussed problems of marriage reforms elaborately, dealing at length with the system of tilak.

Sheonarayan Rai, a Vakil, moved a resolution condemning early marriage and fixing the minimum marriageable age of boys at 16. Considering the horrors of early marriage the resolution was accepted enthusiastically. Another resolution was moved by Ram Dayalu Sinha, another pleader, on the necessity and value of educating girls. Without the education of girls, he pointed out, no community could advance.[2]

According to *The Beharee*, a leading newspaper, "The business of the day was indeed most important and should be stamped in letter of gold in the history of our province." Indeed the meeting proved by the character of the audience "that the good results of the wave of education had thrown their spray not in every part of India, but distinctly in our amidst."[3]

Maithil Brahmans were an intellectual class of people in Bihar noted for their Sanskrit and philosophical learning in the past. But like other communities they had fallen much below their standard. There were many social evils rampant among

1. **Ibid.**
2. **The Beharee**, 25 February 1913
3. **Ibid.**

them. With the advent of new education, Maithils like other communities were also aware of the necessity of adjusting themselves to the modern conditions of life. There naturally came an earnest desire to purge their community of the many social evils which had crept into it and diffusing education widely among the community.

A grand conference of the Maithil Brahmans and Karan Kayasthas of Mithila was held at Madhubani on 26, 27 and 28 March 1910 under the presidentship of Maharaja Bahadur of Darbhanga. Such a huge gathering of Maithils was never witnessed before. The following resolutions were passed—(1) That attempt should be made to spread education amongst the Maithils by establishing schools and granting scholarships to students. (2) That Maithil Brahmans and Kayasthas should avoid polygamy, early marriage and marriage at an old age.[1]

It was resolved that the girls should be married between 8 and 12 years of age and boys between 15 and 16.[2]

In the Mithila Conference held at Supaul in May 1912, the Maharaja of Darbhanga exhorted the Maithils to give priority to the question of education. He asked them to remove the evils which had crept into the marital relations of the community. The Maharaja urged upon the people to improve their material conditions by taking to English education and undertaking commercial and industrial enterprises.[3]

That caste still remained the backbone of the social fabric was shown by the fact that all attempts at social reforms were made through the caste organisations. Even the lower caste people formed sabhas to promote their social status. It is true that some of their organisations did not work regularly and consistently. Many of them were more systematic and active with written constitutions and their own periodical journals. Even the Doms held

---

1. The Beharee, 8 April 1910
2. Ibid.
3. Ibid., 12 May 1911

meetings at Patna in July 1921 and the Mehatars resolved to improve their social condition.[1]

The Dusadhs had a more elaborate organization in the shape of the Dushashan Bansiya Kshatriya Mahasabha founded in 1891 which usually met once a year. There were managing committees in various districts consisting of a president, a secretary and members and the President of the all-India Sabha was elected annually. The spread of education among the caste was the first plank in the platform of the association but it also encouraged the abandonment of evil practices like early marriage of boys and girls.[2]

But the most important and effective Sabha in Bihar was the Gope Jatiya Mahasabha of Ahirs or Goalas founded in 1912. It included members from the whole of North India from the Punjab to Bengal. The association had a monthly journal of its own called the 'Ahir Samachar'. A considerable body of literature was accumulated in support of the claim that the Ahirs had a Kshatriya origin.[3]

The second session of the Gope Jatiya Mahasabha was held on 10,11 and 12 February 1913 at Bankipore. The methods for social and educational advancement were discussed by the delegates. The session adopted resolutions to remove evils of early marriage, extravagant wedding, and other social evils.[4]

Rai Bahadur Nishikant Sen put questions at the meeting of the Bihar and Orissa Legislative Council held on 6 April 1914; asking for proper educational facilities for Ahir students. He claimed that the Ahirs constituted the most numerous caste in Bihar. The Government replied that the number of Goalas exceeded the number of any other Hindu caste but it was less than that of the Mohammedans. Regarding the questions of exemption of fee of the Gope students in the Government and aided schools and of the establishment of schools in Gope villages, the Government replied

1. **Census of India**, 1921, Vol. VII Part, I, p. 236 (Bihar and Orissa)
2. **Ibid.**
3. **Ibid.**
4. **The Beahrae**, 31 January 1913

that the recommendation of the Primary Education Committee was being awaited.[1]

Inter-dining and inter-marriage among different sub-castes of Ahirs was now a settled fact.[2] The Kurmis, the Kahars, the Dhanuks and other low castes claimed the right of wearing sacred thread. The Kurmis also organised their Sabhas, approving inter-dining and inter-marriage. Conferences were perhaps common to almost all the castes in Bihar. A conference of Shaw community to encourage education among its members was held on 28 October 1909. As the caste conferences had become the order of the day, a Sahu Vaishya conference was held at Banaras in December 1912 under the Presidentship of Kartik Prasad, a doctor of Monghyr. It also passed resolutions relating to the spread of education in the community.[4]

A meeting of Sonars was held on 5, 6 and 7 February 1919 at Gaya, attended by 150 Sonars. They claimed a Rajput origin and decided to abandon the dowry system.[4] One Jagannath Prasad a Teli of Bettiah, was reported to be inspired by M. K. Gandhi. He came to Patna in 1918 and tried to start a *Teli Sabha*, with a view to ameliorating the lot of the Telis in Bihar.[6]

In short a process of 'Sanskritization' in all the low castes of Bihar had begun. It was a process by which a 'low' Hindu caste changed customs, rituals, ideology and the way of life in the direction of the high, and frequently in 'twice born' caste. Generally, such changes were followed by a claim to a higher position in the caste hierarchy.

This claim developed tension among high and low castes. When the Ahirs of North Bihar decided to call themselves Kshatriya and donned the sacred thread, the Maithil Brahmans, the Rajputs,

1. Proceeding of Govt. of Bihar and Orissa, 1914, vol. no. 43
2. Census of India, 1921
3. The Beharee, 5 November 1909
4. Ibid., 14 January 1913
5. Bihar and Orissa Police Abstract of Intelligence, vol. VIII, p. 66
6. Bihar and Orissa Police Abstract of Intelligence, vol, VIII, p. 25

and the Bhumihar Brahmans tried to prevent them. This resulted in violence and resort to the law courts.[1]

There was in theory no caste system among the followers of the prophet. But in practice they were divided into distinct groups, which stood socially apart. Just like the Hindu functional castes, the Muslims were divided on the basis of occupations passed on to each group from generation to generation. No intermarriage was permitted between the different groups. There were also restrictions on eating together. Attempts to spread education among Musalmans began quite early in Bihar. With this aim educated groups of Musalmans organised Mohammedan Association in different parts of the province. Anjuman Islamia was established at Bankipore by Ali Hasan, a student of Patna College, in 1855. Its aim was to remove social and religious evils that had crept into Mohammedan society. It was revived in 1909. Anjuman Islamia worked for the social development of Muslims throughout the province.

Ali Imam, while presiding over the All India Muslim League at Amritsar in 1908 said : "I believe that the establishment of Conferences, Associations and corporate bodies in different communities on denominational lines are necessary to give expression to denominational views, so that the builders of a truly national life in the country may have before *them to* crystallize needs and

---

1- M. N. Srinivas, **Social Change in Modern India**, 1966, p. 16

In Several villages of North Bihar the gowalas were implicated in false criminal cases by the higher castes to harass them. The efforts of the lower castes to improve their status led to a considerable friction and occasional disturbance. The cause of the dispute had a more deeper origin than it appeared. The economic exploitation of zamindars erupted in a communal clash and took shape of conflit between upper and lower castes. The main cause of the disputes was that the zamindars insisted on continuing, Begari System'. The zamindars used to employ labour in fields on nominal rates and wished to continue this privilege. The Goals protested by restricting the outdoor employment of their woman folks and curtailing the milk supplies to zamindars. The Sabhas of Goalas, Kurmis, Koeries and other low castes sought to improve the educational prospects of their members. In 1922 Gope Sabha tried to secure representation of their interest in local bodies.

aspirations of all sects.[1] He welcomed institutions as the Kayastha Conference, the Bhumihar Brahman Mahasabha, Rajput Conference and Mohammedan Anjumans.

The *Adivasi* (tribal) population of Bihar derived modern benefit of enlightenment mainly through Christian missionaries. The Christian students of Chotanagpur were first to think of the social development of Adivasis at large. Chotanagpur had witnessed a series of uprising in the nineteenth century.[2] Under the educated leaders like Buddhu Bhagat, Ganga Narain, Birsa and others. But the torchbearers of modern social changes were the educated tribal youths. J. Bartholemen, a Christian student of St. Columba's College organised a Student Union in 1911-12, which included Christian students.[3]

This student organisation developed into a bigger body, which was named 'Chotanagpur Improvement Society' or the 'Chota Nagpur Unnati Samaj'. The membership was restricted to the adivasis of Chotanagpur. Its declared aim and object was the upliftment of Chotanagpur from the backward state, and the improvement of social and political conditions of the adivasis.[4] This organisation successfully carried the work for many years.

Social Changes Through Various Agencies :

The work of social change was taken up by many other agencies. In fact, the first decade of the twentieth century witnessed the formation of many educational and political associations with the work of social change as an important part of their programme. The Bihari Students' Conference was opened in 1906 in Patna College Hall. In Bihar, it was the first organisation of its kind which included educated men of all the communities. It held its annual sessions in different parts of Bihar. The second session of the Bihari Student Conference was held on 28 and 29 September

1. Presidential Address, All India Muslim League, March 1908.
2. See J.C. Jha, **The Kol Insurrection of Chotanagpur;** J.C. Jha **The Bhumij Revolt of 1832-33** and Suresh Singh, **Dust Storm and Hanging Mist.**
3. L.P. Vidyarthi. ed., **Leadership in India**. 1967, pp. 131-32
4. Ibid., p. 132.

1907 at Bhagalpur. This session condemned in its resolution the evils of early marriage, urging upon its members to exert to discourage the practice. It was resolved to create public opinion against local evils.[1]

The other items of social reform which were usually included in the resolution of Bihar Students Conference were female education and foreign travel. In course of his presidential address Syed Husan Imam said to the students that the subject of travels in foreign land deserved their immediate attention.[2] This conference created a favourable atmosphere for sea-voyage. It was primarily because of the public opinion created by this association that the students of Bihar started demanding permission to go to foreign countries.

The establishment of the Bihar Provincial Association in 1907 was a landmark in the modern history of Bihar. It was the first political association in Bihar in the widest sense of the term which was organised by Hindus and Muslims jointly. True, there were political institutions before its advent in Bihar, but they had limited sphere of activity. As the Bihar landholders' Association was restricted to the landed aristocracy of the province, Bihar Association was started with the object of counteracting the agitation which was carried on for the separation of Bihar. But it did not receive response and met its natural death soon.

However, this association also undertook the programme of social reform enthusiastically in its early sessions. It had universal education and economic improvement of the masses as main planks in its programme of nation building. Deep Narayan Sinha presiding over one of its sessions in 1910 declared that the eradication of social evils, like the practice of early marriage and the backward condition of women was one of the main aims of the association.[3]

---

1. The Beharee, 8 October 1907
2. Ibid., 5 November 1909
3. The Beharee, July 1910

The formation of educational societies in Bihar accelerated the trend of social change among the educated classes of the province. Two such associations were established, one each in South and North Bihar. The Patna Board of Education was established in 1910 through the initiative of Purnendu Narayan Sinha, for improving female education in Bihar. It was felt that government and public bodies might spend money on female education, but they could not force guardians to send their girls to schools. Private agencies could do much to popularise female education especially in those pockets where conservatism still persisted. It included mass education and education of depressed classes in its programme. Indeed, education of depressed classes deserved the most sympathetic treatment. It also worked for propagating industrial, agricultural and commercial education.[1] Men like Hasan Imam, S. Sinha, Mazharul Haque, P. P. Sharma and Sheoshankar Sahay were associated with the board.[2]

Another similar organization, 'The Tirhut Education Society' was started under the chairmanship of Parmeshwar Narayan Mehta. The society founded in May 1908 established many primary schools and night schools in North Bihar. A respectable Kayastha lady was so much impressed with the account of the work of the society that she became a life-member and donated a handsome amount to the society.[3]

The Bihar Industrial and Agricultural Exhibition had an association attached to it namely the 'Bihar Industrial and Education Association.' The association established many scholarships for students in Bihar. It promoted foreign travel by providing financial assistance to willing students : it sent two students to England in 1905.[4] Even co-operative credit societies conference at its annual sessions demanded educational facilities in Bihar, adopting resolutions relating to educational and social development.

---

1. The Beharee, 17 July 1910
2. Ibid.
3. Ibid., 20 May 1910
4. Ibid. 15 January 1909

Newspapers and periodicals published in different parts of Bihar in many languages paved the way for social changes. They published articles and comments on the need for social changes in Bihar. They created a strong public opinion against social evils and provided a forum for enlightened people to ventilate their grievances of social change through them. They became a strong weapon in the hands of social reformers of Bihar. Comments like the following were the regular features of the journals: "Our needs are classified under three broad divisions, viz., (1) Social (2) Educational (3) Political...our social structures require change. Much controversy has arisen regarding the sea-voyage. The next point for consideration is early marriage. It has many drawbacks..."[1] The article further discussed the necessity of female education.

Parda was a great hindrance in female education and it attracted the attention of many social change campaigners. Mahatma Gandhi had discussed its removal at Champaran. It formed an important programme of social work at Champaran. A few years later, while performing the function laying the foundation of an orphanage at Darbhanga, Mahatma Gandhi said that the sight of the screen behind his audience (women behind the *parda*) made him sad. He announced that unless women came out of *parda*, India could not advance. He requested to tear down *parda* with one mighty effort.[2]

The call of Mahatma Gandhi sowed the seed of a great social movement in Bihar. In course of time it developed into an anti-*prada* movement in Bihar. Many devoted men and women joined it which gave an impetus to social change in Bihar. For the first time women felt the impact of social change in Bihar.[3]

By the beginning of the third decade of the twentieth century many social evils showed signs of disappearance. Rigidity of caste-

1. The Biharee, 23 July 1909
2. Rajendra Prasad, Atmakatha (Hindi), p. 333
3. About the year 1927 an anti-Parda movement began in Bihar. Sri Ramanand Mishra of Darbhanga had started a compaign against it and went to Mahatma Gandhi's ashram at Sabarmati with his wife to seek blessings.

taboos relaxed and inter-dining among different sub-castes developed. Perhaps too much emphasis on caste-association led to the emergence of loyalty to caste-politics. But during the period under our review all caste-groups were directing their attention to improvements in their social and economic status. Many of the caste associations which were formed initially for non-political purposes later assumed political importance, while retaining their earlier interest in social and economic advancement.[1]

Progress of education and the concerted effort of many organisations raised the marriageable age of boys and girls. Women slowly began to discard *parda*. But there was no sign of any check on dowry system. All conferences, social, Kayastha, Brahman, Kshatriya, Bhumihar and others were unanimous in decrying this evil. This social abuse had been denounced at successive social conference but no one imagined that the custom would be given up without legislation.[2]

Education helped many individuals in raising their social status through marriage. Those who were economically hard-pressed were sometimes forced to delay the marriage of their daughters because of their incapacity to meet heavy expenses. In such cases, child marriage was automatically avoided.

At times caste Sabhas tried to enforce their decisions on the members of the caste. A Kayastha Vakil of Gaya who had pledged a limitation on the acceptance of wedding gifts and took rupees two thousand on the marriage of his son. The caste association exposed his deed and forced him to donate the entire sum to a fund for the education of poor Rayasthas.[3]

But such effective pressures on faltering caste breathen is not frequently recorded, and in any case it shows up limitations of caste reform as a lever for general social advancement; while instituting its own reforms, a caste became increasingly less aware of

---

1. Charles H. Heimsath, op. cit., p. 279
2. S. Natrajan, A Century of Social Reform in India, 1959, p. 136
3. Charles H. Heimsath, op. cit., p. 290

general of social problems, and the possibilities of developing corporate social consciousness among all Indians receded even further.[1]

Caste-organisations were criticised on the ground that they led to an aggravation of social distinctions, to a sense of exclusiveness and animosity and that tended to divide and disunite the Indian people at a time when united action was most needed. But as S. Sinha, while once presiding over the Kayastha Canference noted, "Societies advance, as their component parts advance. As long as Hindu society was divided into castes, whose rules of behaviour were accepted by their members, social advance had to be a function of the progress made by each caste component."[2] He further pointed out that "before there can be a true spirit of nationality in our country each component part of the people must realise that its individualisation has realised a point in self-expression when it is desirable in the interest of further advance or progress to merge itself with other groups or communities."[3]

CHAPTER IX

CONCLUSION

Interaction between education and Social Progress with reference to National Development-Bihar became the Vanguard of National Movement by 1921

Bihar had a glorious past and in the ancient period it stood on the highest pedestal of cultural and political arena. In the later medieval period Bihar receded into the background but again in the nineteenth century she played a significant role in the life

1. Ibid.
2. Charles H. Heimsath, op. cit., p. 242
3. S. Sinha, A Selection from the Speeches and Writings, p. 732

of the nation. No sooner had the British consolidated their authority over the land and a new middle class raised its head, than the rumblings of revolt heard in Chota Nagpur and Santhal Parganas. The successive risings like the Kol Insurrection, the Bhumiji Revolt and the Santhal Insurrection, although directed against the local authorities and caused by petty tyrannies, gave the British an idea of how far the people of a comparatively backward area would go.

During the Mutiny of 1857 Bihar under the leadership of Babu Kunwar Singh waged a relentless war against the Britishers. Bihar was an important centre of anti-British Wahabi movement which, though religious in character, had a social and political face also.[1] In the district of Ranchi the seeds of discontent burst forth in the Sardari Larai and the Birsa revolts. Birsa Munda, a tribal who had received some education at the hands of the Christian missionaries, organised a revolt against the British government. The establishment and possession of the Raj under Birsa was the supreme political end of this Munda revolt.[2]

The post-1859 period in Indian history was marked by the development of some new forces. The reformation movement in India during the period was producing a new awakening. This period also witnessed many new efforts in the spheres of education and with the growing acquaintance, through the medium of English education, new ideas of liberty and freedom came to Indian minds. A new India was born under the rejuvenating influence of the west.[3] Western institutions, like schools and colleges, played an important part.[4] The English education opened the gates of new thought to the mass of educated Indians.[5]

The expansion in the numbers of literate and educated graduates of secondary schools and universities led to the improvements in communication system. The number of newspapers increased

---

1. W. W. Hunter, **The Indian Musalmans**, p. 61. Also See Q. Ahmad, **Wahabi Movement.**
2. Suresh Singh, op. cit., p. 95
3. S. S. Dikshit, **Nationalism and Indian Fducation**, p. 20
4. A. N. Basu, **Education in Modern India**, p. 1
5. Lajpat Rai, **Young India**, p. 114

with a great speed. By the middle of the nineteenth century the press had taken root, and was developing rapidly.[1] The Indian intellectual life developed on modern lines. The local efforts to achieve religious, social and political reform began to combine into organized movements with adherents scattered throughout several provinces.[2] In Bihar even caste organisations organised campaigns against social evils.

The four main currents of religious reformation movement which swept over India in the nineteenth century, as mentioned earlier, while trying to reform religion and society became increasingly aware of the importance of education as a tool of reform and national regeneration. They made signal contributions to the cause of education.[3]

In the early phase of the Indian National Movement the interrelation between religion and politics manifested itself in two different directions : one in the social and religious reform movements which had a political bearing, and the other in the political movement whose leaders made appeals to the religious traditions of the people and to the social institutions connected with them. The social and religious reform movements came first and, in one sense they were a necessary prelude to the political awakening in the country.[4]

The educational policy of the British Government began with Macaulay's minute in 1835. This was perhaps the most momentous decisions in the history of British India.[5] The new educational policy soon began to bear fruit. In Bengal, Anglo-vernacular schools were established in the districts by official agency, while in other provinces, although there was a time lag, missionaries and philanthropists cooperated enthusiastically with the Government in founding new educational institutions. One of the immediate

1. Bruce T. Mcculy, **English Education and the Origins of Indian Nationalism**, p. 233
2. Charles H. Heimsath, **Indian Nationalism and Hindu Social Reform**, p. 131
3. S. S. Dikshit, **op. cit.**, p. 12
4. K. K. Karunakaran, op. cit., p. 22
5. P. Griffiths, **The British Impact on India**, p. 237

results of the considerable intellectual activity now stimulated was the foundation of discussion and debating societies in many places.[1]

A demand for the reform of the social system was created by the enlightened ideas introduced by western thought and by acquaintance with the humanitarian principles of Christianity. In some cases this was connected with religious movements which initiated a social reform movement. In north India many local associations were formed in order to create conditions favourable to reform by the education of public opinion.[2]

In these and similar bodies in other parts of the country attention was at first concentrated on religious and social reform. The new education was, however, almost entirely confined to the well-to-do and high caste sections of the urban population. It did not at that time touch the masses, and the young enthusiasts soon found that their discussions of social reform amounted to little more than beating the air. They therefore, turned to politics, where they were less likely to meet with opposition.[3]

By the middle of the nineteenth century the ground was thus prepared for the growth of various political associations which preceded the Indian National Congress. In its development Bengal led the way.[4] The spread of English education inspired the educated Indians with new hopes and aspirations. Bishan Narayan Dhar, while presiding over the Congress session in 1911 observed :

"English education and a closer contact with the West have raised our intelligence and expanded our vision; the example of English enterprise has given us new ideals of citizenship and inspired us with new conception of national duties."[5]

---

1. P. Griffiths, **The British Impact on India**, p. 254
2. L. S. S. O' Malley, ed., **Modern India and the West**, p. 855
3. P. Griffiths, op. cit., 254
4. Ibid, pp, 254-255
5. Congress Presidential Address, Calcutta, 1911

Education was reviving energies of Indians which had been dormant for so long a time; it was fostering in them a spirit of nationality, lifting them up from the mire of many social perjudices, preparing their mind for the reception of liberal ideas and for the use of political and social progress.[1]

Bihar of the nineteenth century presented a picture different from many other parts of India. There had been many occasions of serious conflict with the rulers in the nineteenth century. So the people of Bihar did not respond enthusiastically to the new education in the beginning. Nevertheless, a change was visible towards the end of the century. Gradually, people began to appreciate the advantages of new education. Soon an inter-action between education and social progress was felt in Bihar : the spread of new education brought social consciousness. The educated men began to organise local association in different towns of the province.

The percentage of literacy in Bihar was still very low, and vast mass of the population was ignorant. But the educated class acquired ascendancy in society through various means. The press and newspapers proved the most effective weapon in the hands of the educated class. The numerous newspapers and journals published both in English and vernaculars provided so many channels through which different sections of opinion found expression. At the same time they assisted powerfully in overcoming the barrier which English education had erected between the educated community and the rest of the population.[2]

The attempt to educate public opinion for social progress and national development was made easy. It moved forward horizontally from the village to the town, from the town to the city, from the city to the capital, and vice-versa, thus travelling through the different strata of native society. Such a chain of relationships played directly into the hands of the educated class whose political influence was enormously enhanced by virtue of its control over the native press which it owned, edited and mana-

1. Bruce T. Mccully, op. cit. p. 288
2. Bruce T. Mccully, op. cit., p. 236

ged. It enabled the intelligentsia to gain a psychological hold upon the masses and, in the long run, to identify its economic grievances and political aspirations of the native community at large. Thus the educated class became the voice and brain of the country.

The educated class of Bihar began to organise a native press towards the end of the nineteenth century. With the beginning of the twentieth century they had well-established organs, and were trying to mould public opinion. In fact during the first decade of this century educated Biharis had powerful organs which influenced the entire population of the province. They were educating public opinion for social consciousness and political awakening. The partition of Bengal provided an opportunity, a propeller to the Bihar leaders to organise a campaign for the separation of Bihar. The credit for the success of this campaign goes to the press of Bihar, likewise the press in Bihar successfully campaigned for educational development and social progress.

There were local associations in almost all advanced towns of Bihar. For example, the Bihar National Improvement Association of Bhagalpur was very active towards the closing years of the nineteenth century. The inauguration of the Youth Club, called the 'Boys' Association' on March 1899 in the Rajmaidan at Darbhanga under the chairmanship of Afak Khan, Bar-at-Law, marked a significant turning point in the rise of political consciousness. Another noteworthy incident at Darbhanga in those days was the establishment of the Saraswati Academy on 1 January 1901.[1]

These associations symbolised the dawn of a new political consciousness in the minds of educated Biharis. Rajendra Prasad even when he was a student in Calcutta, joined the Dawn Society, established in 1902.[2]

The association with this society stirred his thought and his imagination was caught by public and social affairs. He established a Biharee Club at Calcutta, and took an initiative in organi-

---

1. K. K. Datta, History of Freedom Movement in Bihar, Vol. I. 1857-1928
2. Rajendra Prasad, **Autobiography**, p. 42

sing the Biharee student conference, which was opened for the first time in 1906 in the hall of the Patna College under the chairmanship of famous barrister, Shurfuddin.[1] This organisation became the harbinger of social consciousness and political awakening in Bihar a direct result of interaction between educational development and social progress. Many of the leaders of Bihar received their early training in this organisation.

The Students Conference organised with the object of improving the physical, intellectual, moral and social conditions of Bihar students. In its very first conference on 16 September 1906 Sachchidanand Sinha asked the student community not to sit idle, dreaming of their past; but they should be active, and by actions should prove themselves worthy successors of their noble descent. The new spirit of awakening penetrated into the ranks of the students of Bihar who began to play an important role in the Indian battle for liberty. The students in Bihar remained confined to social problems since there was hesitation in participating in politics in the beginning. But eventually, several students in Bihar joined the National Movement with zeal and enthusiasm.

Presiding over the second session of the Biharee Students Conference on 28 and 29 September 1907, Deep Narayan Singh expressed faith in the awakening of the country. He said that a wave of self-reliance and acts of self-sacrifice was stirring in the hearts of the students of Bihar. He further observed : "the rising generation who represent the growing intellect and culture of the province are imbued with the vigour and enthusiasm of youth."[2] The youth of Bihar received the impact of the new wave and reacted to it.

In 1909, Syed Hasan Imam in his presidential address to the Annual Session of the organisation declared boldly that the moral worth of a nation alone entitled it to a political privilege. He said that social obligations preceded politics, and not politics social obligations. Much of the trouble, he thought, was due to the social

---

1. **The Beharee**, 12 October 1906
2. Ibid., 8 October 1907

conditions in Bihar.[1] Through the platform of the students' conference, the educated men of Bihar began a campaign for social progress. This conference was presided over in its annual sessions by eminent personalities like Sharfuddin, Hasan Imam, Sachchidanand Sinha, Parmeshwar Lal, Deep Narayan Singh, Braj Kishore Prasad, Mazharul Haque, Rajendra Prasad, Jadunath Sarkar from Bihar and Mahatma Gandhi, Shrimati Sarojini Naidu, C. F. Andrews, Srimati Sarala Devi and Ganesh Prasad from outside. The advent of this organisation marked the beginning of a new era in Bihar. It infused a new spirit among the Biharis.

In the beginning of the twentieth century almost all the provinces of India had their provincial conferences. Only Bihar was lagging behind. With the spread of education, however, there came a general awakening, and by 1906-07, Bihar was also awakened to look after her political and educational advancement. Bihar now began to assert her existence as a separate and distinct unit among the provinces of India. True, in Bihar there were few political associations, such as Bihar Landholders Association and Bihar Association, and these too had limited activities. The Bihar Landholders' Association's sphere of activity was restricted to the interests of landed aristocracy of the province. The Bihar Association was organised with the object of counteracting the agitation started in Bihar for the separation of Bihar from Bengal. It did not get favour with the public in Bihar, and so it remained defunct. The educated men of Bihar keenly felt the need of a political institution in its widest sense that might reach the masses in their very homely cottages. The people of Bihar need a political training, and an institution which might look after the political, economic, social and educational advancement of the people.

The leading educated men of Bihar assembled at the Bihar Landholders' Association Office on 12 March 1907 to formulate a scheme for establishing a provincial association. A provincial committee with Brahmdeo Narayan as provisional secretary was

1. The Beharee, 5 November 1909

formed. This symbolised the new awakening, and an attempt to equip herself to take proper place in the national development was initiated. Deep Narayan Singh and Sachchidanand Sinha started the formation of the district committees. S. Sinha explained in a meeting on 28 April 1907 the needs of forming a political and social organisation in Bihar.[1]

The Bihar Provincial Conference which was also organised during the period used to hold its annual session, focussing attention on social and political developments of Bihar. This Association was unique as it was organised jointly by the Hindus and Muslims in Bihar. G. K. Gokhale, who attended the fourth session at Bhagalpur, commended this conference. He said that it occupied a unique position among the political institutions of India. It was unique in the sense that it had given body and shape to the ideas of working together to Hindus and Muslims. Indeed, the Bihar Provincial Conference set an example to the rest of the country. At the time of the Morley-Minto Scheme it championed the cause of Hindu-Muslim unity.[2]

The history of modern Bihar is really interesting in as much as other parts of India were rousing themselves up and plunging into vigorous activities while Bihar was sleeping, indifferent to the modern currents. One wondered if Bihar would ever remain the 'Beotia of India.' But this lethargy could not continue as educated men became conscious of social progress.

The hearty co-operation between the Hindus and Musalmans in Bihar was a fact which had been repeatedly acknowledged by all as a unique feature of Bihar's public activities. This cosmopolitanism of Bihar was not a new thing, but was rooted in the historic traditions of the people. Sister Nivedita once wrote : "Bihar has always been, and remains today, the most cosmopolitan province of India. It has doubtless been this close contiguity of highly diversified elements, within her boundaries, that had so often made Bihar the birth place of towering political geniuses. The Great Chandra Gupta, his grandson Asoka, the

1. The Beharee, 3 May 1907
2. Ibid. 16 April 1909

whole of the Gupta dynasty, Sher Shah, and finally Guru Govind Singh, are more than a fair share of the eminent personalities of Indian history for one province to have produced. The policy of the great Akbar himself was determined by the ideas of his predecessor, Sher Shah. Each of the great Biharees has been an organiser."[1]

In the history of Indian nationalism, the foundation of Indian National Congress, in 1885 was an epoch-making event. The Congress movement was largely an out-growth of British rule and English education.[2] The beginning of modern political consciousness can be traced in Bihar from the early Congress days, but some people were also attracted by the socio-cultural movements in the first decade of the twentieth century. The motto and programme of the Servant of India Society appealed to Rajendra Prasad very much. Sri Krishan Prasad of Monghyr went to Poona to study the affairs of the Servants of Indian Society. Ramdayalu Singh of Muzaffarpur was also attracted to this Society.[3]

In the earliest days of the Congress there used to be a great deal of enthusiasm in Bihar about it, and a large number of delegates used to attend the sittings of that body. But after a few years, interest for the Congress dwindled in Bihar. After some time conscious of the changed attitude, some educated and enlightened men of Bihar made efforts for improvement in the situation. At the Sonepur fair in 1908, an important meeting was held under the presidentship of Nawab Sarfraz Husain Khan at which a Bihar Provincial Congress Committee was formed. In the next Congress session at Madras, Bihar was represented by six delegates, namely Syed Hasan Imam, President Bihar Congress Committee, Basant Chandra Sinha, a pleader of Muzaffarpur, Deep Narayan Singh of Bhagalapur, Syed Najmul Huda, Parmeshwar Lal and Sachchidanand Sinha. The Provincial Congress Committee had its headquarters at Patna and the branches in the districts.[4]

---

1. Cited by S. Sinha, **Some Eminent Behar Contemporaries**, Intr., xxxvi
2. Bruce T. Mceuly, op. cit., p. 193
3. K. K. Datta, op. cit., pp. 148-199
4. K. K. Datta, op. cit., p. 150

The lethargy, apathy and indifference of educated classes to the public interests of the early period had disappeared with the advent of agitation for the separation of Bihar from Bengal. Sachchidanand Sinha advanced a theory of 'local patriotism.' It aroused an unprecedented enthusiasm among the Biharis : public meetings began to be organised and the demand for separation gained ground. This agitation brought the question of the prevailing politics to the forefront. Thus the movement took a new shape,[1] and Bihar and Orissa were separated from Bengal. Thus Bihar obtained a distinctive individuality in 1912.

There was evidence of new life in all directions after the creation of Bihar into a separate, self-contained province. The twentyseventh session of the All India Congress in 1912 was held for the first time at Patna, the metropolis of Bihar. Bihar thus attempted to remove the stigma of inactivity. Mazharul Haque was elected chairman of the Reception Committee. The year 1912 has been memorable in the history of Bihar. In his welcome address Mazharul Haque declared that the Congress ideal was throbbing in the heart of Bihar people, and they were not behind anyone in their love for mother India.[2] In fact, new Bihar began to play an active role in the successive phase of Indian nationalism. In 1914 two eminent Biharis, Mazharul Haque and S. Sinha along with B. N. Basu, M. A. Jinnah, B. N. Sharma, N. M. Samarth and Lajpat Rai were elected to serve on a deputation sent to England by the Congress.[3]

The first World War had a tremendous impact on Indian Society and politics. National leaders like Tilak and Mrs. Annie Besant imitated the Home Rule Campaign in 1916. The influence of the Home Rule Movement was felt in different parts of India including Bihar. A Home Rule League was established at Bankipore with Mazharul Haque as president.[4] Mrs. Annie Besant

---

1. R. K. Choudhary, **History of Bihar**, p. 304
2. **Presidential Address at Congress session, Bankipore**, 1912
3. K. K. Datta, op. cit., p. 156
3. Ibid., p. 162

visited Patna, and a big procession with great pomp and show was taken out on this occasion. There were many Home Rulers in different towns of Bihar who held several meetings. Purnendu Narayan Sinha was perhaps the most devoted Home Ruler in Bihar.

The participation of the people of Bihar in the struggle for independence had been so far confined to the nobility and intelligentsia. But with the advent of Gandhiji on the national scene, Bihar's involvement became more intense, as the common mass of the people were more and more drawn into it.

The Champaran experiment marked the beginning of public life in Bihar. Till that time, it was enough to hold a session of the Provincial Conference and pass resolution to attend the annual sessions of the Congress, to donate to the Congress, to write something in the newspapers, and if once happened to be a member of the legislative council, to put some questions and deliver some speeches. Gandhiji did not do any of these things, and yet he left Bihar pulsating with new life.[1]

At the end of the war events moved fast. The British Government began a dual policy of reform and repression. The educational development of nearly two decades had brought an unprecedented social consciousness. Naturally enough, at the country's clarion call for national resistance against repressive policy of an alien Government, Bihar's soul was stirred. The agitation in Bihar against foreign rule was intensified. The educated classes of Bihar began to take interest in national development.

The Provincial Congress Committee of Bihar passed a resolution that the principle of non-cooperation was the only effective means of securing the redress of national wrongs. At the 12th session of the Bihar Provincial Conference, Rajendra Prasad while presiding put a strong plea for non-cooperation movement. There was by this time a profound awakening in Bihar, and a considerable number of delegates attended the special session of the Indian Natio-

---

1. Rajendra Prasad, At the Feet of Mahatma Gandhi, 1967, 70

nal Congress held in Calcutta from 4 to 9 September 1920 under the presidentship of Lala Lajpat Rai.[1]

Indeed, Bihar set herself promptly to act according to this resolution. There was consequently brisk activity in different directions at various places in the province. Many leaders including Rajendra Prasad and Mazharul Haque declared their withdrawal from the forthcoming election. Haque declared that it was impossible to work with a Government whose hands were stained with the blood of Indians.[2]

The non-cooperation movement soon spread throughout Bihar. By the beginning of 1921 Non-cooperation for the country's independence and regeneration had become a popular faith among most of the Biharis.[3] In fact, the Non-cooperation movement in Bihar was more widespread than in Bengal.[4] The impact of the movement was felt most deeply in Tirhut Division. The Chota Nagpur division also did not lag behind. There was also a reform movement known as Tana Bhagat Movement.

The mainspring of this new movement originated with a desire to raise the social position of Mundas, Oraons and other tribesmen to the higher level occupied by the Hindu and Christian converts among their tribe-fellows.[5] The underlying tendency of the Tana Bhagat Movement in its more attractive aspect as reform movement was towards an increased simplicity and purity of life. It is interesting to note that one or two of the main conditions which determined the growth of this movement grew due to dissatisfaction with their economic condition. The Oraons who had become Hindus or Christians were better educated. They had thus a better awareness of the socio-economic maladies, and a greater determination to stand against landlords and money lenders.[6]

---

1. K. K. Datta, **op. cit.**, pp. 302-303
2. **The Searchlight**, 19 September 1920
3. Dr. K. K. Datta, op. cit., p. 329
4. L. S. S. O' Malley, **History of Bengal**, p. 190
5. Sarat Chandra Roy, **"A New Religious Movement Among the Oraon Man in India"**, Vol. 1, 1920, p. 268
6. **Census Report of India**, 1921, Vol. VII, part I, pp. 128-129

Mahatma Gandhi's tour of Bihar in 1920 and 1921 gave a new impetus to the rise of nationalism in Bihar. Liberal nationalism had appeared in India as a reasonably legitimate off-spring of a half-century of English education. By and large the individuals who espoused it belonged to the educated class.[1] Surendra Nath Banerjee had narrated the impact of Mazzini, the greatest champion of Liberal Nationalism in the nineteenth century.[2] But with the advent of Mahatma Gandhi the currents of nationalism were broadened. He converted the national movement into a mass-movement. His impact on Bihar was widely felt by 1921.

Mahatma Gandhi wrote in *Young India* on 2 March 1921: "Bihar is adrovince in which the most solid work is being done in connection with non-cooperation......There were signs on every side of a national awakening in Bihar.[3]" Under Mahatma Gandhi's influence, in the beginning of 1921, national schools were started in Bihar. Besides them, a national college named Bihar Vidyapith was formally opened on 5th January 1921 by Mahatma Gandhi. Mazharul Haque and Brajkishore Prasad were appointed chancellor and vice-chancellor of the Vidyapith respectively. Many patriotic students joined the Bihar Vidyapith.

By 1921 Bihar became the vanguard of national movement. Education came to be closely identified with the struggle for independence. Large number of students left schools and colleges managed or aided by the government. The national schools and colleges provided instructions to students who boycotted the government institutions. This new kind of education prepared them for the service to the country. It threw up many leaders who dedicated themselves to the cause of national liberation. Indeed, it marked a turning point in the history of national movement which assumed a new dimension in Bihar.

---

1. Bruce T, Mc Cully, op; cit., 261
2. Surendra Nath Banerjee, op, cit., p. 43
3. K. K. Datta, **The Writings and Speeches of Mahatma Gandhi in Bihar**, p. 156.

APPENDIX A

BIOGRAPHICAL NOTES

Syed Sharfuddin :

Born on 10 September 1856 at Neora in the Patna District: educated in Patna Collegiate School; joined Middle Temple; was called to the Bar in 1880; began practice in Calcutta Higb Court, came to Patna and finally set up his practice at Bankipore; established a name for himself in Bihar; espoused the Congress cause; a man of many sided activities; took interest in the education of his community; Patna Islamic School was established through his money and energy; held office of vice-chairman of the Patna District Board for three successive terms; was nominated a Fellow of the Senate of the Calcutta University, was the Honorary Secretary of the Bihar Landholders' Association—elected in 1905 to represent that body on the Bengal Legislative Council; was appointed to serve as a Judge to the Calcutta High Court bench, took active part in the public life of the province.

Khuda Bakhsh (1842-1908) :

Born at Chapra in 1842; was educated in Calcutta, struggled to become a lawyer; started practice at Patna in 1868; appointed Government Pleader and went to Hyderabad in 1894 as the Chief Justice of the Nizam's High Court; returned to Patna in 1898 and lived there till his death in 1908, elected the first Vice-Chairman of the Patna Municipality, and of the Patna District Board; founded the Oriental Library at Patna, a great institution containing magnificent collection of manuscripts; spent all his earning on the library which he founded : the Oriental Public Library was opened to the public in 1891 by Charles Elliot, the then Lieutenant-Governor of Bengal, Bihar and Orissa. Curzon took a keen interest in its improvement and visited it in 1903.

Rameshwar Singh (1860-1929)

Born in 1860; educated at home, and at Queen's College, Banaras; was proficient in English, Sankrit and several other Indian languages, was nominated to the newly constituted statutory Civil Service, resigned after serving for some years as a Magistrate, succeeded his brother as the Maharaja of Darbhanga in 1898; appointed a member of the Police Reform Commission in 1905; was intimately connected with various activities and institutions in the country; was President of the British Indian Association, Landholders' Association, Calcutta and Bihar Landholders' Association, Patna, presided over the Lahore session of the Industrial Conference in 1909, was the first non-official Indian to be appointed as Executive Councillor of the new province; elected to the Imperial Legislative Council also returned to the Council of State on the inauguration of Montagu-Chelmsford Scheme in 1920 ; tried to organise Hindu Sabha in Bihar, was generous in donations for religious and educational purposes ; died in 1929 at the age of 70 years.

Lakshmeshwar Singh (1858-1898)

Born in 1858; received liberal education in English, Sanskrit and the north Indian languages at the Queen's College, Banaras, brought up by private tutors, who were eminent British educationists was a man not only of liberal and progressive views in the political spheres, but was also admired for possessing independence and strength of character; was a staunch supporter of Zamindary rights and privilege but was a sympathiser of educated Middle classes; contributed regularly a handsome sum to the Indian National Congress; from 1886 to 1898 presented a sum of Rs. 10,000 to the Congress every year; used to take an active part in the Imperial Legislative Council.

Mahesh Narayan (1859-1907)

Born in 1859; was the father of journalism in Bihar; worked strenuously for the creation of Bihar; was father of Public opinion in Bihar; died suddenly in 1907 at the early age of fortyeight; was secretary of the Bihar Landholders' Association; used his pen successfully to propagate his views; was a successful editor; used to write in *Bihar Bandhu* and *Bihar Herald;* joined the Indian Chronicle; started a paper *Kayastha Gazette* in 1891; felt the need of a suitable organ in Bihar to arouse political consciousness; started in collaboration of Sachchidanand Sinha and Hasan Imam *Bihar Times*; became its first editor and continued as such for the years; was instrumental in advancing social and political movements in Bihar; was a great force in arousing political consciousness in Bihar; edited *the Beharee.*

Srikrishna Sahaya (1866-1921)

Born in village Shorampur in the distrtct of Patna in 1866; educated in Patna Collegiate School and Patna College, graduated in Law 1890; started legal practice in the Patna District Court; served also as a part-time lecturer in law in the Patna Law College, of which he was a co-founder along with Archdale Earle, Commissioner of Patna in 1909; elected member of the Imperial Legislative Council, 1913-16; appointed a member of the Executive Council, 1913-16; appointed a member of the Executive Council of the Lieutenant Governor, and afterwards Governor of Bihar and Orissa, 1910-12; died 1921; was the most prominent Liberal Congressman of Bihar during the pre-non-cooperation period; also interested in social reform.

Siva Sankar Sahaya (1863-1914)

Born at Bhagalpur in February 1863; educated at Bhagalpur Zila School; matriculated in 1881, managed to get a scholarship; passed the pleadership examination; joined the Bhagalpur Bar in July 1886; was connected with the Banaili Raj from 1887; represented the Banaili Raj during the Survey and Settlement Operation in 1898, was elected uncontested to represent District Board of the Bhagalpur division in the Bengal Legislative Council; turned the weekly Biharee into a daily from 13 April 1912; died in 1914 prematurely at the age of fifty-two.

Purnendu Narayan Sinha :

A leading member of the domiciled Bengali Community of Patna; prominent lawyer ; took active interest in social and educational works of the province, established P.N. Anglo-Sanskrit School at Patna, was a leading member of Pre-Montague-Chelmsford Legislative Council of Bihar and Orissa; presided over a special session of the Bihar Provincial Conference 1917; was an enthusiastic theosophist and a foremost Home Ruler in Bihar.

Ganesh Dutta Singh (1868-1943)

Born in February 1868 in the Patna District; matriculated in the first division in 1891; graduated in law in 1897, practised in the district court for seven years; was enrolled as a Vakil in the Calcutta High Court in 1904; became a Vakil of Patna High Court in 1916; was elected a member of the Bihar and Orissa Legislative Councils 1921; was selected as a Minister in March 1923 and served in that capacity till 1937; was one of the greatest philanthropists of his time and did much to further the cause of education through donations etc.; was one of the builders of Modern Bihar; established several hospitals and institutions, both technical and non-technical; Lunatic Asylum and Darbhanga Medical School were established in 1925 during his ministership; created a record in munificence by giving greater part of his income to the cause of education; lived an austre and saintly life; conferred *honoris causa* Doctorate by the Patna University in 1933; died 1943.

Parmeshwar Lal (1874-1919)

Born in 1874; after taking his M. A. degree went to England; devoted much of his time to Indian Public life; was elected vice-President of the London Indian Society; returned to India in 1906; soon presided over a session of the Biharee Students Conference; died prematurely in 1919.

Nand Kishore Lal (1866-1918)

Born in 1866; belonged to the earlier batch of English educated Biharis; passed M. A. and graduated in Law; worked for the separation of Bihar; presided over the Bihar Brovincial Conference in 1915; did an immense amount of highly useful public work in rousing the political consciousness of the Piharees.

Deep Narayan Singh (1875-1930)

Born in 1875 at Bhagalpur; educated in Calcutta; left for England in 1891; was called to Bar in 1891; returned to India in 1897; engaged himself in public activities from the very beginning; was elected Chairman of the Reception Committee of the session of the Bengal Provincial Conference in 1901, in 1907 became its President in 1916 he organised a fight to the Patna University amounting to Rs. four lakhs; donated all his life's savings for the good of the future generations of Bihar; was elected a member of the Bengal Legislative Council; met Mahatma Gandhi in 1920, and formally joined the non-co-operation movement; took active part in the Civil Disobedience Movement of 1930; was arrested and imprisoned for three months; was elected a member of the Indian Legislative Assembly, was ever ready to extend a helping hand to the students; was specially interested in the education of girls; gave large sums to educational institutions including the College at Bhagalpur, founded by his father.

Sachchidanand Sinha (1871-1950)

Born on 10 November 1871; the first Bihari Hindu to go to England for study in 1890; refused to perform *prayaschitta;* opened the door for sea-voyage; was pioneer of Social Reform in the Kayastha Society; called to Bar in 1893; married a lady of a distinguished family of Lahore in 1894; started in the same year at Patna, the seat of his activities, a weekly English newspaper called the *Bihar Times* with Mahesh Narayan as its editor; started a movement for the separation of Bihar from Bengal; took an active part in the Indian National Congress and attended its annual meetings; was associated with All India Kayastha Sabha and edited its journal the *Kayastha Samachar*, which he later renamed as the *Hindustan Review;* was returned to the Central Legislative Council on the inauguration of the Morley-Minto Reform, 1910; had an effective hand in the creation of the Separate Provincial Government of Bihar and Orissa and the annulment of the partition of Bengal in 1912; and was later the President of the Bihar Provincial Congress Committee; was a member of the Executive Council of the Government of Bihar and Orissa; 1921; presided over the All-India Kayastha Conference at Delhi, 1929; Vice-Chancellor of Patna University, 1936-45; presided over the first meeting of the Constituent Assembly of India, 1846; died in 1950; was man of aristocratic tastes, elegant literary style, immense social respectability and undoubted political influence; a great lover of books and founded out of his personal collections, beautiful library and reading room at Patna, called the Sinha Library and Radhika Sinha Institute; published works: *Some Eminent Bihar Contemporaries* (1944), *A Selection from the Speeches and Writing of Sachchidanand Sinha* (1942).

Kulwant Sahay (1873-1940)

Born in 1873 in the Gaya district, took B. L. degree; was enrolled as a Vakil in the Calcutta High Court in 1898; transferred his practice to Patna in 1916; appointed Judge of the Patna High Court in 1922; and died in 1940.

APPENDIX-B

TABLE OF NUMBER OF PRIMARY SCHOOLS AND BOYS ATTENDING THEM : 1916-17 to 1921-22

Name of Districts	Population.	Number of PRIMARY Schools for Indian boys.		Number of Pupils in Primary Schools for Indian Boys		Percentage of children of school to those of School going		No. of literates as shown in the Census	Percentage of literates to population.
		1916-17	1921-22	1916-17	1021-22	1916-17	1921-22		
1. PATNA	1,574,287	1 284	1,279	35,267	35,740	23.1	21.2	137,038	8.70
2. GAYA	2,152,930	1'537	1,634	45,560	47,780	17.8	18.2	112,528	5.23
3. SHAHABAD	1,816,821	'959	1,002	29,186	30,400	15.2	15.4	89,551	4.92
4. SARAN	2,339,953	1,088	783	31,880	22,169	12.0	9.1	101,237	4.32
5. CHAMPARAN	1,940,841	810	619	20,444	16,180	9.6	8.9	59,013	3.04
6. MUZAFFARPUR	2,754,945	1,239	1,229	35,139	35,845	11.3	10.9	110,612	4.01
7. DARBHANGA	2,913,529	1,438	1,396	50,564	40,339	15.8	12.4	122,742	4.21
8. MONGHYR	2,029,965	1,345	1,339	34,495	38,200	14.8	16.9	100,668	4.95
9. BHAGALPUR	2,033,770	1,096	1,096	31,550	32,561	13.5	15.0	100,493	4.92
10. PURNEA	2,024,608	990	1,202	25,806	31,696	11.2	13.2	63,527	3.12
11. SANTHAL PARAGANAS	1,798,639	992	1,088	30,042	35,047	14.04	16.4	52,099	2.89
12. HAZARIBAGH	1,276,946	663	644	17,230	16,602	11.3	10.6	38,804	3.03
13. RANCHI	1,344,473	1,142	1,100	28,238	29,158	17.8	19.2	46,445	3.48
14. PALAMAU	733,394	380	283	9,049	6,918	11.3	8.1	20,302	2.76
15. MANBHUM	1,548,777	1,036	1,033	39,013	31,175	15.4	16.0	81,327	5.89
16. SINGHBHUM	759,438	382	347	11,135	11,004	14.0	13.2	30,067	3.90
Total including District of Orissa,	34,002,189	23,274	22,443	646,345	629,59	16.3	15,7	1,586,257	4.66

APPENDIX C

Table showing the number of students in Each High English School in Bihar in 1915

Serial Number	Name of Schools	Number of Students
1.	Patna Collegiate School	323
2.	Bihar National Collegiate School	459
3.	Bankipore Female High English School	82
4.	Ram Mohan Roy Seminary	318
5.	T. K. Ghosh's Academy	486
6.	Anglo-Sanskrit Academy	452
7.	Patna City School	184
8.	Mohammedan Anglo-Arabic H. E. School	311
9.	Dinapur High English School	199
10.	Khagole E. I. Railway H. E. School	222
11.	Barh Bayley H. E. School	157
12.	Bihar H. E. School	353
13.	Arrah Zila School	308
14.	Arrah Town H. E. School	512
15.	K. J. Academy	447
16.	Dumraon Raj H. E. School	368
17.	Buxar H. E. School	321
18.	Sassaram H. E. School	261
19.	Gaya Zila School	282
20.	Gaya Town School	565
21.	Gaya Sahebganj H. E. School	221
22.	Tikari Raj H. E. School	256
23.	Chapra Zila School	432
24.	Chapra Collegiate School	632
25.	Saran Academy	701
26.	Foley Rajput H. E. School	130
27.	Swan H. E. School	262

Serial Number	Name of Schools	Number of Students
28.	Hathwan Eden H. E. School	153
29.	Gopalganj V. M. H. E. School	215
30.	Motihari Zila School	258
31.	Bettiah Raj School	319
32.	Muzaffarpur Zila School	400
33.	Mukherjee's Seminary	583
34.	B. B. Collegiate School	712
35.	Sitamarhi H. E. School	327
36.	Hajipur V. M. H. E. School	219
37.	Northbrook H. E. School	379
38.	Darbhanga Raj H. E. School	331
39.	Saraswati Academy	261
40.	Madhubani Watson H. E. School	373
41.	Samastipur H. E. School	264
42.	Monghyr Zila School	323
43.	Monghyr Training Academy	523
44.	Begusarai H. E. School	263
45.	Jumui H. E. School	156
46.	Bhagalpur Zila School	268
47.	T. N. Jubilee Collegiate School	509
48.	Adampur C. M. S. H. E. School	301
49.	Barari H. E. School	143
50.	Supaul H. E. School	128
51.	Shirres Institute	205
52.	Banka M. K. H. E. School	237
53.	Purnea Zila School	294
54.	Araria H. E. School	191
55.	Kiseanganj H. E. School	305
56.	Dumka Zila School	203
57.	Sahebganj H. E. School	192
58.	Pakur H. E. School	180
59.	Godda Cornoration H. E. School	154
60.	Deoghar H. E. School	251

Serial Number	Name of Schools	Number of Students
61.	Madhupur H. E. School	157
62.	Jung Bahadur H. E. School	233
63.	Hazaribagh Zila School	227
64.	St. Columba's Collegiate School	260
65.	Giridih H. E. School	257
66.	Giridih High School for Girls	68
67.	Ranchi Zila School	444
68.	St. Pauls' H. E. School	361
69.	St. John's High School	420
70.	G. E. L. Mission	289
71.	Palamu Zila School	261
72.	Purulia Zila School	238
73.	Manbhum Victoria School	589
74.	Raghunathpur H. E. School	167
75.	Pandra H. E. School	129
76.	Chirkunda H. E. School	167
77.	Jharia H. E. School	167
78.	Chaibassa Zila School	345

APPENDIX D

Table 1

EDUCATION BY CASTE[1]

Castes	No. Per 1,000 Literate Persons	Male	Female	Number per 10,000 Literate in English Persons	Male	Female
Kayastha	332	603	56	551	1072	19
Brahman	168	317	18	81	156	6
Babhan	102	187	14	16	31	—
Kalwar	100	201	3	20	40	1
Rajput	91	176	6	23	44	—
Kurmi	30	60	1	4	8	—
Teli	39	77	2	4	7	—
Koiri	22	43	1	3	5	—
Jolaha	20	41	2	7	14	2
Kahar	17	34	2	7	15	—
Tanti	16	32	1	3	6	—
Hajam	14	27	1	7	9	5
Lohar	14	27	1	3	5	—
Goura	14	27	1	1	3	—
Kumhar	13	26	1	3	6	—
Dhanuk	13	27	1	1	2	—
Goala (Ahir)	12	24	1	2	4	—
Dhobi	8	17	1	1	2	—
Munda (animist)	5	10	1	2	3	—
Santhal (animist)	5	8	1	1	1	—
Santhal (Hindu)	4	7	—	—	1	—
Dusadh	4	7	—	—	1	—
Mushahar	1	2	—	—	1	—

1. Census of India, 1911, Vol. 1, p. 314.

Table 2

Number of Literate per mile

	1911 M.	1911 F.	1901 M.	1901 F.	All ages progress of Education since 1901-1911
Bihar & Orissa	76	4	63	4	
India	106	10	98	7	
Bengal	140	1	127	8	

Table-3

EDUCATION BY CASTE[1]

Castes	Number Per 1,000 Aged 5 and over who were literate					
	1921			1911		
	Persons	Males	Females	Persons	Males	Females
1	2	3	4	5	6	7
Babhan	139	249	23	114	210	16
Brahman	180	339	21	190	358	20
Kayastha	385	657	95	375	680	63
Rajput	124	231	10	103	197	6
Kurmi	44	85	3	35	68	1
Koiri	29	57	2	25	49	1
Chamar	5	10	1	4	8	3
Teli	54	106	3	45	89	2
Goala	15	29	7	23	49	3

1. Census of India, 1921, vol. VII, (Bihar and Orissa), Part-I Report Subsidiary Table VI, p. 204.

BIBLIOGRAPHY

1. Unpublished Sources :

(i) Curzon Papers : Microfilm reels of the correspondence of Curzon ; vol. 1-14
- (a) Curzon to Secretary to State for India.
- (b) Secretary of State for India to Curzon.
- (c) Private letters of Curzon.

— Preserved in the National Archives, New Delhi.

(ii) Bundles of Files : Files of the Government of Bengal, General Department (Education) nos. 12, 13, 14 (1901)

— Preserved in the Bihar State Central Record Office, Patna.

(iii) Manuscript of the 'History of Bihar Arya Pratinidhi Sabha' —prepared by Patna Arya Samaj.

2. Unpublished Theses :

(i) J. S. Jha, Education in Bihar, 1813-1854 (1961-P.U.)

(ii) S. R. Singh, Nationalism and Social Reform in India, 1885-1920 (1963-P.U.)

(iii) R. R. Singh, The Growth and Evaluation of Education Administration in Bihar (1964-P.U.)

(iv) M. Razi Ahmad, Indigo Unrest in Champaran and Mahatma Gandhi 1867-1918 (1966-P.U.).

3, Proceedings, Addresses, Resolutions & Memorials :

1. Proceedings of Imperial Legislative Council 1911 and 1916.
2. Proceedings of the Government of Bengal, General Department (Education), 1899, 1900, 1901, 1902, 1903, 1904, 1905, 1906, 1907, 1908, 1909, 1910.

3. Proceedings of the Government of Bihar and Orissa, Education Department, 1911, 1912, 1913, 1914, 1915, 1916, 1917, 1918, 1919, 1920 and 1921.

4. Proceedings of Bihar and Orissa Legislative Council, 1913, 1914, 1915, 1916, 1917, 1918, 1919, 1920 and 1921.

5. Presidential Address of Indian National Congress, 1904, 1911, 1912, 1916.

6. Presidential Address of All India Muslim League, Amritsar, 1908.

7. Presidential Address of the Bihar Students Conference 1906 and onwards.

8. Presidential Addresses of the Bihar Provincial Conference 1908 onwards.

9. Resolutions by the Government of India, Home Department, nos. 199-221, dated the 11 March 1904.

10. Proceedings of Simla Conference, 1901.

11. Memorial of the inhabitants of Saran to the Secretary of State for India, 10th July 1870.

4. Published Reports, Records and Gazetteers :

1. W. Adam, Report on Vernacular Education in Bengal and Bihar, submitted to the Government in 1835 and 1838, edited by Rev. J. Long (1868).

2. Francis Buchanan : (i) Account of the District of Purnea.
   (ii) Account of the District of Patna and Gaya.
   (iii) Account of the District of Shahabad
   (iv) Account of the District of Bhagalpur. (Published by Bihar Research Society, Patna).

3. H. Sharp, Selections from Educational Records.

4. W. W. Hunter, Statistical Account of Bengal, London, 1875.

5. Charles Wood Despatch, 1854.

6. The Report of the Indian Education Commission, 1882.

7. Report of the Indian Universities Commission, 1902.

8. University Act of 1904.

9. Education in India (Quinquennial Reviews)

10. Report on Public Instruction in Bengal, (1899-1900, 1900-1901, 1901-1902, 1902-1903, 1903-1904, 1904-1905, 1905-1906, 1906-1907, 1907-1908, 8908-1909, 1909-1910).

11. Moral Material Progress Report (Annual).

12. Report on the Administration of Bihar and Orissa, 1911, 1912, 1913, 1914, 1915, 1916, 1917, 1918, 1919 1920 and 1921.

13. Report on the Progress of Education in Bihar and Orissa, 1912, 1913, 1914, 1915, 1916, 1917, 1918, 1919, 1920 and 1921

14. The First Quinquennial Review on the Progress of Education in Bihar and Orissa (1912-1917).

15. The Second Quinquennial Review on the Progress of Education in Bihar and Orissa (1917-1921).

16. Report of the Patna University Committee.

17. The Patna University Bill.

18. Reports on the Calcutta University Commission, 5 Vols.

19. Selected Chapters on the Reports of the Calcutta University Commission.

20. Report on Indian Constitutional Reforms, 1918.

21. Indian Statutory Commission, 1919 (Interim Report).

22. Report on Technical and Industrial Education in Bengal (1888-1908)

23. Report of the Rowlett (sedition) Committee 1918.

24. Report of Royal Commission on the Public Service, 1917.

25. Report on the Vernacular Newspapers of Bihar and Orissa, no. 26, 1916.

26. Report on the Census of India, 1901.

27. Report on the Census of India, 1911, vol V. Part-I (Bengal, Bihar and Orissa).

28. Report on the Census of India, 1921, vol VII Part I (Bihar and Orissa).

29. O' Malley, (ed.) Bengal District Gazetteers.

30. Imperial Gazetteers of India, Bengal, vol. II.

31. O' Malley, Hallet and Tallents (ed.), Bihar and Orissa District Gazetteers.

32. P. C. Roychoudhary, (ed) Bihar District Gazetteers.

33. Calendars of the Patna University (1918 to 1921).

34. Patna University Minutes of the Senates, Syndicates and Faculties (1918 to 1922).

35. Patna University Silver Jubilee Souvenir Volume, 1944.

36. Bihar and Orissa Primary Education Act 1919.

37. Bihar and Orissa Police Abstract of Intelligence, Vol. VIII, 1919.

38. Bihar Provincial Association Tracts, nos. 1 & 2.

39. The General Report of Ram Krishna Math and Mission, 1926.

40. Report of the Ramkrishna Mission Ashrama, Patna (1966-1967).

41. First Decinnial Review (1912-1922) of the Administration and Development of the Province : Bihar and Orissa.

42. P. C. Roychoudhary, (ed.), Gaya Old Records.

43. Bihar and Orissa, Gazette, 1919.

44. The Report of the University Education Commission (December 1948-August 1949).

45. Statistical Abstract of British India (annual).

4. Published Books :

1. Ahmad, M. M. Zuhuruddin — *Present Day Problems of Indian Education* (With special reference to Muslim Education), Bombay, 1935

2. Ahmad, Q — *Wahabi Movement*, Calcutta, 1967

3. Andrew, C. F. — *The Renaissance of India*, London, 1912

4. Aurobindo — *A System of National Education*, Calcutta, 1924

5. Aziz, K. K. — *The Making of Pakistan*, London, 1957

6. Agrawala, R. C. — *Constitutional History of India*, Delhi, 1964

7. Banerjee, Surendra Nath — *A National in Making*, London, 1925

8. Baman, Behram, B. K. — *Educational Controversies in India*, Bombay, 1943

9. Basu, B. D, — *Education in India Under the Rule of E. I. C.*, Calcutta

10. Basu, A. N. (ed.) — *Adams Reports on Education* (1835-1838) Calcutta, 1941

11. Besant, Annie — *Essentials of an Indian Education*, Madras, 1912

12. Bewan, Edwyn — *Indian Nationalism*, London, 1913

13. Blunt — *Caste System of Northern India*, — 1931

14. Chatterjee, Ramanand — *Ram Mohan Roy and Modern India*, Calcutta, 1918

15. Chintamani, C. Y. — *Indian Social Reform*, Madras, 1901

— *Indian Politics Since Mutiny* London, 1940

16. Choudhary, V. C. P. — *The Creation of Modern Bihar*, Patna, 1954

17. Choudhary, R. K. — *History of Bihar*, Patna, 1958

18. Coupland, R. — *The Indian Problem*, (1833-1935)

19. Curzon, Marquess of Kedleston. — *Leaves from a Biceroy's Note Book*, London, 1926

20. Datta, K. K. 1— *Renaissance, Nationalism and Social Changes in Modern India* (1965)

2— *The Writings and Speeches of Mahatma Gandhi in Bihar* (1917-1947)

3— *Dawn of Renascent India*, Nagpur, 1950

4— *Biography of Kunwar Singh and Amar Singh*, Patna, 1951

5— *History of Freedom Movement of Bihar* (1858-1928), Vol-I

6— *A Survey of Recent Studies on Modern Indian History*, 1963

7— *Introduction to Bihar*, 1946

21. Datta, N. K. — *Origin and Growth of Caste in India* London, 1931

22. Das, M. N. — *India, under Morley and Minto*, London 19ɔ4

23. *Dayanand Commemoration Volume*, Ajmer (1933)

24. Dayal, Har — *Our Educational Problems*, Madras, 1922

P25. Desai, A. R. — *Social Background of Indian Nationalism*, 1959

26. Diwakar, R. B. (Ed.) — *Bihar Through the Ages*, Patna, 1958

27. Dikshit, S. S. — *Nationalism and Indian Education*, Delhi, 1966

28. Dodwell, H. H. (ed.) — *The Cambridge History*, vol. vi. 1958-1932.

29. Durrani, F. K. Khan — *Education in India*, Graphic Presentation) New Delhi, 1951

30. Farquhar, J. N. — *Modern Religious Movements in India*, New York, 1915

31. Fraser, Lovat — *India Under Curzon and After*, London, 1911

32. Fazlur, Rahman — *Future of Education In India* (A Symposium), New Delhi, 1954

33. Gokhale B. G. — *The Making of the Indian Nation*, 1960

34. Gokhale, G. N. — *Practical Education*, Madras

35. Ghurye, G. S. — *Caste and Class in India*, Bombay (1952)

36. Griffiths, P. *The British Impact on India*, London, 1952

37. Gopal, S, — *Viceroyalty of Lord Ripon*, London, 1953

38. Hartog, P. — *Some Aspects of Indian Education Past and Present*, London, 1929

39. Heimsath, Charles, H. — *Indian Nationalism and Hindu Social Reform*, New York, 1964

40. Hennesy, Jossleyan, — *Indian Democracy and Education* Bombay, 1965

41. Hunter, W. D. — *The Indian Musalmans*, London, 1871

42. Hutton, J. H. — *Caste in India*, London, 1951

43. James, H. R. — *Education and Problems of Statesmanship in India*, London, 1911

44. Jha, J. C. — *The Kol Insurrection of Chota Nagpur*, 1964

45. Jha, J. C. — *The Bhumij Revolt*, New Delhi, 1967

46. Karim, Abdul — *Muhammedan Education in Bengal*

47, Kabir, Humayun — *Education in New India*

48. Karunakaran — *Religion and Political Awakening in India*, 1965

49. Kedleston, Marquess Curzon — *Leaves From A Viceroy's Note Book*, London, 1926

50. Ketkar, S. V. — *History of Caste in India*, New York, 1909

51. Kellock, James — *Mahadeva Govind Ranade*, 1926

52. Khan, Syed Sirdar 1 — *Lord Curzon's Administrations of India*, Bombay, 1905

2— *Life of Lord Morley*, London, 1923

53. Kulyar, S. P. — *Swami Dayanand Sarswati*, Patna, 1938

54. Lovett, Sir Verney — *A History of the Indian Nationalist Movement*, London, 1929

55. Lord Meston — *Nationhood for India*, London, 1931

56. Macdonald, J. Ramasway — *The Awakening of India*, London, 1910

57. Machicol, Nicol — *The Making of Modern India*, London, 1924

58, Mackenzie, Dewitt — *The Awakening of India*, London, 1917

59. Mccully, Bruce T. — *English Education & Origins of Indian Nationalism*, New York, 1940

60. Mahmood, Syed — *A History of English Education in India*, Aligarh, 1895

61. Mary, Countess of Minto — *India Minto and Morley*, 1905-1910, London, 1934

62. Majumdar, B. B. — *Militant Nationalism in India*, (1897-1917).

63. Majumdar, R. C. (Ed.) — *The History and Culture of The Indian People*, Vol. X, Part-II

64. Majumdar, B. B. and Majumdar, B. P. — *Congress and Congress Men in the Pre-Gandhian Era*, (1885-1917), 1907

65. Mayhew, Arthur — *The Education of India*, London

66. Meston, W — *The Indian Educational Policy: Its Principles and Problems*, Madras, 1936

67. Misra, B. B. 1— *The Indian Middle Classes*, Oxford, London, 1962

2— *Selected Document on Mahatma Movement in Champaran*, Patna, 1903

68. Misra, J — *Jewels of Bihar*

69. Mookerjee, R. K. — *Ancient Indian Education*, London, 1947

70. Monk, F. F. — *Educational Policy in India*, Bombay, 1934

71. Mukherjee, S. N. — *History of Education in India*, Baroda, 1957

72. Narayan, Mahesh, and Sinha, S. — *The Partition of Bengal or the Separation of Bihar*, Patna, 1906

73. Natrajan, S. — *A Century of Social Reform in India*, 1959

74. Nurullah, S. and Naik J. P. — *History of Education in India during the British period*, 1943

75. Nehru, J. L. — *Discovery of India*, Calcutta, 1946

76. Oak, V. V. *England & Educational Policy in India*, Madras, 1925

77. O' Donnel, C. J. — *The Failure of Lord Curzon.*

78. O' Malley, L. S. S. 1— *Bengal, Bihar and Orissa and Sikkim*, Cambridge, 1917

2— *History of Bengal, Bihar and Orissa*, Calcutta, 1925

3— *India's Social Heritage*, Oxford, 1934

4— *Modern India and the West*, London, 1941

79. Owen, G. E. — *Bihar and Orissa*, 1921

80. Panikkar, K. M. — *Essays on Educational Reconstruction in India*, Madras, 1920

81. Pal, B. C. — *The Spirit of Indian Nationalism*, London, 1910

82. Pavitranand, Swami — *A Short Life of Swami Vivekanand*

83. Philips, C. H. (ed.) — *Politics and Society in India*, London, 1963

84. Prasad, Rajendra 1— *Autobiography* (in Hindi and English)
2— *Satyagrah in Champaran*
3— *Mahatma Gandhi and Bihar* 1949

85. Rai, Lajpat. 1— *The Arya Samaj*, London, 1915
2— *Young India*, New York, 1916
3— *National Education in India*, London, 1920

86. Releigh — *Lord Curzon in India.*

87. *Ram Mohan Centenary Commemoration Volume.*

88. Risley, H — *The People of India*, London, 1915

89. Ronaldshay — *The Life of Lord Curzon*, 2 Vols 1928

90. Roychoudhary, P. C. 1— *Inside Bihar*
2— Sarkar Saran.

91. Sahaya, B. — *History of Education in Bihar under British Rule*, Bhagalpur, 1928

92. Sarker, J. N. and Jha J. C. — *History of Patna College* (1863-1963) Patna, 1963

93. Sarda, Har Bilas — *Life of Dayanand Saraswati*, Ajmer 1946

94. Sastri, Sivanath 1— *The Mission of the Brahmo Samaj*, Calcutta, 1910
2— *History of Brahmo Samaj*, 2 Vols. Calcutta, 1912

95. Sen, A. N. — *Educational Reorganisation in India*, Calcutta, 1944

96. Smith, William Roy — *Nationalism and Reform in India*, London, 1938

97. Siqueira. J. N. — *The Education of India* (History and Problem) Mysore, 1939

98. Sinha, Sachchidanand 1— *Some Eminent Contemporaries*, Patna, 1944

2— *A Selection From Speeches and Writings.*

99. *Sachchidanand Sinha Commemoration Volume*

100. Singh, Suresh — *Dust Storm and Hanging Mist*, Calcutta, 1966

101. Singh, G. N. — *Land Mark in Indian Constitutional and National Development*, Vol. I, 1952

102. Singh, V. R. (ed.) — *Economic History of India*, (1857-1956), 1965

103. Singh, Baljit and Singh, V. B. — *Social and Economic Change*, 1967

104. Singh, R. P. — *Bihar Ka Nav Ratna* (Hindi), Patna, 1947

105. *Srikrishna Abhinandan Granth (Hindi)*

106. *Sri Ramlochan Sharan Ki Swarna Jayanti* (Hindi)

107. Srinivds, M. N. — *Social Changes in Modern India*, 1967

108. Tendulakar, D. G. 1– *Gandhi in Champaran*, Calcutta, 1957

2— *Mahatma, Life of Mohan Das Karm Chand Gandhi, Vol. I*, (1869-1920), Bombay, 1951

109. *The Collected Works of Mahatma Gandhi*, Vol. XII

110. Trevelyan, C. E. — *On the Education of the Indian People*, 1830

111. Tinker, Huge — 1— *Local Self Government in India, Pakistan and Burma.*
2— *India and Pakistan.*

112. Uma Shankar — *Bihar Ke Nirmata* (Hindi), Dumka, 1963

113. Vakil, K. S. — *Education in India*, Lucknow, 1948

114. Varm, Kamla Prassd — *Bhulti Bhagati Yaden* (Hindi), Patna 1957

115. Vidyavachaspati, Indra — *Arya Samaj Ka Itihas* (Hindi), Delhi, 1957, 2 Vols.

116. Vidyarthi, L. P. (ed.) — *Leadership in India*, 1967

117. Wadia. A. R. — *History and Philosophy of Social Work in India*, Bombay, 1961

118. Waheéd, A. — *The Evolution of Muslim Education, Lahore.*

119. Wasi, S. M. — *President Prasad*, Calcutta, 1962

120. Wasti, Syed Razi — *Lord Minto and Indian Nationalist Movement*, London, 1964

121. Wilson, Minder — *History of Bihar*, Calcutta, 1908

122. Zachariaa, H. C. E. — *Renascent India from Ram Mohan Roy to Mohan Das Gandhi*, London, 1933

123- Zutshi — *Education in British India*, Allahabad, 1910

5. *News Papers and Journals.*

1. *Bihar Times*
2. *Kayastha Samachar*
3. *Kayastha Messenger*
4. *The Beharee*
5. *The Bihar Herald*
6. *The Express*
7. *The Hindustan Review*
8. *The Calcutta Review*
9. *The Modern Review*

10. *The Searchlight*
11. *The Leader*
12. *The Times of India*
13. *The Journal of Bihar Research Society*
14. *Man in India*
15. *The Illustrated Weekly of India*
16. *The Cambridge Historical Journal*, Cambridge

GLOSSARY

Ahimsa	—	Nonviolence
Ashram	—	A condition of life or hermitage
A'tu	—	Muslim lady teacher
Bazar	—	Market
Bidar	—	Pewter inlaid with Silver
Guru	—	Teacher
Gurukul	—	School based on Indian tradition
Hartal	—	Strike
Izzat	—	Prestige
Kachchi	—	Uncooked
Madarasa	—	A kind of Muslim School
Maktab	—	A kind of Muslim Primary School
Mantra	—	A hymn of invocation or form of prayer in the Sanskrit language
Maulvi	—	A learned man or a muslim teacher
Mufussil	—	Interior Area
Pandit	—	A learned man
Patwari	—	Accountant (village)
Pathsala	—	A Hindu School
Parda	—	Veil
Parda nashin	—	A Lady with a veil

Prayaschitta	—	Expiation
Puranas	—	Traditional History of India in Sanskrit
Ryots	—	A tenant or a farmer.
Sadhu	—	A Hindu ascetic or holyman
Sati	—	Widow self immolation by fiire
Shastrath	—	Religious discourse
Shradha	—	An obsequial or funeral sacrifice
Suddhi	—	Reconversion to one's own religion
Satyagrah	—	Peaceful non-cooperation
Swadeshi	—	The Introduction and use of home manufactured.
Swaraj	—	Self rule
Samaj	—	A Society
Samiti	—	A Society
Tols	—	Sanskrit School
Vakil	—	Pleader
Vidyapith	—	A kind of indigenous School
Zenana	—	A women's section of house.

INDEX